Gender, Violence and the Social Order

Gender, Violence and the Social Order

Jayne Mooney
Senior Lecturer
Centre for Criminology
Middlesex University
Enfield

palgrave

Published by PALGRAVE
Houndmills, Basingstoke, Hampshire RG21 6XS and
175 Fifth Avenue, New York, N. Y. 10010
Companies and representatives throughout the world

PALGRAVE is the new global academic imprint of
St. Martin's Press LLC Scholarly and Reference Division and
Palgrave Publishers Ltd (formerly Macmillan Press Ltd).

Outside North America
ISBN 0–333–73480–7 hardcover
ISBN 0–333–91886–X paperback

In North America
ISBN 0–312–23157–1

This book is printed on paper suitable for recycling and
made from fully managed and sustained forest sources.

A catalogue record for this book is available from the British Library.

Library of Congress Catalog Card Number: 99–088131

10   9   8   7   6   5   4   3   2
08   07   06   05   04   03   02   01

Printed and bound in Great Britain by
Antony Rowe Ltd, Chippenham, Wiltshire

For Faith Martin and a future free from violence

Contents

List of Figures and Tables

Acknowledgements

My thanks must first go to all the people who agreed to take part in the research component of this book, especially the women who had the courage to talk or write about their experiences of violence. I hope that by highlighting the problem of domestic violence more support and resources will be available for women in future.

I received a great deal of help and encouragement with this project from friends, colleagues at Middlesex University and those working in the area of violence. Special mention, in no particular order, must go to Shona Elrick, who also helped with the fieldwork for the survey; Kate Peach, who along with Shona put up with our home being taken over by questionnaires and reams of computer print-out; Edward Whelan, who displayed amazing patience whilst helping me to decipher the vast quantities of data collected; Claire Martin, Jeanne Gregory, Sue Lees, John Lea, Susanne MacGregor, Colin Francome, Shiona McArthur, Sandra Walklate, Nigel South, Susan Edwards, Trevor Jones, Derek Sawyer, Michael Pollak, Rubina Akhar, Bonnie Miller, Kate Painter, Stephen Parrott, Thalia Nettleton, Juliet, Anny and Jesse Ash, Jenny Pearce, Ian Taylor, Ruth Jamieson, Chris Hale, Jalna Hanmer, Mai Kennedy, Christine Daley, Jill Cannon, Davina James-Hanman, Collette Paul, Liz Davies, Keir Sothcott, Faith Martin, Lucien Martin, Karen Duke, Robin Norton, Russell Dobash, Catherine Itzin, Catriona Woolner, Ruth Hall, Women Against Rape, Jill Radford, Rights of Women, Nicola Harwin, National and London Women's Aid, the Metropolitan Police (Tottenham, Kilburn, West Hendon and Holloway Divisions) and the Crown Prosecution Service (Wood Green).

Finally, I would like to thank Stewart, Joseph and Fintan for always being there for me.

Introduction

Sara Dylan: I can't go home without fear for my safety. I was in such fear of him that I locked doors in the home to protect myself from his violent outbursts and temper tantrums ... He has struck me in the face injuring my jaw.

(Heylin, 1991: 295)

The New Criminology, the classic text of radical criminology of the early 1970s, starts with a quotation from Bob Dylan. I choose to start with one from Sara – erstwhile wife of Dylan and the muse of 'Sad Eyed Lady of the Lowlands' and 'Forever Young'. The freewheeling libertarianism of the time pervades *The New Criminology*, and the oppressive violence of authority is a constant theme throughout. Yet nowhere is violence between intimates considered, and in particular, as so many writers have pointed out, the violence of men upon women – 'the other side' of Bob Dylan, if you like.

Violence by a man against a woman within the safe haven of the home and in the midst of a close relationship is a tragedy which has occurred throughout history, engendering a spectrum of emotions from abhorrence to male self-congratulation. Such violence also generates a series of important questions. The family is seen as the basic building block of liberal democratic society, politicians of all persuasions lament its erosion and attribute all sorts of social evils, including crime itself, to its supposed decline. But if the family is a guarantee against crime, how can it be that a particularly unpleasant crime is fostered by close relationships within the family itself? The answers to this question are various, from those liberals who guard their fundamental tenets by stressing the rarity of domestic violence, to radical feminists who view it as central to the maintenance of male power, to

1

the increasingly fashionable band of evolutionary psychologists, who maintain that because such violence is widely prevalent, it must bestow a Darwinian advantage – what is bad for the wife may be good for the species. All these theories I shall examine, but let us note how domestic violence demands an answer from all of them.

Much of this discussion must revolve around empirical evidence. How prevalent is domestic violence? Is the home as dangerous as the streets for a woman as some would suggest; or is it *more* dangerous and are the mass media representations of 'stranger danger' for women a fiction which creates unnecessary fear in public and displaces anxieties on the wrong people and places? Is the image of domestic violence as over-whelmingly man against woman wrong, or is violence as likely in both directions as Murray Straus and his colleagues in the United States, and Erin Pizzey and a recent Home Office report in the UK, maintain? Indeed, what is the level and seriousness of such violence? Is it, in fact, no more than the inevitable minor frictions of family life and only rarely as serious as conflicts outside of the home? The answers to such questions are surprisingly sketchy and frequently contradictory. This study attempts to sort this out, involving as it does one of the largest pieces of research in this area carried out in Europe. But this in turn generates a series of methodological questions. How does one best conduct research in such a sensitive area? Why do the published data vary, sometimes by as much as ten times? How can one develop research tools which generate reliable data and at the same time test the major competing theories which claim validity in the field? Lastly, and most importantly, what policies does such a discussion of theory and examination of data suggest? This book aims to take us from theory to methodology and from method to policy. Its intent is didactic yet, however important it is to clarify the debate and set down firm guidelines for policy, we must never lose sight of the reality of human suffering which such violence causes.

The need for research

Domestic violence has, since the 1970s, been increasingly recognised as a serious social problem. There is, of course, a great deal of historical evidence to show that women have always suffered violence from their husbands and partners (see Martin, 1976; Tomes, 1978; Dobash and Dobash, 1979; Freeman, 1979; Smith, 1989; Clarke, 1992; Doggett, 1992). However, it is a problem that has only become publicly evident at times when there has been a strong feminist movement, enabling collective organization against its occurrence (Freeman, 1979;

Brokowski *et al.*, 1983; Wilson, 1983). Thus, it was an issue in the first wave of feminism in the nineteenth century, as it is in the second wave of the late twentieth century. Today few weeks pass without there being a programme on television or the radio or an article written on the subject. Domestic violence has, in addition, become a priority for many local authorities and police divisions around the world.

Despite current public concern, little is known about domestic violence, and it has been recognized as an area which needs detailed and in-depth research, particularly on the general population (Smith, 1989). The true extent of domestic violence, for example, is generally agreed to be unknown. Indeed, many commentators consider it to have one of the highest hidden figures of any crime (Dobash and Dobash, 1979; Hanmer and Stanko, 1985; Worrall and Pease, 1986; British Medical Association, 1998). Figures derived from agencies such as the police and women's refuges are necessarily selective and encompass only a small proportion of victims. It is well documented that police statistics suffer from the problem of the 'hidden figure of crime' – that is, the non-reporting of crime to the police, and the failure of the police to record all the crime that is reported to them. The problem of the hidden figure of crime has been recognized throughout the history of social statistics. Indeed, it was first delineated in the 1830s by Adolphe Quetelet, the Belgian mathematician, astronomer and developer of social statistics. Agency figures, therefore, represent merely the tip of the iceberg and, in some cases (for instance, those derived from women's refuges) point more to the limited availability of such resources than to the overall extent of the problem. The reasons for both the lack of reporting and its variation by subgroup remain speculative.

Victimization surveys, which typically involve asking a sample of the population about crimes that have been committed against them in the previous year, have made a considerable contribution to the knowledge of the hidden figure of many crimes, the social and geographical pattern of problems, the potential levels of demand on relevant agencies and the degree of satisfaction with them.[1] While they have their own figure of non-response, this is much smaller than that of police statistics. However, in the area of domestic violence, they are seen to have severe limitations. The researchers themselves frequently recognize their data to be under-representative and there are doubts as to whether mass surveys covering the whole gamut of crime are sufficiently sensitive to pick up on all but a fraction of the actual incidence of domestic violence. Levels of non-reporting are thought to be considerable for various reasons: fear of reprisals (the assailant may be nearby during the interview), embarrassment, psychological blocking, and so on (Walklate, 1989). Domestic violence is often unknown to anyone outside the immediate family and it is unlikely, therefore, that a victim will choose to reveal her experiences to a disinterested interviewer, a stranger, standing on the doorstep with a clipboard. Incidence figures uncovered by such surveys are 3 per cent in the Merseyside Crime Survey (Kinsey, 1985), 8 per cent in the second Islington Crime Survey (Crawford *et al.*, 1990) and 3 per cent in the 1992 British Crime Survey (Mayhew *et al.*, 1993).

Surveys conducted by feminists, in contrast, have pointed to much higher figures, as in the pathbreaking work in Britain of Jalna Hanmer and Sheila Saunders (1984) and Ruth Hall and Women Against Rape (1985). Feminist researchers have generally been aware of the profound methodological inadequacies of conventional surveys, most notably in the definition of what constitutes domestic violence, and have employed more sensitive research strategies (for example, with respect to interviewing techniques and the use of self-complete questionnaires).[2] Unfortunately, this body of work has been restricted by a lack of funding and has come under criticism for the use of small or biased sampling methods which prevent the results being generalized to the population as a whole (MacLean, 1985; Jones *et al.*, 1986).

It has been suggested that the lack of authoritative statistics on domestic violence serves to limit the ability to take preventative or remedial action to alleviate the problem (London Strategic Policy Unit, 1986; Smith, 1989). This book is concerned, therefore, to create a methodology which can generate reliable data on the extent of domestic violence. But it must be stressed that it does not focus on methodology alone, it also seeks to test theory with regard to the causation, and hence distribution, of domestic violence in the population. There is, for example, considerable debate over hypotheses generated with respect to its class-based nature (for example, Gelles and Cornell, 1985; Young, 1986; Schwartz, 1988; DeKeseredy and Hinch, 1991) or its uniform distribution throughout the population (for example, Russell, 1982) which needs thorough examination. Finally, both methodology and theory allow the development of a socially-based policy and an evaluation of which agencies are involved in tackling domestic violence and the limits of their effectiveness.

The research project

The research project at the core of this book was formulated in response to the need for better information on domestic violence in the general population. As the survey is the only method of gaining mass data that is considerably better than police or other agency statistics, a variation of the victimisation survey was used, adapted to deal with the specific problems involved in researching such a sensitive area. Trained, sympathetic interviewers and carefully worded questionnaires were employed, together with the incorporation of various methodological innovations, for example, supplementary self-report questionnaires (the 'piggy-back' method), in-depth interviews and vignettes detailing 'conflict' situations which could lead to violence. The method is discussed in detail in Chapter 5. The survey was random, with a final sample size of 1,000 individuals. This is considerably larger than that required for statistical significance; but such a large sample size is necessary to facilitate the cross-tabulation of the data by age, class and ethnicity. The main focus was on women's experiences of violence from husbands and boyfriends, although the investigation was extended to other forms of domestic and non-domestic violence. Of great interest is the opinions of men, for, as we shall see, it is they who commit the majority of the violence. The male half of the sample were, therefore, asked their opinion on violence, when it was justified – if ever – and if they had ever been violent to their partners. At the very least this allowed us to compare the rates of violence as reported by men and women, as well as to contrast attitudes across the sexes. The purpose of the survey was to investigate the incidence and prevalence of domestic violence; its variation by subgroups of the population; the nature, context and impact of the violence; levels and patterns of reporting to various agencies and satisfaction with the help received; attitudes to domestic violence; the relationship of domestic violence to stranger violence, and the location of violence in terms of public and private space.

The survey was conducted in an area of North London. Lorna Smith (1989), in her overview of the research on domestic violence, advocated the use of local surveys as these are less expensive than national surveys and are just as capable of generating detailed information. Despite the local focus the sample was large: 1,000 individuals were interviewed covering a wide age range and mixed in terms of both ethnicity and class. Thus just under half the population were from England, Scotland and Wales, and there were substantial Irish and African Caribbean populations as well as those of Cypriot, Asian and African origin. The survey location was a typical inner-city area where, although housing is predominantly council-owned, there has been a considerable process of gentrification, with one in five houses being owner-occupied.

The importance of theory

> Theoretical perspectives provide us with an image of what something is and how we might best act toward it. They name something this type of thing and not that. They provide us with the sense of being in a world of relatively fixed forms and content. Theoretical perspectives transform a mass of raw sensory data into understanding, explanations, and recipes for appropriate action.
>
> (Pfohl, 1985: 9–10)

Popular theories of domestic violence

As various commentators have pointed out, crime has always and inevitably been the subject of popular theories with regards to its causation. Thus Lilly, Cullen and Ball, referring to the American public, write:

> Most Americans have little difficulty in identifying the circumstances they believe cause people to engage in wayward conduct. When surveyors ask citizens about the causes of crime, only a small percentage of the respondents say they 'have no opinion.' The remainder of those polled usually remark that crime is caused by factors such as unemployment, bad family life, or lenient courts.
>
> (1989: 9)

Domestic violence is no exception to this. When women were asked in pilot studies, and in the main survey which forms the research base to this book, what they thought caused men to use violence against their wives or girlfriends, very few said they 'didn't know'. Below are some of the explanations that were suggested. As can be seen, they range from a focus on individual factors (alcohol, mental instability, emotional insecurity) to the wider culture (representations of women in the mass media, pornography) and social structure of society (unequal power relations between men and women, social pressures such an unemployment).

Individual factors

> They could have been exposed to the very same behaviour when they were a child and their subconscious mind is therefore conditioned into reacting with violence when faced with problems, etc.

> Some men become violent when intoxicated with alcohol or drugs.

Mentally unstable. They have to take it out on someone and as women are the weaker, they are the easy target.

Because women provoke men. ... and jealousy through insecurity stops men from behaving rationally and reasonably.

They find it difficult to express anger through words, lack of communication skills.

Cultural and social structural factors

Because society, TV, popular press, adverts, porno mags, etc. present a picture of women as subordinate objects for men's pleasure. I think it is extremely difficult for women to assert themselves within a male/female relationship.

Because they feel this is 'macho' conduct and it is how men should behave.

The stresses of poverty, unemployment.

Some men are conditioned into thinking that violence is acceptable within a domestic environment. The woman should obey his demands and when she doesn't is punished. In this society men and boys are taught that violence equals strength. Men go to war and kill people and are then given medals and hailed as heroes for their bravery. Therefore why should this not apply on a smaller scale?

I think that perhaps men who use physical violence in this way do so in order to gain a feeling a power, or superiority over their partner. Perhaps they do this because they are downtrodden in other aspects of their lives (for example, employment) and need to feel 'respected' as they see it by someone; and inflicting violence is the only way they see they can achieve any level of superiority in their eyes over anyone.

To give them a feeling of power and control over the woman. Men feel by threatening the woman, she will remain under their influence.

Because society allows them to get away with it – poor sentencing.

Popular explanations and criminology

Jock Young in *Thinking Seriously about Crime* points out that there are important differences between 'popular theories' of crime – such as those presented on domestic violence above – and criminological theory, in particular, the latter:

> a) attempts to ground itself in an empirical knowledge of the patterns, incidences and variations in criminal behaviour, drawing on more systematic information;
>
> b) attempts to build a theoretical position systematically, so that the different parts of the theory fit coherently, ironing out inconsistencies and contradictions of position;
>
> c) attempts to be as comprehensive as it can – dealing with the different aspects and drawing these into a systematic account.
>
> (1981: 248)

Furthermore, popular theories tend to be contradictory, for example, with respect to the factors involved in causation and between these and the policy implications that are drawn. The theoretical section of this book (Chapters 1–4) will examine the theories of classicism and new administrative criminology; positivism, including the 'family violence' approach and evolutionary theory; feminism and left realism in relation to domestic violence. It will systematically examine a series of questions which an adequate theory of domestic violence should be able to answer. These are:

1. **Definition:** What is domestic violence and how should it be defined?
2. **Extent and distribution:** How frequent is the incidence and prevalence of domestic violence, and how is it distributed within the social structure (that is, by age, class and ethnicity)?
3. **Causes:** What are the causes of domestic violence?
4. **Impact:** What is the impact on women of domestic violence and how does this vary within the social structure?
5. **Methods:** How should one best investigate the extent and distribution of domestic violence and elaborate its causes?
6. **Policy:** Which policies, involving which agencies, are most effective in tackling the problem and what is a satisfactory outcome?

These questions will be asked of each of the theories under consideration. It should be noted that the answers to each question should display a consistency within the particular theory whilst being aware that omissions and contradictions are as important as commissions and coherence. The discussion of each theory will begin with an historical overview and a description of its conception of human nature and social order, for this will predicate its approach to the questions listed above.[3]

The book falls into four main parts. The first (Chapters 1–4) takes the major criminological theories, systematically discusses their main tenets and details how each attempts to explain, research and tackle domestic violence. The theoretical limitations and insights of each tradition are explored. On examination the work of radical feminists and left realists are singled out as having the greatest purchase on the phenomenon and a synthesis of these approaches, *feminist realism,* is demarcated. In Part II (Chapters 5–7) the empirical study of the prevalence of domestic violence is detailed, informed as it is by the methodological approaches of radical feminism and realism. The predictive capacity of each theoretical tradition is tested in Part III (Chapter 8), where the parameters of domestic violence and non-domestic violence are documented with an emphasis on the spatial distribution of violence. Finally, in Part IV, the theoretical, methodological and policy implications of the empirical findings and the theoretical discussion are elaborated.

Part I

1
Classicist Criminology: Liberal Explanations of Violence

Classicist theories of crime are the criminology of liberal democracy. The fundamental notions of free will, equality and responsibility to the community are the same as those that govern liberal conceptions of politics and, indeed, economic behaviour. They concern the core rules of citizenship and their tenets are enacted in every major judicial court in the western world.

Classicist theories of crime first emerged in the latter half of the eighteenth century derived from the philosophy of the Enlightenment, which forms the basis of modern liberal democracy. Their concern was not so much with the causes of crime as with developing a legal system which would justify and effectively control it. It was for this reason that George Vold characterized the classicist school as 'administrative criminology' (1958: 23). Indeed, the impact of these theories was such that within a century the majority of the legal and penal systems of administration in Europe were reformulated to reflect classicist principles. Within academic criminology, classicist theory is best displayed in deterrence theory which has recently witnessed something of a resurgence. This can be found in the work of van den Haag (1975), Ehrlich (1975) and James Q. Wilson – particularly his earlier work, for example *Thinking About Crime* (1975) (see Roshier, 1989: 47–9). In recent years a modified version of classicist ideas, a 'new administrative criminology', has emerged in all the advanced industrial societies. In Britain this has been associated with Home Office researchers under the directorship of Ron Clarke, particularly in the early 1980s. This has exerted considerable influence on official crime prevention policy (Clarke, 1980; Clarke and Cornish, 1983; Heal and Laycock, 1986) and has subsequently developed into a flourishing 'rational choice' school of criminology (see Clarke and Felson, 1993; Felson, 1994), which stresses the voluntaristic nature and opportunism of the criminal act.

Classicism

The philosophy of the Enlightenment reflects the political and social overthrow of the *ancien régime* of feudalism and absolute monarchs who maintained the divine right to intervene in all aspects of life, that is, in all political, financial and personal affairs. Its impetus was the reaction of the emerging capitalist class to the constraints of feudalism, for example, with respect to property, finance, manufacture, travel, and so on, which were seen as severely limiting the development of trade and industry. The *ancien régime* was superseded by a politics based on a radical reconceptualization of the nature of the individual and the formation of society, which found its most concrete expression in the American Declaration of Independence and the French Declaration of Man and Citizen. Central to this were the notions of *freedom, equality* and the *social contract*.

In Enlightenment thought the individual was presented as rational and governed by free will. All 'men' were considered to be formally equal in that all were endowed with these attributes. Human behaviour was seen as purposeful and founded on hedonism: the individual rationally calculated the drawbacks and rewards of 'his' actions, thus avoiding that which gave pain and seeking that which resulted in pleasure. Individuals were described as originally living in the 'natural state' where they were governed by what John Locke called 'the law of nature', in which 'no one ought to harm another in his life, health, liberty or possessions' (1690: II.6). However as transgressions of this law occurred, 'men' were described as giving up some of their natural freedom to 'contract' together to protect their rights and thus prevent the 'natural state' degenerating into war and chaos. The basis of society is, therefore, the social contract, that is the 'contracting' together of free and equal individuals to form a state for their individual and mutual benefit.

Anne Phillips has commented that, for most liberals, the state is a 'necessary evil' existing because 'individuals cannot be trusted to regulate themselves, and the state must therefore play a referee role' (1987: 13). As the creation of the state involved placing restrictions on individual freedom, it was deemed that its power should be contained by carefully delineating the boundaries in which it could operate; in particular distinctions were made between the public and private spheres of life. Regulation was to be permitted in the public sphere but not the private. The private sphere was seen to include the family; it represented the personal side of life. Other areas immune from state control included freedom of speech, of worship and the right to own private property.

Classicist principles have had, as previously indicated, a considerable influence on legal and criminological thinking. The notion of contract forms the basis of modern civil law: individuals are seen as replicating the original social contract when they enter into employment, property and marriage contracts. Cesare Bonesana Marchese de Beccaria (1738–94), an Italian mathematician and economist, was the key figure in the classical school of criminology, bringing eighteenth-century liberal ideas to the subject of criminal justice. Classicist scholars began from the position that, just as the individual was governed by reason, so should the criminal justice system. Individuals were seen as 'free' to act in whatever way they wished in so far as they did not interfere with the freedom of others. If transgressions occurred, then punishment should be proportional to the social harm inflicted, 'punishment to fit the crime', not to the social, psychological or physical characteristics of the offender. Further, as classicist thought presents all individuals as formally equal, they are therefore considered to merit equal treatment before the law. To ensure that this occurs and that the law is not open to interpretation, crimes and punishment were to be defined in a fixed legal code. Punishment was to be swift and inevitable. For it was deemed important that the workings of the criminal justice system should be irrefutable and predictable. Citizens could then calculate the 'benefits' and 'costs' of any crime. In support of its notion of legal equality, it was, in addition, argued that crimes should be judged by a jury of one's peers, that is by other rational and equal individuals.

The new administrative criminology

In Britain the new administrative criminology developed in the late 1970s and early 1980s at the Home Office research unit particularly around the notion of situational crime prevention. The timing here, as in the rest of the western world, was scarcely random. As Adam Crawford puts it:

> As in the USA and Australia, this … coincided with a political, as well as an academic, shift. The installation of governments committed to a neo-liberal ideology – emphasising the free market, a minimal state and individual free choice and responsibility – dovetailed with and promoted criminological ideas which shared the same basic presuppositions.
>
> (1998: 65; see also O'Malley, 1992)

This theory, then, involved a revival of neoclassicist theories of crime and was concomitant with the world-wide re-emergence of neoliberal politics and economics (see Taylor, 1997). It developed, in part, as a reaction to the perceived failure of social democratic positivism, which had argued that the major cause of crime was poor social conditions. Social democratic positivism had been the main theory of postwar establishment criminology. Situational crime prevention reversed this: in the place of a determined actor propelled by adverse conditions was a voluntaristic offender seeking gain and searching out opportunities. Crawford describes this well:

> At the heart of situational crime prevention is a rational choice theory of human decision-making. Rational choice theory connects with a wider renewed interest within criminology in neo-classical understandings of crime. Following Beccaria and Bentham this neo-classicism emphasises the rationality and voluntary thought processes of individuals in the commission of crime. It conceptualises the decision-making process on which choices – as to whether or not to engage in criminal activity at any given moment – are premised, as the product of calculation on the basis of the relative balance between the perceived risks and effort involved as against the potential rewards offered. Here, the potential criminal is perceived as a self-maximising decision maker who carefully calculates the advantages and disadvantages associated with certain activities. Prevention therefore is aimed at altering the decision-making process in order to increase the risks or effort involved in the commission of a crime and decrease any rewards associated with it.
>
> (1998: 70)

The classicist roots of new administrative criminology are indicated in its disinclination to explain crime in terms of causes – such as those presented by individual and social positivists (see Chapter 2) – and its critique of what Ron Clarke (1980: 137) calls the 'dispositional bias' of much criminological theory. Instead, it views crime as the product of wilful, rational action. The criminal is presented as having rationally weighed up the costs and benefits of the criminal act. People, therefore, are seen as liable to commit crime when there is little to prevent them from doing so. Crime is viewed as opportunistic, in that it mainly occurs when situations arise which present possibilities for criminal advantage. Yet the traditional classicist emphasis on the use of the criminal justice system as a deterrence is considered palpably ineffective. Prisons merely encourage recidivism whilst policing has little

proven record of effectively apprehending offenders (Clarke, 1980).
Thus, the emphasis in the new administrative criminology has been on
restricting the opportunities for crime, rather than looking at the moti-
vations of the criminal, and by building up new social control mechanisms. This has involved target-hardening and increasing levels of
surveillance. With this in mind, various situational crime prevention
measures have been proposed: better locks and bolts on houses, improv-
ing environmental and architectural design, creating defensible spaces,
Neighbourhood Watch, and so on. This strategy has been very influential and, as Downes and Rock have commented, is in accord with their
perception 'of criminals as reasoning people implicated in chains of
decision' for 'rational criminals confronting critical choices are fairly
readily susceptible to intelligent control strategies' (1988: 229). In addition, this approach has stressed that it is the responsibility of each individual citizen to prevent crime:

> Promoting responsibility for crime prevention is a key issue.
> Responsibility does not mean criminal culpability, but rather
> invokes the notion of a general duty on the part of the citizen to
> take steps to prevent crime. Individuals and organisations may con-
> tribute to the growth of crime either by unwittingly creating oppor-
> tunities or by failing (for a variety of reasons) to take reasonable
> actions to limit them.
>
> (Hope, 1985: 6)

Finally, in line with classicist thought, the focus of new administrative criminology has been on the public sphere and the protection of
private property. What occurs in the private sphere has tended to be
overlooked. As Gordon Hughes points out, the crime prevention initiatives pursued by the Home Office were characterized by the imagery of
'outsiders' whom one must protect oneself against. He contrasts this
with the stress in France on creating solidarity within the community
and in a crime prevention based on this premise. Here

> we find two consistent themes, namely 'solidarity and partnership'
> and 'integration' (unlike the central government policy in the UK
> with its themes of consumerism, individualism and self-reliance).
> The *Bonnemaison* approach thus carried social imagery of the people as
> one community of 'insiders' in contrast to the imagery of 'outsiders'
> in much UK central state-sponsored 'community' crime prevention.
>
> (1998: 101)

Human nature

In classicist thought human nature is perceived as rational and governed by free will. Until recently it has been customary to suggest that classicism presumed a notion of volition untrammelled by determinacy. But, as Piers Beirne has shown in his pathbreaking *Inventing Criminology* (1993), this was certainly not the case. Classical thinkers such as Beccaria saw no contradiction in the notion that people make choices in determinate situations. Perhaps the important element to stress is that the majority of human beings are seen in classicism as able to transend the circumstances which surround them and make choices. It is only in the minority of cases, such as acute mental illness where such forces are ineluctable, that choice and, hence, responsibility are negated. Therefore, from this perspective, a man who is domestically violent will generally be seen, not as someone who is severely mentally ill or experiencing insurmountable social pressures, but as a rational individual. The violent act, its timing and intentions, is considered as planned and voluntaristic rather than the result of psychological or social determinants. Indeed, contemporary manifestations of classicism, such as that of the new administrative criminology, although not denying pathological and social explanations in extreme situations, consider such determinacy to be greatly exaggerated and, moreover, largely impossible to tackle (Clarke, 1980).

Social order

Social order is based on the social contract. Free and rational individuals 'contract' together to create a state in order to protect their rights. Society is divided into public and private spheres. The private sphere is usually understood to be the family. Marriage or the formation of live-in relationships are seen as contractual, a replication of the original social contract. Men and women freely choose to live together, to form the heterosexual, nuclear family. Government or state interference, including the rule of law, is to be kept at a minimal level in the private sphere so as not to interfere with the rights of the individual. Stinchcombe has commented that the legal distinction between the private and the public spheres in the modern liberal state is 'the main source of the capacity of small social systems (for example, the family) to maintain their boundaries and determine their own interaction without interference from the outside' (1964: 151) and further that 'a primary function of the criminal law is the limitation of coercion within small social systems' (*ibid.*: 153). Formal legal intervention is seen as risking 'undermining … the stability of the family, the weakening of family bonds, the atomising of individual family members, and the destruction of the family as a political bulwark against excess of state power' (O'Donovan, 1985: 14–15). Any disputes within the private sphere should, therefore, preferably be resolved by using non-legal methods, for example, through marriage guidance counselling. The division of society into public and private spheres is clearly a problem for classicism in developing a theory of domestic violence as it is in the private sphere that this form of violence is located.

Definition

Crime is defined as that which is against the law. Those behaviours that are deemed to violate the social contract are set down in advance in a fixed legal code. In traditional classicist thought, if the act is not prosecutable in court, then it is not a crime. Theoretically, the criminal law covering domestic violence is the same as that covering violence by strangers and is largely contained in the Offences against the Person Act 1861. Lorna Smith (1989) has commented that whilst this Act deals with all forms of assault, from common assault to murder, the four sections most commonly applicable to domestic violence are: common assault (s. 42), assault occasioning actual bodily harm (s. 47), malicious wounding (s. 20) and grievous bodily harm (s. 18). The new administrative criminologists in the British Crime Surveys (see Hough and Mayhew, 1983; Hough and Mayhew, 1985; Mayhew *et al.*, 1989; Mayhew *et al.*, 1994; Mirrlees-Black *et al.*, 1996; Mirrlees-Black *et al.*, 1998) also apply legal definitions in the classifying and counting of crimes. In the report of the 1992 survey, Mayhew *et al.* indicate 'that they do not simply accept respondents' definitions of what is crime', but use what they term a 'nominal' definition of crime: 'a count of incidents which according to the letter of the law could be punished, regardless perhaps of the value of doing so, and regardless always of whether a layman would really see the incident as "crime" as such' (1993: 4; see also Mirrlees-Black, 1998: 76–7). Thus behaviours such as mental cruelty, which fall outside the legal categories, would not be seen by traditional classicists or the new administrative criminologists as 'crime'. Domestically, violent acts are those that the law designates as being violent.

Extent and distribution

For classicism the crime rate in a nation governed by the rule of law is a problem, but involves only a minority of people either as offenders or victims. It is not an endemic problem extensively affecting and involving the majority of the population. The social contract, after all, is formed precisely because of this: to minimize the war of all against all. On this premise alone the prevalence of domestic violence would be reckoned to be limited, not widespread. But there is a further and important reason why domestic violence would be viewed as a minority phenomenon. For classicists, marriage and the forming of close personal relationships replicate the original social contract and, moreover, the union between husband and wife, like that between parents and children, is seen to represent a more or less unquestioned unity of interest. When crime does occur it is, therefore, deemed more likely to be from strangers – those individuals with whom no personal contract has been formed.

As crime is defined as that which breaks the legal code, classicists would traditionally look to the official criminal statistics to determine the extent and distribution of crime. Indeed, some would argue that official statistics are the only 'true' crime rate as they are the only statistics to represent cases which have been prosecuted by the courts and adjudicated as crimes (see Tappan, 1947). Such a position has two well-known problems: it too readily accepts that legal categorization reflects the social reality of crime; and it ignores the 'hidden figure' of crime (those unknown to the police and the courts). I shall explore the problem of legal categorization later in this chapter, but let us note in passing that the official statistics provide us with little information with regards to domestic violence. They only tell us the number of violent offences overall, not the number that were 'domestic', as 'domestic violence' does not exist as a separate category. Information is available on domestic homicides only.

The new administrative criminologists are well aware that not all crime that infringes the legal code is reported to or recorded by the police, and will, therefore, not appear in the official statistics. For this reason they have used national crime surveys to investigate the extent and distribution of crime (Hough and Mayhew, 1983; Chambers and Tombs, 1984; Hough and Mayhew, 1985; Mayhew *et al.*, 1989; Kinsey and Anderson, 1992; Mayhew *et al.*, 1994; Anderson and Leitch, 1996; Mirrlees-Black *et al.*, 1996; Mirrlees-Black *et al.*, 1998). From their results they argue that:

1. the risk of crime is generally low;
2. violent offences are low in comparison to crimes against property;
3. violence is more commonly against men than against women; and
4. violence is more likely to occur in public space.

Indeed, the authors of the report of the 1982 British Crime Survey commented:

> That a 'statistically average' person age 16 or over can expect:
>
> – a robbery once every five centuries (not attempts)
> – an assault resulting in injury (even if slight) once every century

– the family car to be stolen by joyriders once every 60 years
– a burglary in the home once every 40 years.
... and a very low rate for rape and other sexual offences.

(Hough and Mayhew, 1983: 15, 21)

Subsequent survey work has seemingly corroborated this view; thus the 1992 British Crime Survey indicated that the risk of violence was greater for men than for women (1.83:1), that public violence was much more common than private violence (2.44:1), that despite women being more likely to have violence committed against them in the private sphere this was not dramatically so (1.32:1), and that, although women experienced a higher rate of domestic violence than men, their overall risk of domestic violence was low (just under 1 per cent, and this includes all household members as offenders not merely partners or ex-partners). The findings are presented in Tables 1.1 and 1.2.

New administrative criminologists explain much of the rise in the official crime statistics as the result of an increase in the reporting of petty offences to the police, greater efficiency in police recording of crime and more opportunities to commit crime (Clarke, 1984; Mayhew and Hough, 1988). Mayhew *et al.* (1993) suggest, with respect to violent crimes, that the police are upgrading common assault to wounding

Table 1.1 Risk of violence from the 1992 British Crime Survey (incidence rates per 10,000)

	Private	Public	All
Men	113	702	815
Women	254	192	446
All	367	894	1261

Table 1.2 Ratios of violence from the 1992 British Crime Survey

	Ratio of incidents
Men	1.83
Women	1
Public	2.44
Private	1

Source: Derived from Table A6.3 in *The 1992 British Crime Survey*, Mayhew *et al.*, 1993.

and giving a higher priority to certain types of violent crime, for example, domestic violence. Further, the rise in the reporting of rape and domestic violence is seen as due to the public's perception of a more sensitive police response. The most recent survey (1998) continues with this theme: the risks of violence are played down compared to property crime (4.7 per cent compared to 34 per cent overall) and domestic violence is calculated as affecting 0.9 per cent of the population (Mirrlees-Black *et al.*, 1998). Changes in perspective are, however, manifest as the influence of the new administrative criminology in the Home Office begins to wane. Thus the markedly unequal focus of crime in certain social groups and areas becomes a major theme and in the 1996 survey (Mirrlees-Black, 1999) a concerted effort was made to tackle the problem of low domestic violence figures. I shall return to this in more detail in Chapter 6.

Causes

Crime is not caused; it is willed where the opportunities to benefit oneself undetected occur (Clarke, 1980). From this perspective crime between strangers would have a greater benefit than that between family members, as detection is less likely and the presumed coincidence of material interests in the family would militate against possible advantage. For classicists the family in its private sphere is viewed almost as an individual person: crime in this area is crime against oneself. Domestic violence, when it occurs – and it is seen to be infrequent – should be dealt with by the law, but resolved in institutions such as marriage guidance where the underlying 'unity' of interests between husband and wife are made clear through counselling.

Impact

As classicists generally see the crime rate as low although deplorable, its overall impact on society is minimized. On an individual level its impact is likewise not going to be great since the new administrative criminologists describe the 'typical' victim as 'very much like the typical criminal – not old, female and wealthy, but male, young, single, a heavy drinker, and involved in assaulting others' (Slattery, 1986). Indeed, new administrative criminologists regard fear of crime as being more of a problem and as having a greater impact than actual crime, particularly for women and the elderly. It is fear of crime that affects the quality of people's lives by, for example, reducing their use of public space. As a result, new administrative criminologists have seen it as their role to reduce exaggerated fear of crime (Mayhew and Hough, 1988).

Methods

As we have seen, traditional classicism, with its emphasis on the legal code, would use only those cases that were convicted by a court to investigate the extent and distribution of crime (Tappan, 1947). Crime is that which is adjudicated by the courts. The problem here is, of course, the hidden figure of crime. For this reason new administrative criminologists utilize the survey method, although retaining, as we have seen, legal definitions. They use structured questionnaires and face-to-face interviews to gather information from a sample of the population about crimes that have been committed against them in the previous 12 months in order to be comparable with the criminal police statistics, although some 'have ever' questions are asked in the more recent surveys. To date there have been seven sweeps of the British Crime Survey measuring crime rates in 1981, 1983, 1987, 1991, 1993, 1995 and 1997. (The reports rather confusingly are named after the year of the survey rather than the year measured so the 1992 British Crime Survey measures crime in 1991 and the 1998 survey that in 1997.) In each sweep a representative sample of more than 10,000 people aged 16 years and over are interviewed. New administrative criminologists have also been involved in three international victimization surveys in which interviews were conducted by telephone (Van Dijk and Mayhew, 1993; Mayhew and Van Dijk, 1997). Analysis of domestic violence occurred in the reports of the 1992 and 1996 British Crime Surveys (Mayhew *et al.*, 1993; Mirrlees-Black *et al.*, 1996). Of most relevance to our discussion is that, faced with what was correctly perceived as the unrealistically low domestic violence figures, new techniques have been developed to tackle the problem. Chief of these is Computer-Assisted Self-Interviewing (CASI) in which, following the main interview, the respondent is handed a laptop computer and, reading questions from the screen, inputs his or her responses directly into the computer (Mirrlees-Black, 1999).

Policy

The focus of classicist criminal policy is on the criminal act; the conditions which lead up to the act and previous convictions of the offender are deemed irrelevant. The individual should be punished proportionally to the act and to that offence alone. Thus, the perpetrator of domestic violence would be judged only in relation to the act which had come to the attention of the authorities; a past history of domestic

violence would not be taken into consideration. Furthermore, the classicist distinction between the private and public spheres has implications for policy. As previously stated, classicists argue that government
or state intervention should be kept to a minimum in the private
sphere in order to protect the rights of the individual; any disputes
that do occur are better resolved by employing non-legal methods.
Policy is, therefore, more likely to be directed towards the development
of mediation and/or counselling strategies so as to limit disruption of
the private sphere. On those occasions when legal intervention is necessary it is considered important that sets of procedures are adhered to

> which guarantee that the autonomy of individuals and small social
> systems will be restored as quickly as possible if a crime has not in fact
> been committed. And … that the process of investigating and legally
> establishing the existence of a crime shall not so far damage the small
> social system that they cannot function after being found innocent.
>
> (Stinchcombe, 1964: 153)

The policy recommendations of the new administrative criminologists are based on the findings of the British Crime Surveys. Indeed,
according to Mayhew and Hough, the argument for the conducting of
a national survey was founded on its potential value to policy-makers:

> it would offer a more comprehensive picture of the crime problem,
> and would thus be a useful contribution to the process of setting
> priorities and allocating resources. Information about the groups
> most at risk was expected to prove of practical value in the search
> for solutions – in crime prevention programmes, for example.
> … Information on crime risks was also expected to demonstrate
> the comparatively low risks of *serious* crime, and puncture the inac-
> curate stereotypes of crime victims. In other words, the survey
> promised a more informed picture of crime which might help create
> a more balanced climate of opinion about law and order.
>
> (1988: 157, original emphasis)

The focus of new administrative criminology has, therefore, been on
crime in public space, property crime and reducing fear of crime. There
has been little advice for women experiencing violence in the home,
and guidelines have tended to be directed at avoiding 'stranger danger'.
Hence, as Betsy Stanko documents, in the Home Office crime prevention campaign of 1988–9, women were instructed: to avoid short-cuts

through dimly-lit alleys; not to hitch-hike; to cover up expensive-looking jewellery; to buy a screech alarm ('their piercing noise can frighten off an attacker'); to sit near the driver or conductor on buses and, when driving, to park in a well-lit, preferably busy area, and so on (1990: 86–8). Crime is presented as 'opportunistic' and, because of this, it is the public who have a central role to play in controlling crime, not the police. Thus Hough and Mayhew point out:

a substantial body of research indicates that it is difficult to enhance the police effect on crime … For many sorts of crimes, people themselves might take more effective preventive action, either acting individually or together with others. The police could do more to promote preventive action of this kind, while the trend to putting more officers on the beat may have the desirable effect of reducing fear of crime.

(1983: 34)

What is important is the development of situational crime prevention measures to reduce opportunities for crime. These include target hardening (for example, more locks, bolts, burglar and car alarms) and greater public surveillance (for example, through Neighbourhood Watch schemes).

Criticisms

Criticisms have been directed at both the fundamental principles on which classicism is based and the methodological and policy implications of contemporary classicist thinking.

Human nature and social order: sex and class bias in classicist thought

Various writers have documented the sex and class bias of classicist thought (Mitchell, 1987; Pateman, 1988; Naffine, 1990; Bryson, 1992; Donovan, 1997; Phillips, 1998; Okin, 1998). For whilst Enlightenment thought used the language of universal rights, these 'rights' were not extended to women or the poor. The word 'man' was not employed in a generic way: 'man' was a property-owning male. And it was this bourgeois male who was endowed with the attributes of free will and rationality; it was he who had formal equality, that is with other bourgeois men. Indeed, with respect to women, there was general agreement amongst the principal Enlightenment thinkers that women's biological make-up was such that they could not be considered rational individuals (Bryson, 1992). In the writings of Voltaire, Diderot,

Montesquieu and Rousseau, for example, we find women described as governed by their emotions and passion. Women are seen as having an important function as wives and mothers, but their biology is presented as rendering them unfit for life in the public sphere. Women, therefore, did not have the 'capacities' for citizenship in the liberal state and as such were excluded from full participation in society and deemed subject to man's authority. Thus Rousseau wrote in *Emile*:

> [a woman] cannot fulfil her purpose in life without [a man's] aid, without his goodwill, without his respect; she is dependent on our feelings, on the price we put upon her virtue, and the opinion we have of her charms and her deserts. Nature herself has decreed that women, both for herself and her children, should be at the mercy of man's judgement.
>
> (rpr. 1974: 328)

John Locke, having overthrown the old patriarchs as represented by the absolute monarchs of the *ancien régime*, still accepted that in so far as the husband is 'the abler and the stronger' (*Second Treatise of Government*, 1690: IV.22) he has natural authority over his wife and children. As Carole Pateman has pointed out, these theorists constructed 'sexual difference as a *political* difference, the difference between man's natural freedom and women's natural subjection' (1988: 5, original emphasis). It is not surprising, therefore, that Mary Astell, writing on marriage in 1700, questioned the assumptions of early classicist thought,

> If Absolute Sovereignty be not necessary in a State, how comes it to be so in a Family? or if in a Family why not in a State? since no Reason can be alleg'd for the one that will not hold more strongly for the other?
>
> For if Arbitrary Power is an evil in itself, and an improper Method of Governing Rational and Free Agents, it ought not to be Practis'd any where; Nor is it less, but rather more mischievous in Families than in Kingdoms, by how much 100000 Tyrants are worse than one. What tho' a Husband can't deprive a Wife of Life without being responsible to the Law, he may however do what is much more grievous to a generous Mind, render Life miserable, for which she has no Redress, scarce Pity which is afforded to every other Complainant.

If all Men are born free, how is it that all Women are born slaves? as they must be if the being subjected to the *inconstant, uncertain, unknown, arbitrary Will* of Men, be the *perfect Condition of Slavery?*

(rpr. 1986: 76; original emphasis)

More recently, Phillips remarked, 'denied entry by the front door, patriarchy crept in at the back' (1987: 14). It can, of course, be argued that the logical extension of the liberal/classicist project is the extension of equal rights to women and the poor. Indeed, Jaggar has commented with regards to women:

The overriding goal of liberal feminism always has been the application of liberal principles to women as well as men. Most obviously, this means that laws should not grant to women fewer rights than they allow to men.

(1983: 35)

This however leaves untouched what Young has described as the 'classicist contradiction' (1981: 264) – the contradiction between formal and substantive equality. Classicism ignores the material conditions that govern people's lives, the inequalities caused by differences in gender, class and ethnicity. Whilst these differences exist, equality between women and men cannot be assumed. For substantive inequalities make women financially dependent on men and/or the welfare state, and compound their problems in domestically violent relationships. Even if, for example, violence committed against men and women were treated equally by the law, the impact of such violence would be greater against women than men because of their economically more vulnerable situation. Women are forced by such dependence to remain in violent relationships; they are tied by both lack of finances and, very often, the needs of their children. Thus, it is the view of many feminists that the main suppositions made by male theorists in the development of liberal theory may not be adequate or appropriate when it comes to discussing women's needs and experiences (see Bryson, 1992; Donovan, 1997; Okin, 1998; Phillips, 1998).

Further, the enactment of legislation seeking to protect women within the liberal project does not necessitate its just implementation. For, as repeated studies of the service delivery of the criminal justice system have shown, the less powerful, whether they be women, ethnic minorities or the working class, have unequal access to the law and to legal protection. It is not just that substantive inequalities are ignored by laws that seek to guarantee formal equality, but that formal equality is denied because of substantive inequalities in power.

Social order: the distinction between the public and the private spheres

The division of society into public and private spheres is inherently problematic in constructing a theory of domestic violence. Women's 'natural' role is seen as that of a wife and mother, they are defined in terms of their family relationships; the private sphere is thus their domain. And it is, of course, in this private sphere that domestic violence largely occurs. As the private sphere is designated by the liberal state as the sphere of the least state interference, this has profound implications for women. First, power relations in the family have remained unchallenged; that is, the state has left power with the husband and father (O'Donovan, 1985); and second, as a consequence, women historically have had little formal legal protection against domestic violence. For example, in the past, police officers were often reluctant, or would even refuse, to intervene in an incident of domestic violence. Indeed, Roberts (1984) has commented that in Victorian England, if the police responded to a domestic violence call, they would not enter the house unless invited to do so by the man and it was left to others living in the house to throw him out – making it a public matter – which might, then, result in an arrest. Thus feminists have repeatedly suggested that the poor treatment traditionally given to women experiencing violence in the home is the result of the division of the world into public and private spheres in which the private, the home, is equated with the personal and with a policy of non-interference (Pahl, 1985; Hanmer and Maynard, 1987; Edwards, 1989; Hague and Malos, 1993; Harwin, 1998). As Susan Edwards comments, this division has also meant that 'it is no accident that a man who beats his wife on the street is more likely to be prosecuted than the man who behaves in exactly the same way in his own home' (1989: 32). Mabel Sharman Crawford, a first-wave feminist, noted: 'a labouring man at Wigan who...stood calmly by whilst a collier kicked his wife to death, said at the trial he did not interfere as it was not for him "to step in between man and wife"' (1893: 297).

Lastly, it should be noted that whilst women are not excluded from the public sphere today, they are still unable to participate fully because of inequalities in the private sphere (Pateman, 1989). Child-rearing, for example, is still largely seen as women's responsibility and a private matter. Women have never been fully incorporated into civil society as individuals and citizens, but only as members of the family. We see this reflected in many areas of the law, for example, divorce law, welfare law and immigration law (see Edwards, 1985). Men are still seen as having power over, and responsibility for, their families and can move much more freely between the public and private spheres (O'Donovan, 1985).

Definition: the problem of legal categorization

To define crime as being that which is against the law creates difficulties in so far as not all forms of domestic violence are covered by the legal categories (for example, mental cruelty). Indeed, there are many forms of anti-social behaviour which are not covered by the criminal law and are considered too trivial for the courts. Petty vandalism, graffiti and 'minor' sexual and racial harassment are examples. However, the accumulation of 'incivilities' such as these can make people's lives a misery, often more so than a single and relatively infrequent 'real' crime, such as burglary.

Until recently, with respect to domestic violence, this legal tolerance extended to very severe incidents. For, prior to a House of Lords judgment on 23 October 1991, it was regarded as impossible for a man to rape his wife because of the assumption that sexual intercourse in marriage could not be unlawful. Thus Archibold's *Criminal Law: Practice and Proceedings* states: 'it is [a] clear and well settled ancient law that a man cannot be guilty of rape upon his wife' (cited in Kennedy, 1992). What was known as the 'married man's exemption' is usually attributed to Sir Matthew Hale, an eighteenth-century legal commentator, who justified it in terms of the language of contract. Marriage was seen as a contract, formed in the same way as the original social contract, and sexual intercourse was part of the marital contract. Indeed, Pateman remarks, 'until 1884 in Britain, a wife could be jailed for refusing conjugal rights and, until 1891, husbands were allowed forcibly to imprison their wives in the matrimonial home to obtain their rights' (1988: 123). Hence, according to Hale,

> The husband cannot be guilty of a rape committed by himself upon his lawful wife, for by their mutual matrimonial consent and contract the wife hath given up herself in this kind unto her husband, which she cannot retract.
>
> (1778: 628)

Furthermore, the use of objective definitions – such as legal categories – cannot convey the subjective impact of the act and the context of the violence. What is classed as a 'common assault' will mean different things in different situations – it can, for example, be the result of a fight between two adolescent boys on a football pitch, the result of a psychiatric patient hitting a nurse or part of a long-term history of violence against a woman by her husband or boyfriend. Indeed, as Young has pointed out:

> Violence, like all forms of crime, is a social relationship. It is rarely random: it inevitably involves particular social meanings and occurs in particular hierarchies of power. Its impact, likewise is predicated on the relationship within which it occurs... the very impact of the offence depends on the relationship between victim and offender.
>
> (1988a: 174)

The underlying problem of legal categorization stems directly from the classicist contradiction: that is, an attempt to delineate social harm in terms of formal categories. For we must be aware that social harm will be proportional to the substantive degree of vulnerability of the person so afflicted. The legal notion of judging objectively similar offences as if they were equal in harm and inflicted on equal victims ignores the substantive differences, of an economic, emotional and psychological nature, between victims. I will return to this later in this chapter, but suffice to say that, of all offences, domestic violence highlights the weakness of classicism in this respect. For the use of objective legal categorization and a concentration on the criminal act, rather than on the events which lead up to the act, and the inherent male bias of the law also create problems in constructing legal defences for battered women who kill (see Edwards, 1985; O'Donovan, 1991; Kennedy, 1992; Rights of Women, 1992; Radford, 1993; Nicolson and Sanghvi, 1993; McNeill, 1996).

The denial of causes

Classicism does not relate the causes of crime to substantive problems within society. Crime is merely seen as willed where opportunities occur and deterrence is low. Domestic violence is seen as an infrequent crime because of the supposed unity of interest between husband and wife; thus there is no discussion of the wider causes of such violence which lie in patriarchy and gender inequality. This leads to a paradox, for it is, of course, in the home, relatively immune from interference because of the classicist notion of its sanctity, that opportunities for violence regularly occur and deterrence is low. Indeed, Barbara Laslett (1973) has commented that in the twentieth century the family became less susceptible to informal social controls over behaviour. She sees the family as more private today due to changes in household composition (for example, there has been a decrease in the number of the children born, it is less likely to comprise of extended family members (grandparents), lodgers, apprentices, servants, and so on) and developments in architectural styles and practices. Thus behaviour is less visible and less prone to detection that it was in the past.

Problems of method: the minimization of the extent and distribution of domestic violence

The traditional classicist method of using official statistics to determine the extent and distribution of crime is not a useful tool, particularly in the case of domestic violence. Generally speaking, as noted previously, official police figures are beset with problems of accuracy caused by the hidden figure of crime. With respect to domestic violence, it is known from the work of others (Dobash and Dobash, 1979; Walker, 1979; Horley, 1988) that domestic violence is a crime that is rarely reported to the police. There is a patterning here: in general, crimes against property are reported less than those involving violence, and crimes committed by strangers more than those against family members.

Certainly in the past, domestic violence was frequently under-recorded by the police. For example, Susan Edwards' 1986 study conducted in Islington and Hounslow, found that only about 12 per cent of all reported cases of domestic violence were made the subject of a crime report by the police and, of these, more than 80 per cent were subsequently 'no-crimed', that is, not proceeded with or officially recorded as a crime.

The conventional victimization survey method employed by the new administrative criminologists, whilst an improvement on the use of official statistics, is also problematic. Women who are experiencing or have experienced domestic violence in the past are likely to be too fearful or embarrassed to talk about their experiences. Further, it is possible that the perpetrator may be near to the interview situation, which will obviously inhibit response. Interviewers may also make mistakes, misread questions, lead or mislead respondents, fail to probe when appropriate, lose questionnaires or falsify responses (Walklate, 1989). In the case of the international victimization surveys, the use of telephone interviews accentuate the above problems, with the exception of interviewer falsification. It is, for example, more difficult to judge the situation in which the interview is being conducted (for example, the presence of another person or an inconvenient time) or the response of the interviewee to questioning and to probe or modify questions accordingly. Questions are also more likely to be misinterpreted or misunderstood, and interviewees have been known to be either over-reserved or over-compliant, the latter giving rise to what is known as the 'easy' answer, particularly in yes/no questions (see Barnett, 1991).

More recently, the introduction of Computer-Assisted Self-Interviewing (CASI) seeks to create a situation of greater anonymity. On the face of it, the method is successful in that it produces much higher figures. In the 1996 British Crime Survey the rate of domestic violence against women indicated by the CASI was over three times that using conventional interviewing techniques (Mirrlees-Black, 1999: 15). In Chapter 6 I discuss whether this figure, although manifestly higher, is high enough, but suffice to say at this point that the two major problems with CASI are these:

1. The use of a computer is a deterrent to those less technically minded, particularly older people.
2. The presence of others in the room during completion is bound to create an atmosphere where anonymity is perceived to be threatened. Interviewers were obviously present in 100 per cent of the cases but, even more relevantly, someone else was present in the room in a third of cases, 40 per cent in the case of women aged 16 to 29 years (Mirrlees-Black, 1999: 97) – indeed in the case of 14 per cent of women the spouse or partner was present. Further, in 12 per cent of cases the interviewer assisted with the inputting of data.

The method used in the research undertaken for this book was to employ a questionnaire, which was to be completed privately by the respondent in their own time (see Chapter 5). My feeling is that this guarantees a much higher level of anonymity and security; it is, however, a much more costly procedure and the use of CASI has obvious benefits of economy which are attractive to government departments.

The minimization of the impact of crime and domestic violence

The methods used by classicists have led to an underestimation of the extent and impact of crime. Thus they argue that most crime is petty, and that the public, especially women and the elderly, have an exaggerated perception of their risk rate. However, left realists and feminists, by means of local surveys, have shown with regards to crime in public space that fear of crime is based on a realistic assessment of risk (for example, Hanmer and Saunders, 1984; Hall, 1985; Stanko, 1985; Jones *et al.*, 1986; Crawford *et al.*, 1990; Hester *et al.*, 1996). Further, left realists have pointed out that there is no such thing as an equal victim, people who are victims of crimes tend to experience other social problems and as such this has a compounding effect. Thus a major problem with classicism is that it abstracts crime rates from the predicaments which people face. With respect to women, Young has argued that official statistics and the British Crime Surveys conceal crime risk rates and that the impact of crime must be seen as 'a function of *risk, compounding, vulnerability* and *relationship'* (original emphasis); he expands this in the following way:

Concealment of risk: the invisible victim

Domestic violence and sexual crimes are less likely to enter the statistics than property crimes, which leads to the systematic underestimation of violence against women...The actual impact of known crime on women is underplayed by designating much of their victimisation as trivial.

Compounding

Women do not only suffer crime *per se* but also an undertow of incivilities and harassment which men do not experience. The impact of crime on women cannot be assessed without taking into account these incivilities.

Vulnerability

The relatively powerless situation of women – economically, socially and physically – makes them more unequal victims than men.

Relationships

Crime is a relationship. And as fifteen years of feminist research has indicated, crime against women is about patriarchy. Crime in the home occurs within a relationship of economic dependency: the woman – particularly if she has children – cannot walk away. It occurs within an emotional bond, which gives it all the more hurtful poignancy. Crime and incivilities against women in the streets reflect the overbearing nature of particular values. What a dramatic indictment it is, in the inner cities of Europe, men can quite happily walk the streets at night, yet a huge section of women are curfewed because of fear of crime.

It is easy to see then how crime has a greater impact on women as well as, at the same time, women are more sensitive to violence. For in the last analysis many women react to the adversity of the world by creating a female culture which is opposed to violence, whilst men frequently react to adversity by creating a culture of *machismo* which is insensitive to violence and, indeed, in some groups glorifies it.

(Young, 1988a: 175)

Policy

The minimization of the extent of domestic violence, the misunderstanding of its impact combined with the denial of causes has led classicism to focus upon stranger violence. There is, therefore, a tendency to play down domestic violence in the crime prevention literature. As Jill Radford and Elizabeth Stanko put it:

> Crime prevention advice stems primarily from a perspective that rests prevention on situational deterrence. The 'locks and bolts' solution to crime suggests that adequate security, vigilance, and common sense reduce the likelihood of experiencing crime.
>
> Moving the responsibility for crime prevention to the individual through adequate security and reasonable precaution, means that approaches to preventing crime necessarily focus on the danger of the unpredictable stranger who awaits opportunities for criminal enterprise. (This approach leads up to woman-blaming when protection fails. Not having taken self-defence classes is deemed provocation or negligence inviting attack.) Take for example the £11 million Home Office crime prevention campaign. Now in its fourth edition, *Practical Ways to Crack Crime* includes a special section advising women about safety. Although there is a paragraph about domestic violence, it appears at the end of a four-page litany addressing women's precautions at home, while on the street, and driving. (The fact that the heading for the section, *Special Advice for Women*, is subsumed under the heading *Your Family* does deserve more than a passing mention.) Women are advised to take care, to protect themselves outside the home and inside the home from outside intrusion.
>
> If one assumes that it is women's safety that is important, then the Home Office campaign on crime prevention misses the mark by a wide margin.
>
> (1991: 198)

Finally, such policy tends to be patronizing. As Elizabeth Stanko indicates:

> the crime prevention advice is devoted to teaching adult women how to walk in the street, sit on public transport, park their cars and lock their doors. What is ... more extraordinary about the crime prevention literature, is that it is seemingly unaware of all empirical evidence which shows women take more precautions for their safety than do men.
>
> (1992: 3)

2
Positivism: Scientific Explanations of Violence

Positivism, as a theory of crime, developed in the nineteenth century, influenced by the general enthusiasm for science that dominated the time. It challenged the traditional classicist notions to such an extent that it was seen by both positivists and social commentators as an intellectual revolution. Indeed the principles of positivism are posed as the opposite of classicism: free will is replaced by determinism, equality gives way to natural differences between individuals, and the knowledge of the expert becomes paramount. Scientific positivism thus turns the armchair musings of classicism, so to speak, on its head. Or at least that is how early pioneering positivists such as Enrico Ferri described their mission. Yet to an extent such a characterization, although widely accepted, is an exaggeration for, as I noted in the last chapter, classicism did have a notion of determinacy, and the widespread image of classicism as a theory of unhampered volition is probably a creation of positivists. Indeed, as Piers Beirne acidly puts it, 'perhaps classical criminology is no more than the retrospective invention of distorted scholarly self-aggrandizement' (1993: 22–8). Yet classicism in theory, and certainly in legal practice, has held that in *most* circumstances a person can morally assess a situation and make free and rational choices. Furthermore, positivism certainly holds the notion of total determinacy for all else would preclude science, so the notion of 'inversion' and 'revolution' is only slightly overdrawn. Positivism's focus is on the criminal and the causes of crime rather than the criminal act. It presents crime as something that individuals are driven to by forces that are largely beyond their control and exhorts the use of the 'scientific method' to identify and investigate those factors that differentiate between criminals and non-criminals. It is for this reason that positivism is closely linked with empiricism, the collection of 'hard' data (see Jupp, 1989) and the search for causes.

Theorists have variously classified these determining factors as biological, psychological or social – or simply multi-factorial, combining elements of each. Historically, there are two positivistic traditions within criminology: a sociological perspective, which dates from the work of Adolphe Quetelet and A.M. Guerry in the early to mid-nineteenth century, and one which is individualistic – although social factors are inevitably also brought in to its analysis. The most frequently cited examples of early individualistic positivistic thought are those of the Italian school of criminology, as presented mainly in the writings of Cesare Lombroso, Enrico Ferri and Raffaele Garofalo, which emerged in the late nineteenth century.

In this chapter the focus will be mainly on the development of individualistic positivism. I shall first illustrate the basic tenets of this form of positivism and proceed to show how such an approach is evidenced in the study of domestic violence. The problems inherent in the positivist method are then subject to a critique based on the grid of questions developed in the Introduction. Finally, I turn to two contemporary accounts of domestic violence, those of evolutionary theory, and the work of Murray Straus and his colleagues in the United States, known as the 'family violence' approach. Both of these attempt to circumvent the limits of individualistic positivism by introducing, to a much greater extent, social factors into their analysis whilst confronting the fact that domestic violence is much more widespread than traditional positivism would countenance.

Positivist theories of crime in general

The Italian school of criminology

Vold and Bernard have described Cesare Lombroso (1835–1909) and his followers Enrico Ferri (1856–1929) and Raffaele Garofalo (1852–1934) as all 'self-conscious positivist[s], rejecting the doctrine of free will and supporting the position that crime can be understood only where it is studied by scientific methods' (1986: 43).

Lombroso

Lombroso has been frequently portrayed as the founding father of biological positivism. Thus Ferri credited him with 'demonstrating...that we must first understand the criminal who offends, before we can study and understand his crime' (1912: 15). Despite being referred to in this way, or more grandly as 'the father of modern criminology' (Wolfgang, 1960: 168), various commentators (Quinney and Wildeman, 1977; Savitz *et al.*, 1977; Vold and Bernard, 1986; Lilly *et al.*, 1989) have been at pains to point out that Lombroso was not the first to employ biological explanations of criminal behaviour. Savitz *et al.*, for example, cite the studies of Franz Joseph Gall (1758–1828) and the phrenological school, and Lilly *et al.* (1989), the even earlier work of John Caspar Lavater (1741–81). Further, in refutation of the description of Lombroso as 'the father of modern criminology', biological positivism was, as noted previously, preceded by sociological positivism, although as Savitz *et al.* remark:

> Criminology textbooks and volumes purportedly surveying the historical development of criminological theory and research usually blithely leap from the armchair speculations of the 'classical' theorists to the research of Lombroso and his school. The early 19th century ... environment research of A.M. Guerry, Quetelet and others seem never to have existed.
>
> (1977: 41–2)

With respect to this, as we shall see, it is of interest that Lombroso himself was well aware of nineteenth-century environmental research, and both Ferri and Garofalo refer to Quetelet in their major works. It is the historians of criminology not the criminologists of the time who suffer from such amnesia.

In *The Criminal Man*, first published in 1876, Lombroso argued that male offenders were biological throwbacks to an earlier evolutionary stage of development; they were seen as more primitive and less highly evolved than non-criminals. In the introduction to his daughter, Gina Lombroso Ferrero's summary of *The Criminal Man*, Lombroso discusses performing a postmortem examination of an Italian criminal, the famous brigand Vilella, during which he realized the criminal was one who 'reproduces in his person the ferocious instincts of primitive humanity and the inferior animals' (1911: xv). This clearly derives from Darwin's *Descent of Man*:

> injurious characters ... tend to reappear through reversion, such as blackness in sheep; and with mankind some of the worst dispositions, which occasionally without any assignable cause make their appearance in families, may perhaps be reversions to a savage state, from which we are not removed by very many generations. This

view seems indeed recognized in the common expression that such men are the black sheep of the family.

(1874: 134)

Individuals were, therefore, 'born criminals'; Lombroso used the word 'atavistic' to characterize them. By comparing criminals with non-criminals he claimed to have identified a number of physical anomalies which indicated a criminal propensity. For example,

The born criminal shows in a proportion reaching 33% numerous specific characteristics that are almost always atavistic. Those who have followed us thus far have seen that many of the characteristics presented by savage races are very often found among born criminals. Such, for example, are: the slight development of the pillar system; low cranial capacity; retreating forehead; highly developed frontal sinuses; great frequency of Wormian bones; early closing of the cranial sutures; the simplicity of the sutures; the thickness of the bones of the skull; enormous development of the maxillaries and the zygomata; prognathism; obliquity of the orbits; greater pigmentation of the skin; tufted and crispy hair; and large ears.

(1918: 365)

In addition to such physical characteristics, many of which have obvious racist connotations, Lombroso noted in the born criminal other factors such as: a lack of moral sense (for example, vanity, cruelty, idleness), various sensory and functional peculiarities (for example, greater sensibility to pain and touch, more ambidexterity, greater strength in the left limbs), the use of criminal slang and a proclivity for tattooing. Lombroso did, however, modify his theory following criticism and more extensive investigation. He later conceded that not all criminals were born criminals and classified them into various types: 1) born criminals, 2) insane criminals, 3) criminaloids (occasional criminals), and 4) criminals of passion who commit acts that arise out of 'anger, platonic or filial love, offended honour'. He also gave more attention to factors in the physical and social environment of the male offender. Indeed Lilly *et al.* note that 'the modern search for multi-factorial explanations of crime is usually attributed to Cesare Lombroso' (1989: 27). Thus, as early as the second edition of *The Criminal Man* (1878), he makes use of London data from Mayhew's *Criminal Life* (1860) and Brace's *Dangerous Classes of New York* (1874) and emphasizes several environmental conditions that cause or have an effect on criminality, including that of poverty; the relationship between prices of wheat, rye, grain, potatoes and other staple foods, and minor violations, arson, crimes against property and crimes against the person; the influence of alcohol; the effects of criminal association in prisons that are not built on the cellular system, and so on (See Gina Lombroso Ferrero's summary, 1911). Moreover, Lombroso's last book *Crime: Its Causes and Remedies* (1899) opens with the words:

> Every crime has its origin in a multiplicity of causes, often inter-wined and confused ... This multiplicity is generally the rule with human phenomena, to which one can almost never assign a single cause unrelated to others ...

and proceeds to discuss many factors related to crime causation, the majority of which are environmental. Nevertheless, Lombroso remained convinced that the major determining factors are biological and thus he continued to view the criminal as a degenerate, inferior being.

Lombroso's theory attracted much controversy and was widely criticized by the leading social scientists of the day: Gabriel Tarde, Henri Joly, Georg von Mayr and W.A. Bonger. Herbert Bloch and Gilbert Geis commented: 'the best criticism of Lombroso remains that of the French anthropologist Paul Topinard (1830–1911) ... who, when shown a collection of Lombroso's pictures of asymmetric and stigmatic criminals, remarked wryly that the pictures looked no different than those of his own friends' (1970: 89). However, despite being widely criticized and ridiculed at the time, Rose *et al.* have noted how such presentations of the criminal man found their way into mass culture. They cite the example of Agatha Christie:

> In an early book (*The Secret Adversary*, 1922) we find her clean-cut young upper-class English hero secretly observing the arrival of a Communist trade unionist at a rendezvous: 'The man who came up the staircase with a soft-footed tread was quite unknown to Tommy. He was obviously of the very dregs of society. The low beetling brows, and the criminal jaw, the bestiality of the whole countenance were new to the young man, though he was a type that Scotland Yard would have recognised at a glance.' Lombroso would have recognised him too.
>
> (1990: 54)

Today his theories of the criminal man are variously dismissed as 'bizarre' (Jupp, 1989: 2), 'fanciful' (Heidensohn, 1985: 114), 'simple

and naive' (Lilly *et al.*, 1989: 29) and 'an amusing and slightly unfortunate episode in the development of criminology' (Smart, 1976: 32),
although a biological positivist stance has persisted in criminology (see
Eysenck, 1964; Rushton, 1995). Indeed, 'the slightly unfortunate
episode' has re-emerged as a considerable and threatening school of
thought in the present day. There has been a resurgence of the belief
that the criminal is wicked by nature (see, for example, Wilson and
Herrnstein, 1985) and Darwinian ideas with respect to domestic violence involving resort to evolutionary theory (see Burgess and Draper,
1989; Wilson, 1989; Wilson and Daly, 1992; Daly and Wilson, 1994;
Wilson and Daly, 1998; Dutton, 1995).

Women offenders

Lombroso's work, unlike much traditional criminology (see commentaries by Heidensohn, 1985; and Morris, 1987), was not confined to
the male offender.[1] In 1893 he published *The Female Offender*, written
in collaboration with his son-in-law, Guglielmo Ferrero. In this work,
women criminals were investigated in a similar way to men, that is
the emphasis was placed on uncovering the various physiological
and pathological anomalies associated with criminality. However, whilst
certain physical characteristics were apparent (for example, Lombroso
and Ferrero noted, 'certain wrinkles, such as the fronto-vertical, the
wrinkles on the cheek bones, crow's feet and labial wrinkles are more
frequent and deeply marked in criminal women of mature age' (1895:
72, English trans.), they found much less variability amongst women.
All women (criminal and non-criminal) were described in terms
that, although derogatory, reflect the attitudes of the time towards
respectable and 'other' women. Thus women were generally presented
as less developed than men, for example, more like children and less
sensitive to pain. As such, all were seen as having the potential to commit crime, 'the ... semi-criminal present in the normal woman' (*ibid.*:
151). In the 'normal' woman these deficiencies were usually kept in
check by piety and maternity. Women, therefore, had low offending
rates and Lombroso and Ferrero found them more likely to be occasional rather than born criminals ('the natural form of retrogression in
women being prostitution and not crime. The primitive woman was
impure rather than criminal' (1895: 152)). But when a woman was a
born criminal – for example, born criminals were found to be more frequent amongst prostitutes – she was presented as much worse than a
man: 'they are often much more ferocious ... a monster' (1895: 150, 152).

The following quotation summarizes Lombroso and Ferrero's position on women and the woman offender:

> We have seen that the normal woman is naturally less sensitive to pain than a man, and compassion is the offspring of sensitiveness. If one be wanting, so will the other be.
>
> We also saw that women have many traits in common with children; that their moral sense is deficient; that they are revengeful, jealous, inclined to vengeances of a refined cruelty.
>
> In ordinary cases these defects are neutralised by piety, maternity, want of passion, sexual coldness, by weakness and an undeveloped intelligence. But when a morbid activity of the psychical centres intensifies the bad qualities of women, and induces them to seek relief in evil deeds; when piety and maternal sentiments are wanting, and in their place are strong passions and intensely erotic tendencies, much muscular strength and a superior intelligence for the conception and execution of evil, it is clear that the innocuous semi-criminal present in the normal woman must be transformed into a born criminal more terrible than any man.
>
> (*ibid.*: 150–1)

Frances Heidensohn has noted the duality of such an analysis: 'women are both wicked and saintly, whores and mothers' (1985: 112). And, as Carol Smart has put it, ' "true" female criminals are biologically abnormal, because first they are rare and second they are not fully female.' This 'produces a situation in which female offenders are doubly damned for not only are they legally sanctioned for their offences, they are socially condemned for being biologically or sexually abnormal' (1976: 34). Moreover various feminist writers (for example, Smart, 1976; Heidensohn, 1985; 1994; Carlen, 1985; Morris 1987) have argued that biological positivist theories have particularly dominated the study and treatment of women offenders, more so than those of men. As Smart commented: 'variations on the belief in biological determinism, both of crime and the nature of women, on sexist beliefs in the inferiority of women and an implicit support of double-standards of morality, along with the failure to take account of the socio-economic, political and legal context in which "crime" occurs, all appear in later works on female criminality' (1976:36).[2] Indeed, Pat Carlen has demonstrated that they have had a detrimental effect on the treatment of female offenders by the criminal justice system: 'in the nutshell of

Lombroso and Ferrero's theory of 1895...are all the elements of a penology for women which persists in misogynous themes' (1985: 3). As we shall see, this is of relevance to the present study of domestic violence, not just in terms of the treatment of battered women who kill (see Nicolson and Sanghvi, 1993; Radford, 1993; McNeill, 1996), but more generally with respect to the presentation of women victims.

Contemporary positivism

In recent years, as previously noted, there has been a resurgence of positivist ideas that focus on individual and biological factors. The most well-known example of this is James Q. Wilson and Richard J. Herrnstein's *Crime and Human Nature* (1985). Wilson was an adviser to the Reagan and Bush administrations and as such was a particularly influential figure in the 1980s.[3] In *Crime and Human Nature* Wilson and Herrnstein state: 'our intention is to offer as comprehensive an explanation as we can manage of why some individuals are more likely than others to commit crime' (1985: 20). Although their approach is broadly multi-causal, involving, for example, family rearing and cultural factors, they lay great stress on what they term 'constitutional factors', which they suggest predispose individuals to become criminals. The biological positivist stance of their approach is self-evident:

> The existence of biological predispositions means that circumstances that activate behaviour in one person will not do so in another, that social forces cannot deter criminal behaviour in 100 per cent of the population, and that the distribution of crime within and across societies may, to some extent, reflect underlying distribution of constitutional factors. Crime cannot be understood without taking into account predispositions and their biological roots.
>
> (*ibid.*: 103)

It is, therefore, not surprising that Young has described their work as 'the new scientific revolution of the "born again" Lombrosians' (1994: 70) and Lilly *et al.* comment that 'Wilson and Herrnstein's perspective harkens back to the theories of Lombroso, Hooton, Sheldon and the Gluecks' (1989: 196). Indeed, in *Crime and Human Nature* they lend support to the notion that criminals can be differentiated from non-criminals by body type:

> Wherever it has been examined, criminals on average differ in physique from the population at large. They tend to be more mesomorphic (muscular) and less ectomorphic (linear), with the third

component (endomorphy) not clearly deviating from normal. Where it has been assessed, the 'masculine' configuration called andromorphy also characterizes the average criminal.

(1985: 89)

They reproduce William Sheldon's 1949 photographs of body types which distinguish the criminal from the non-criminal and cite evidence from twin and adoptive studies to support their belief that there is a genetic basis to crime: 'the criminality of the biological parents is…more important than that of the adoptive parents, suggesting a genetic transmission of some factor or factors associated with crime' (*ibid.*: 96). As regards exactly how constitutional factors affect criminality, Wilson and Herrnstein suggest they affect the ability to consider future and immediate rewards and punishment. Thus, young men who are aggressive, impulsive and of low intelligence are more at risk than those who have developed 'conscience', by which they mean an 'internalized constraint against certain actions, the violation of which causes feelings of anxiety' (*ibid.*: 217). Conscience is seen to indicate a higher level of cognitive and intellectual development. The family is seen as able to 'moderate and magnify any natural predispositions' (*ibid.*: 217) through early conditioning. Thus we also have in tandem the 'bad families produce bad children' argument. Lilly *et al.* have described Wilson and Herrnstein's work as 'representative of a growing trend to root crime in human nature' and refer to various studies to support this (1989: 199). They present it as a product of the ethos of individualism which has been prevalent in the United States:

> 'Failure' – whether by being poor, or perhaps by being criminal – is seen either as a matter of choosing a profligate lifestyle or as a product of defects in the individual's character or endowment. The danger of such thinking is not only that it erroneously overlooks the social sources of human behaviour but also that it eases social conscience: Because individuals are to blame for their actions, no need exists to question the justice of the prevailing social arrangements or to support policies that call on citizens to share their advantages with the less fortunate.
>
> (*ibid.*: 194–5)

Positivist theories of domestic violence

The first theories of domestic violence to emerge in the late 1960s and 1970s were presented by clinicians, psychiatrists and psychologists.

As Mildred Pagelow has commented, this is hardly surprising, 'since people in related fields of medicine were most likely to come in close contact with victims and their abusers sooner and with easier accessibility than any others in the social and behavioral sciences' (1984: 112). Positivist approaches to domestic violence to a large extent mirror those of crime in general. Thus, this early work individualized the problem: it focused on the pathological and deviant characteristics of the male perpetrator and frequently also of the woman victim. Those involved in violent relationships are presented as certain 'types' who are different from 'normal' members of society. Their behaviour is presented as being caused by factors which reside within them, although, as previously mentioned, certain social factors were inevitably also seen as relevant. The implication of these theories, however, is that *not* anyone will become a batterer or be battered and those who do are a minority.

The male offender

The male offender is variously classified in this literature, as in the psychological positivist approach to crime in general, as 'mentally ill', 'psychopathic', 'sociopathic', 'neurotic', 'disturbed', 'sick' with an 'inadequate personality' and with a history of drug or alcohol misuse, or other intra-individual abnormalities (see Freeman, 1979; Gelles and Cornell, 1985; Pagelow, 1985; Smith, 1989; Dekeseredy and Schwartz, 1996). As various commentators have remarked, such descriptions were commonly used for the myriad forms of family violence: 'all types of family violence, beginning with child abuse in the 1960s, were initially viewed as rare occurrences engaged in by psychopathological individuals, the most depraved persons who suffered from some sort of "mental illness"' (Pagelow, 1985: 111). Or, as David Finkelhor has put it:

> they were analyzed as extremely pathological behaviours. Incest offenders were seen as backward, degenerates and feebleminded freaks. Child beaters were seen as depraved. Wife beaters were seen as alcoholic rogues and psychopaths and were considered to come from only extremely lower class and disorganized families.
>
> (1981: 12)

Thus Faulk in his study of 23 men remanded in custody for charges of serious assault on their wives or co-habitees, found:

> At the time of the offence, 16 were found to have a psychiatric disorder ... When compared with the age of the subjects it was found

that 7 of the 8 over 40 years of age had serious psychiatric illness. Four had depression which was diagnosed by a marked lowering of mood, loss of hope, and suicidal feelings. One had dementia as shown by a deterioration in intellectual activity. Three suffered from delusional jealousy, one associated with depression and the other with a paranoid personality. Of the 15 below 40 years of age, 7 had a psychiatric disturbance. Of these, 2 had a marked disturbance of personality, 2 had a severe anxiety state, and 1 a post head injury syndrome. Only 2 had the more severe forms of mental illness, i.e., 1 was depressed and the other suffered from a paranoid illness.

(1974: 180).

Indeed, Erin Pizzey, one of the founders of Chiswick Women's Refuge in the early 1970s, wrote: 'no one likes the word psychopath, but that is exactly what he is – aggressive, dangerous, plausible and deeply immature' (Evidence to House of Commons Select Committee on Violence in Marriage, quoted in Freeman, 1979: 137). Likewise, Gayford (1975) showed the husband to be pathologically jealous, badly brought up, spoiled and indulged as a child. Gambling and drinking were also cited as major contributory factors. He commented: 'a picture emerges of men with low frustration tolerance, who often completely lose control under the influence of alcohol' (*ibid.*: 196). There is frequent reference to the influence of biophysical factors such as alcohol (Snell *et al.*, 1964; Dewsbury, 1975; Fojtik, 1977; Roy, 1977; Rounsaville, 1978; Labell, 1979; Appleton, 1980; Stewart and deBlois, 1981) and more recently drugs, particularly 'crack' cocaine (Gelles and Cornell, 1985). Contemporary psychological positivists have linked personality defects with the more extreme forms of violence. For example, O'Leary has commented:

it is clear that as the level of physical aggression increases, the greater the likelihood that some personality style, trait or disorder will be associated with physical aggression ... In samples of men who engage in severe acts of physical aggression and coercive factors against a partner, the likelihood of finding that an individual has a significantly elevated score on a scale that assesses personality disorder is very high.

(1993: 25)

Furthermore, the transmission of violence from one generation to the next has proved a popular explanation within this framework: witnessing or being subjected to violence as a child is said to result in a violent individual (Roy, 1977; Flynn, 1977; Gayford 1978; Fitch and Papantonio,

1983). Here, the 'sick' individual is seen as the product of the 'sick' family.

The woman victim

This approach has additionally looked for predisposing factors in the woman victim. Thus she is presented as abnormal and variously described as 'masochistic', 'paranoid', 'depressed', 'neurotic', 'mentally ill', 'sexually inadequate'. Frequently, and somewhat contradictorily, the woman is portrayed as she is in positivistic accounts of women offenders (Lombroso and Ferrero, 1895) – that is, as once again deviating from the conventional gender role expectations, in so far as she is 'aggressive', 'masculine' and 'over-sexual'. As such she is regarded as having caused her own victimisation. Indeed, it should be noted that victim precipitation theories were commonly used at this time to explain all forms of violence against women (see, for example, Amir, 1971, with respect to rape). A particularly deplorable example of this in terms of domestic violence is found in the work of John Gayford (1975, 1976, 1978, 1979) who interviewed 100 women at the Chiswick refuge. In his 1976 article 'Ten Types of Battered Wives' he categorized victims into misogynistic stereotypes such as 'Downtrodden Dorothy', 'Tortured Tina', 'Fanny the Flirt', 'Go Go Gloria' and 'Neurotic Nora'. As Pagelow points out, this is 'hardly the kind of writing expected in scientific journals' (1985: 115), although a similar approach is to be found in the literature describing the wives of alcoholics (Lewis, 1954; Snell *et al.*, 1964). In a later piece Gayford comments: 'there are many ways in which women can be provocative and so cause friction in a marital relationship' (1979: 501) and cites factors such as the wife's inadequacy, an over-controlling nature and sexual provocativeness. He describes the 'provocative wife' in the following way:

> This type of woman has always enjoyed the company of the opposite sex, even in childhood. Not only does she know how to seek attention but also often enjoys the game of offsetting one man against another. She is generally vivacious and energetic, with many of the qualities of the stimulus seeker who is constantly looking for excitement … Both she and her husband tend to have extramarital sexual relationships, but nevertheless they often have an exciting sexual relationship within the marriage in spite of the violence.
>
> (*ibid.*: 501)

Perhaps more controversially, in view of her work at Chiswick, Erin Pizzey (writing with Jeff Shapiro, 1981; 1982) advanced the hypothesis that some women are biochemically addicted to violence – they need to be hurt – and when one violent relationship ends they find another violent partner. This argument, as Smith has remarked, whilst outraging many of Pizzey's early supporters, 'was sympathetically received by many psychiatrists and therapists' (1989: 24). Neither earlier research (Walker, 1979; Gayford, 1979) nor subsequent studies (Andrews, 1987) have substantiated Pizzey and Shapiro's position. Pizzey (1998) has recently attracted further controversy by arguing that women are as violent, indeed may be more violent, than men (see Chapter 8).

Beginning with the positivist conception of human nature and social order, let us now turn to those questions which a theory should answer and assess the adequacy of positivism as an explanation of domestic violence.

Human nature

In individual positivism human nature is determined by forces inherent in the individual which affect the degree to which the individual is socialised into the values of society. Thus violence is not seen, as in classicism, as a rational choice but one that is caused by psychological, biological or social factors, or a combination of these. As Gelles and Loseke have noted, not only is this the oldest framework on domestic violence, 'it is the commonsense perspective of everyday life in modern day ... society, where we tend to think that problematic behaviours of all sorts are created by individual pathology' (1993: 1).

Social order

For individual positivists social order is presented as consensual. Society is seen as a balanced system underwritten by consensual values into which 'normal' individuals are socialized. Successful socialization is necessary to preserve the workings of the system. It is assumed, therefore, that there is general agreement within society over what is conventional behaviour and what is deviant, with the majority of the population seen as conforming to behavioural norms and a small minority as deviant. The family is considered to be the prime site of socialization. Thus, in this account, domestic violence, as indicated by Finkelhor (1981), is a breakdown of order within the major locus of socialization and is the result of pathologies in the make-up of individual men and women. In support of the disordered family hypothesis, Gayford found in his study 23 cases in which there had been more than one marriage or co-habitation, that the women, 'tended to come from large families and to have plenty of children, even though most interviewed had not finished their reproductive life' and most of the children were disturbed (1975: 195).

Domestic violence as functional to the social order

Domestic violence may, paradoxically, be seen within individual positivism to be functional to the maintenance of social order, in so far as the social order is patriarchal in structure. It can be regarded as a response by the man to 'readjust' the maladjusted woman to the 'normal' family role. Thus Elizabeth Wilson notes:

> some theoreticians of the family explicitly state that violence or its threat are crucial to the maintenance of the structure of the family. Research has therefore tended to concentrate on the battered woman's 'deviance' from the accepted norm of submission to her husband – and that *is* how the norm is defined in the research ... The message in the end is always the same: that *wives* are to blame for their husbands' violence. If they let themselves be dominated it would not happen, nor would it happen if husbands had their rightful higher status – if women are in better jobs than their husbands, this will frustrate their menfolk and so explain and justify their violence.
>
> Other forms of 'provocation' which 'cause' male violence are said to be 'verbal attacks' (nagging), the 'liberated woman' who attacks her husband's 'male chauvinist' attitudes and verbal abuse as a response to a husband's drinking or sexual deficiencies. So-called provocation is used as a powerful tool to justify the husband's bullying and brutality. He is simply reasserting his 'rightful status'.
>
> (1983: 92; original emphasis)

Definition

In line with its emphasis on scientific procedure, positivists have always insisted that the experts must define the terms used and not directly employ 'legal' definitions. This is, of course, in sharp contrast to classicists, who insist on using legal terminology. As noted in the preceding chapter, an inherent problem for classicism is that the formal categories of the law do not correspond to the substantive social harm which offences cause. In the case of domestic violence, then, legal statutes do not reflect the social harm which women experience. For example, continual minor violence, which might generate considerable harm, would be seen as discrete acts of minor violence. Mental cruelty would not even fall within the legal rubric.

Positivists, in contrast, wish to construct definitions which reflect scientifically the 'reality' of the problem. In doing so, they are forced to assume that there is a general consensus on what constitutes domestic violence. This assumption of a consensus is necessary in that, in its pursuit of scientific objectivity and measurement, positivism needs a yardstick by which to measure the phenomenon (see Taylor *et al.*, 1973: 17). If crime is defined differently by different groups, then there can be no possibility of uncontested measurement (see Eysenck and Gudjonsson, 1989). This need for objectivity and quantifiability tends to lead to a focus on obvious and blatant physical violence where everyone would agree that domestic violence has occurred and measurement is unproblematic. Much of the early literature, therefore, focuses on that violence which is visible (that is, physical injuries) and can be described physiologically (for example, 'most injuries are found on the head and neck, with a periorbital haematoma being the commonest' [Gayford, 1979: 500]). Thus, we find mental cruelty and sexual violence are rarely referred to. Further, Gayford distinguishes between aggression and violence in his research – violence being seen as easier to define as problematic behaviour:

> Aggression is an unprovoked attack whereas violence is the exercise of physical force so as to inflict injury or damage to person or property. Thus aggression may be verbal but violence is always physical; aggression can be constructive but violence is always physically damaging.
>
> (*ibid.*: 496)

However, in reality, violence is a social construction and its definition will vary according to the values of the individual doing the defining; these will be affected by such variables as gender, age, social class and education. With respect to definition, individual positivism, therefore, does not overcome the problems of classicism. It merely substitutes the scientific expert for the lawyer and fails to reflect the various definitions used by the women involved (see Kelly, 1988a). Where it goes beyond classicism, however, is that it is not merely concerned with the *act* but with the *actors* involved.

Extent and distribution

Individual positivists view domestic violence as a minority problem engaged in by a few psychologically disturbed individuals.[4] Those involved in violent relationships are presented as certain types, they are different from other so-called normal members of society. Such a belief would suggest that the 'normal' family is immune from such transgression. The implication of this has been highlighted by Gelles and Cornell, who point out that with respect to American society:

> One way of upholding the image of the nurturant and safe family is to combine the myth that family violence is rare with the myth that only 'sick' people abuse family members. Combining the two myths allows us to believe that, when and if the violence does take place, it is the problem of 'people other than us'. An example of this is the manner in which family violence is portrayed in literature, television, or the movies. The sociologists Murray Straus and Suzanne Steinmetz reviewed American fiction, television shows, and movies for examples of family violence. First, they found violence between family members infrequently portrayed. When there was an incident of violence, it almost always involved a violent act committed by someone who was a criminal (the violent son in the movie *The Godfather*), foreign (the comic strip Andy Capp), or drunk (Rhett Butler in *Gone with the Wind*). The message conveyed by the media is that normal people do not hit family members.

(1985: 14)

Further, Gelles and Cornell suggest the reason why such individualistic explanations of domestic violence have remained popular lies

> paradoxically, in the fact that family violence is so extensive in society that we do not want to recognise it as a pattern of family relations. Somehow, we do not want to consider our own potential to abuse or even consider that some of the acts we engage in (pushing a wife, slapping a child) are violent or abusive. If we persist in believing that violence and abuse are the products of aberrations or sickness and, therefore, believe ourselves to be well, then our acts cannot be hurtful or abusive.

(*ibid.*: 112)

With respect to its distribution, individual positivists hold that, in the main, it is women who are the victims and men who are the perpetrators of domestic violence. Indeed, in the early literature, the term 'battered wife' is used more frequently than 'domestic violence' or 'family violence', so emphasizing its gendered distribution. Rarely was a man found to be the victim, and on the few occasions when a woman lashed out she was regarded as likely to be injured. As Dewsbury comments:

> Why never battered husbands? In this study we looked for but failed to find battery of any husband in the practice. There were two injured

males, one before and one after the period of observation... An alcoholic psychopath knifed her husband. The other case was from an increasingly violent homosexual relationship.

(1975: 293)

And Gayford remarks, 'women may attack men and with the aid of weapons may kill them, but it is very rare indeed for them to batter men' (1979: 496). These findings, as we shall see, are in contrast to those of the family violence researchers who controversially show men to be as much at risk of violence from their wives as women are from their husbands (Straus *et al.*, 1980; Straus and Gelles, 1988).

When domestic violence is related to class, whilst it is acknowledged that such background inadequacies, as identified by individual positivists, may occur in a minority of instances throughout the class structure, it is suggested by many that the lower working class, with their 'weak and disturbed' family structure, will give rise to an exceptional proportion of inadequates.[5]

Ethnic variation is also suggested by several researchers. For example, Gayford claimed that, in the UK, 'both immigrant men and women from the Republic of Ireland and the West Indies appeared to be over-represented' (1979: 498), and Dewsbury reported that his Birmingham-based study showed that 'there is a raised incidence of cases from cultures foreign to the Midlands' (1975: 293) and, like Gayford, referred to West Indians and Irish Catholics. Again, the implication is that domestic violence is a problem for people 'other than us', that is, not for the predominantly white, male, middle-class medical or psychiatric professionals who conducted these studies.

Causes

Crime is viewed as determined; individual positivism reduces criminal or deviant behaviour to forces which reside within the individual. It is the task of scientific experts to identify these causal factors. Such a perspective conjures up, as Elizabeth Wilson remarks,

a picture of white-coated experts who know more about the problem than the victims, in this case the women themselves. It is 'scientific', based on 'facts', free from the contamination of feelings and emotions that women bring to their testimony.

(1983: 89)

As we have seen, the causes of domestic violence are frequently presented by positivists as stemming from psychological defects that are located in both the offender and the victim. Research, however, has indicated that fewer than 10 per cent of instances of family violence are attributable to personality traits, mental illness or psychopathology (Straus, 1980). Mildred Pagelow (1984) has pointed out that, given that domestic violence is a social problem of immense proportions, it cannot be explained away as the misbehaviour of a few maladjusted individuals. Thus the main problem of this theory is that it 'seeks an exceptionalistic explanation of a universalistic problem' (Freeman, 1979: 137–8). Furthermore, concerning the personality traits of women victims, Gelles and Cornell (1985) point out that these are often diametrically opposed: some researchers have described women victims as unassertive, shy and reserved (Weitzman and Dreen, 1982), whereas others present them as aggressive, masculine, frigid and masochistic (Ball, 1977; Snell *et al.*, 1964). Feminists have constantly argued against such derogatory, and often misogynistic, stereotypes. Bograd has noted that 'not all abusive men evidence psychopathology and those who do reveal no consistent psychological patterns, while women of all sorts may become victims of their husband's abuse' (1989: 17). Feminist researchers have, moreover, shown that many of the personality traits found among samples of battered women are not pre-existing contributory factors, but are the consequences of being subjected to violence (Graham *et al.*, 1988). Elizabeth Wilson has suggested, with respect to the men:

> Far from being abnormal behaviour, the violence of men towards the women they live with should rather be seen as an extreme form of normality, an exaggeration of how society expects men to behave – as the authority figure in the family. The search for causation then becomes, in a sense, a wild-goose chase, because it is concerned with wider issues to do with the control of women by men, to do with power and inequality, and to do with how we perceive manhood.
>
> (1983: 95)

Impact

For individual positivists, the overall impact of crime, including domestic violence, on society is not seen as great, since it is viewed as a minority problem. On an individual level, however, domestic violence is generally considered to have a detrimental and long-term effect on those involved. The rehabilitation of women and children is considered to be 'a long and complicated process' (Gayford, 1979: 503). Children were found to be frequently disturbed and, as previously indicated, domestic violence is presented as having the potential of being passed on from generation to generation:

> it is a sad fact that many of their children will take marital violence into the next generation. Cases have been seen where this condition has passed through three generations.
>
> *(ibid.*: 503)

Gayford also reported that attempted suicide amongst the women was not uncommon and, again revealing his sexist attitudes, described them as having difficulties finding new partners, 'at an age of 30 and with these handicaps [disturbed children] she cannot afford to be selective about her partners' (1975: 197).

Methods

Individual positivism stresses the importance of scientific investigation often by conducting studies designed to compare criminals with non-criminals. Overall there is an emphasis within positivism on empiricism and the collection of 'hard' facts. In letting the 'facts' speak for themselves, however, we frequently find in positivist work a lack of reflection and contextualization of research findings. Furthermore, even if we were to accept such an approach, much of the research conducted in the area of domestic violence uses small, biased samples, such as clinical samples or those drawn from women's refuges. Unlike many conventional positivist studies, comparison and control groups have seldom been used; thus the results cannot be generalized to the population as a whole. Moreover, much of the work has relied on victim reports; very few researchers have examined the offender himself (Freeman, 1979). Faulk's (1974) small-scale study of men in prison is one of the rare exceptions. Subsequent research has, therefore, not surprisingly, failed to support many of the hypotheses generated by this perspective (see Gelles and Cornell, 1985; Smith, 1989).

Policy

> Sooner or later, society will have to replace its happy-go-lucky, unreasoning ways of dealing with offenders by rational, scientific methods, firmly founded on painstaking observation and empirically based theory.
>
> (Eysenck, 1964: 204)

Individual positivists follow the logic of their own position and recommend the replacement of the jury system – an important element within classicism – with 'a team of experts…to investigate the causes propelling the individual into crime, diagnosing him and prescribing an appropriate therapeutic regime' (Taylor *et al.*, 1973: 22). If criminals are determined, then they cannot be held responsible for their actions. It therefore makes no sense to punish crime. Indeed for positivists the punitive response, as advocated by classicist theorists, is not only inappropriate, it makes things worse. Thus in a situation of domestic violence, therapy would be recommended for both the men and women involved; the emphasis is on rehabilitation. As Pizzey commented in her evidence to the House of Commons Select Committee on Violence in Marriage in 1974: 'I feel that the remedies lie in the hands of the medical profession and not in the court of law, because the men act instinctively, not rationally' (Freeman, 1979: 137).

Individual positivist arguments are, furthermore, dangerous in that by locating the causes within individuals, they imply that there is no need to question society and its social policies. Thus, in Britain, it is perhaps no accident that these theories were predominant in the late 1960s and 1970s for, as Elizabeth Wilson points out:

> After 1945 the expanding Welfare State and much new legislation represented in large part an attempt to improve the quality especially of working-class family life. It was widely believed for some years that the Welfare State and full employment had made poverty avoidable; and families who remained in poverty therefore came to be seen as poor because of their own inadequacy. They became 'problem families'. In that context wife-beating became just part of a general picture of slovenly behaviour, associated with drunkenness, and squalor of the wife's own making, and it was quite customary to portray such wives as bad mothers, bad managers, slatternly and probably nagging or vituperative wives. Increasingly, all were encouraged to see the family as the one great source of happiness and fulfilment, and social workers and the Welfare State were at all costs to prevent family breakdown.
>
> (1983: 87)

Finally, let me turn to two contemporary positivist explanations of domestic violence which freely acknowledge the widespread nature of domestic violence and introduce a more social aspect to the explanation of its occurrence.

Evolutionary theory

Darwinian evolutionary theory[6] has been used to explain domestic violence, as part of the recent interest in what has been described as socio-
biological or evolutionary psychological theory (see Daly and Wilson,
1988; Burgess and Draper, 1989; Wilson, 1989; Wilson and Daly, 1992;
Daly and Wilson, 1994; Dutton 1995; Wilson and Daly, 1998). Indeed,
it is notable that Burgess and Draper's 1989 article is the only theoretical contribution to Lloyd Ohlin and Michael Tonry's edited collection,
Family Violence. Evolutionary theory suggests that human behaviour,
like that of the rest of the animal kingdom, is the product of natural
and sexual selection. As Daly and Wilson note:

> The contribution of Darwinism ... resides in the recognition that selec-
> tion (differential reproductive success or, more precisely, differential
> success in replicating genes) has been the arbiter of adaptation, with
> the result that our most basic motives and emotions, appetites, aver-
> sions and modes of information processing are interpretable as con-
> tributors to relative reproductive success and hence genetic posterity
> (sometimes called 'fitness') in the environment in which we evolved.
>
> (1994: 255)

Evolutionary theorists, unlike the individual positivists discussed
above, acknowledge the non-random and widespread nature of domestic violence and, as such, argue that it must be viewed as having been
adaptive in past environments. Indeed, all violence is seen in this way:
'In the spirit of the classical examples of adaptions such as the verte-
brate eye, the answer [to violence] must be apparent functional
"design" ... violence has been shaped by a history of selection' (*ibid.*:
264). Men are presented as the main offenders and thus have 'evolved
the morphological, physiological and psychological means to be effective users of violence' (*ibid.*: 274). If, as has been suggested, violence
was merely a pathology, it would, from an evolutionist's perspective,
have been selected out. For as Wilson and Daly point out:

> To an evolutionist, pathologies are failures of anatomical, physiolog-
> ical and psychological mechanisms and processes, such that the
> compromised mechanisms and processes exhibit reduced effective-
> ness in achieving the adaptive functions for which they evolved.
> Pathologies may be divided into non-adaptive failures due to
> mishap or senescent decay, and failures due to subversion by biotic

agents with antagonistic interests. Violence cannot be dismissed as either sort of pathology.

(ibid.: 263)

In order to understand how domestic violence is an adaptive function, marriage is shown to be primarily a reproductive alliance, and the arguments of Trivers (1972) and Dawkins (1976) with respect to parental investment and paternal certainty are evoked. Burgess and Draper have argued that parental investment 'is central to our understanding of family violence' (1989: 72). A major threat to a man's evolutionary fitness, it is argued, is the possibility that his 'mate' will become pregnant with another man's child, an event which will prove costly in terms of parental investment should he fail to detect what has happened and accept the child as his own, for this will prevent the passing on of his genes. Only women can have the certainty of parenthood. As Barash comments:

> The one commonality shared by Alaskan Eskimos, Australian aborigines, African Bushmen and Wall Street businessmen is their biological heritage; one aspect of that heritage is that males of virtually all animal species must have less confidence in their paternity than females have in their maternity.

(1977: 300)

Males in species where parental investment is high and long-term are, therefore, seen as having been selected to be intolerant of cuckoldry. Thus, to avoid wasting parental investment on children that are not genetically related, men insist on female chastity. This is presented as setting the stage for domestic violence. As Burgess and Draper put it: 'in comparison to other pair-bonding mammals, humans seem to be "borrowing trouble" by combining sexually exclusive partnerships with all the temptations of group life' (1989: 78). Men are likely to direct threats or actual physical violence at their rivals, their wives or both. As Daly and Wilson note: 'the use of a credible threat of violence ... can ... deter a wife from pursuing courses of action that are not in the man's interests' (1994: 269). Thus violence is related to male sexual proprietariness (see Wilson and Daly, 1992) and has clearly been successful in terms of monopolizing female reproductive capacity and increasing the possibility of confidently identifying offspring. Hence Wilson and Daly argue that whereas 'the use of violence by men against wives is ubiquitous', there are only a few contexts in which it occurs: 'in response to a wife's sexual infidelity (or cues thereof), or a wife's unilateral decision to terminate the relationship (or cues thereof), as well as to "discipline" a "too independent" wife, and in response to other factors (perhaps his own infidelity or paranoia) that activate male sexual jealousy mechanisms' (1994: 269). They also suggest that this provides an explanation for why such practices as the

Veiling, chaperoning, purdah and the literal incarceration of women are common social institutions of patrilineal societies, and it is only women of reproductive age who are confined or chaperoned ... Man's inventive imagination has produced countless designs for chastity belts ... (And the occurrence of) genital mutilations designed to destroy the sexual interest of young women ...

(1992: 301–2)

Women, however, are presented as having evolved different psychologies since, 'if there is a corresponding threat to a woman's fitness, it is not that she will be analogously cuckolded, but rather that her mate will channel resources to other women and their children' (Wilson and Daly, 1992: 292). Thus men are concerned with sexual infidelity, women with the allocation of their mates' resources and attention.

Further evidence of adaptation can be seen in other forms of violence against women, particularly rape, the 'obvious context of sexual conflict' (Daly and Wilson, 1994: 269). Here, it is pointed out:

Perhaps the most costly threat to a woman's fitness throughout history was loss of the opportunity to choose who is likely to sire her offspring, thereby depriving her of the opportunity both to have her children sired by a man with desirable phenotypic qualities and to have her children benefit from the time, effort and resources of a father. Since these are substantial costs, the sexual psychology of women may be expected to manifest adapted design features reflecting the past costs and benefits of accepting or rejecting particular sexual partners. Undesired sexual encounters are resisted by women, and use of violence by men can be a very effective means of controlling the reluctant victim. The fitness costs of any single act of sexual intercourse have always been less for men than women, which suggests that the evolved sexual psychology of men is less likely to be discriminating regarding choice of partner for a single sexual opportunity than that of women. Another design feature of male sexual psychology which is relevant to the occurrence of rape is the apparent disregard of women's unwillingness as indicated by the use of coercion to achieve copulation. The ability of the male to remain sexually competent in such circumstances presumably reflects the past fitness benefits of pursuing and achieving copulation in the face of female resistance.

(ibid.: 269–70)

Wilson and Daly, in line with the majority of evolutionary theorists (see Sayers, 1982), support their argument for the functional design for violence by reference to the adaptation of other species to cuckoldry, for example, swallows and dunnocks, 'a drab little bird found lurking in hedges of English gardens', (1992: 295), and note:

> The utility of using violence to protect, defend or promote fitness in past environments can be discerned by an analysis of the complex functionality of morphology and psychology, as illustrated by stag's antlers which serve no other function than competition amongst rivals for access to females, the male scorpionfly's 'rape' clasper used solely to restrain uncooperative females and the mitigated fear of the male three-spined stickleback in defence of his young.
>
> (1994: 268)

There have been strong criticisms of the application of evolutionary theory to social behaviour (see Sayers, 1982; Rose *et al.*, 1990; Cameron 1997/8). On the most empirical level it does not explain why one of the most typical scenarios where domestic violence is enacted is when the woman is pregnant (see Bewley and Gibbs, 1997; Mezey, 1997; Chapter 6 below). How evolutionary psychology could explain such violence which endangers the genetic stock of the man is a mystery. As a theoretical explanation of domestic violence, it is just a short step away from 'blaming the victim': the implication of evolutionary theory is that if in the past women had not been unfaithful and cuckolded their husbands into accepting and rearing children that were not theirs then domestic violence would not have evolved as an adaptive function to prevent this from occurring in future generations. Moreover, the simple reductionism of evolutionary theory in general presents a very depressing picture of human nature. As Rose *et al.* point out:

> By arguing that each aspect of the human behavioral repertoire is specifically adaptive, or at least was so in the past, sociobiology sets the stage for legitimation of things as they are. We are the products

of eons of natural selection. Dare we, in our hubris, try to go against
the social arrangements that nature in its wisdom has built into us?
There is a reason why we are entrepreneurial, xenophobic, territorial.

(1990: 264)

In this context, domestic violence is an inevitable part of human
existence; as an 'evolved adaptation' there is little that can be done
about it. Men cannot help their violence! However, as Sayers (1982)
notes, people are constantly changing and constructing their own
destinies. Further, Rose *et al.* comment:

Many of the mental objects that are said by sociobiologists to be units
undergoing evolution are the abstract creations of particular cultures
and times ... Is 'violence' real or is it a construct with no one-to-one
correspondence with physical acts? What do we mean, for example,
by 'verbal violence' or a 'violent exception'? ... Sociobiologists commit the classical error of reification by taking concepts that have been
created as a way of ordering, understanding and talking about human
social experience and endowing these with a life of their own, able to
act on the world and be acted upon.

(1990: 248–9)

Sayers, in addition, points out that evolutionists, when using examples from other species to support their thesis, rely on circular reasoning:

It uses terms derived from present human society to characterize animal behaviour and then uses this characterization to justify, in biological terms, the human society from which that characterization
was derived in the first place. [Thus] Trivers and Dawkins describe
sexual behaviour among animals in terms of 'philandry', 'coyness',
and 'dishonesty'; that is, in terms derived from our own particular
human society and from the sexual double standard that obtains in
it. They then use this description of animal behaviour in order to
attempt to legitimate in biological terms the social order and its sexual double standard, from which this description was itself derived.

(1982: 58)

The 'family violence' approach: the development
of multi-factorial positivism

The 'family violence' approach is associated with Murray Straus (of the
Family Research Laboratory at the University of New Hampshire) and

his colleagues, most notably Richard Gelles and Suzanne Steinmetz. The family violence researchers are extraordinarily prolific, having published over the last two decades numerous books, articles and research reports on this subject (see, for example, Straus, 1973; Steinmetz and Straus, 1974; Straus *et al.*, 1980; Gelles, 1987; Hotaling *et al.*, 1988; Straus and Gelles, 1990; Straus, 1998). As Schwartz and DeKeseredy have noted, their work receives widespread attention in North America:

> Within much of the popular press or mainstream sociological press … it has become commonplace to cite Straus and Gelles as a primary authority. North American sociology textbooks aimed at general education courses such as Introduction to Sociology or Social Problems do not always discuss violence in the family. When they do, however, the norm is to base their discussion heavily or essentially on Straus and Gelles.
>
> (1993: 249)

Family violence researchers are, as their name implies, interested in the myriad forms of violence that occur within the family. Violence between husbands and wives – generally called 'spousal violence' or more recently 'partner violence' to cover cohabiting couples – is seen as part of a pattern of violence occurring amongst all familial members. Family violence research is an attempt to look at the whole picture of family violence. As Gelles and Cornell have commented, 'while it is important to understand the nature and causes of … wife abuse, concentrating on just one form of violence or abuse may obscure the entire picture and hinder a complete understanding of the causes and consequences of abuse' (1985: 11). To emphasize this further, they cite the following case-study, which is also suggestive of the importance given to the role of the expert within positivist thought,

> [An] example of the problems produced by narrowly focusing on just one type of abuse is illustrated by the experience of a hospital-based child abuse diagnostic team. The team was discussing the case of a 6-month-old child who had received a fractured skull. After reviewing the medical reports and results of interviews with both parents, it was concluded that a 5-year-old sibling had caused the damage by striking the infant. All in the room breathed a sigh of relief. Now, they concluded, they would not have to file a child abuse report. Just as they were about to break up, satisfied with the consensus they had arrived at, a physician commented, 'But how do

you suppose the 5-year-old learned to be violent?' Back they went to the table for a two-hour discussion about whether or not the violence of a 5-year-old was cause for a child abuse report.

This...dramatically illustrates that one form of family violence may be closely connected to other acts of violence in the home...one can only understand, explain, treat and prevent family violence by understanding the operation and function of the entire system.

(*ibid.*: 11–12)

The family, as a whole, is viewed as a violence-prone institution, and family violence is acknowledged to be widespread. Indeed Straus, Gelles and Steinmetz (1976) suggest that violence in the family is more common than love. The family, it is argued,

with the exception of the military in times of war and the police, is society's most violent institution. The likelihood of being a victim at the hands of a stranger or on the streets is measured in terms of risk per 100,000, but the risk of family violence is measured in terms of a rate per 100 individuals.

(Gelles, 1993: 35)

In terms of causation, family violence is presented as multi-factorial, each variable or factor is considered to provide only a partial explanation to the problem. However, unlike individual positivism, its emphasis is not on factors that reside within the individual – although it is acknowledged these may be relevant – but those arising from social institutions, that is, the family, and the social structure. Indeed the family violence approach is characterized by such a wide explanatory framework that its work is frequently contradictory. This, as Schwartz and DeKeseredy note, 'makes them difficult targets to attack, since they have at one time or another made themselves many of the arguments of their opponents' (1993: 250).

In Straus's work three main theoretical strands have been identified (Okun, 1986). The first involves an analysis of the various cultural and structural factors that contribute to family violence. Norms of violence in the culture, the various forms of social stress (for example, unemployment, financial insecurity and social isolation), sexism and features of the individualistic model (for example, psychopathology, alcohol use and the inter-generational transmission of violence) are all seen to have some relevance (Straus, 1976; Gelles and Straus, 1979; Straus and Hotaling, 1979). Straus *et al.* (1980) developed a profile of wife-beating from an analysis of the various factors: 20 characteristics were found to be relevant, some of which clearly imply a degree of victim-precipitation:

1. the husband is employed part-time or unemployed;
2. the family is on low income;
3. the husband is a manual worker (if employed);
4. both husband and wife are very worried about economic security;
5. the wife is dissatisfied with the family's standard of living;
6. two or more children;
7. frequent disagreements over the children occur;
8. husband and wife have grown up in families where the father hit the mother;
9. couples married less than ten years;
10. the husband and wife both under 30 years of age;
11. couples who are members of a non-White racial group;
12. above-average marital conflict;
13. very high levels of family and individual stress;
14. the wife or husband dominate family decisions;
15. the husband verbally aggressive to his wife;
16. wife verbally aggressive to her husband;
17. both get drunk frequently, but are not alcoholics;
18. couples who have lived in a neighbourhood less than two years;
19. couples who do not participate in organised religion;
20. the wife is a full-time housewife.

If none of these factors was present, there was no incidence of violence against the wife; more than 12 indicated a 60+per cent likelihood of wife-beating in the previous year (see Gelles and Cornell, 1985). The negative consequences of false labelling through the use of such a profile were later acknowledged: 'three in ten families with all the wife abuse characteristics do not have wife abuse' (*ibid.*: 108). However, in terms of its distribution within the social structure, violence remains consistently correlated in the family, violence literature with those in the younger age groups (18 to 30 years), low socio-economic status and black or Hispanic families, for it is here that social stress is perceived to be greatest (Gelles and Straus, 1988; Hampton, Gelles and Harrop, 1989; Straus and Smith, 1990; Gelles, 1993; West, 1998).

The second strand is characterised by a General Systems Theory (Straus, 1973). The family is viewed as changeable and adaptive, rather than as a stable social system. Violence in this context is perceived as a system product or output, rather than an individual pathology. This theory allows all the major factors influencing family violence, either positively or negatively, to be incorporated, as well as the contribution of interventional sources. Where 'positive feedback' processes, such as those already identified, exist there will be an upward spiral of violence, 'negative feedback' will maintain, dampen or reduce the level of violence. Negative feedback, for example, occurs when the violence is not consistent with the goals of the family members involved and the system, there is a low community tolerance for violence, the act of violence comes to public attention and the close presence of control agencies.

The third strand in Straus's (1977) work focuses on women victims. The subordinate position of women in the sexist structure of the family and society is considered to create the conditions for wife-beating. Husbands, it is argued, use violence against their wives in order to maintain their dominant positions in the household. Further, the sexist division of labour in the household, in which women are primarily responsible for child care, and the economic system, which discriminates against women in the workplace, is seen to result in women being dependent on men; thus increasing their vulnerability to violence and trapping them in violent relationships. Other factors cited include the effects of gender socialization and the male orientation of the criminal justice system. In this strand Straus's position seems to be in line with feminist thought. However, as several commentators (Okun, 1986; Bograd 1988) have pointed out, the family violence approach – unlike feminist work – views the subordinate position of women as simply *one* of many contributory factors and, at other times, Straus is drawn into direct conflict with feminists, and also his own theories, in interpreting his research as showing wife-on-husband violence to be as common as husband-on-wife (Straus *et al.*, 1980; Straus and Gelles, 1988).

In an attempt to answer the question 'how violent are American families?' Straus and his colleagues conducted two national surveys in 1975 and 1985, respectively (Straus *et al.*, 1980; Straus and Gelles, 1986; Straus and Gelles, 1988). In order to measure the violence the so-called Conflict Tactics Scale was used. This is a quantitative measure consisting of 19–21 items and scores three ways of resolving interpersonal conflict in families: reasoning, verbal aggression and physical violence. Respondents were asked to think of situations in the past year when they had had a disagreement or were angry with a family member and how often they had engaged in each of the acts included in the Conflict Tactics Scale. The theoretical basis for this scale is said to derive from conflict theorists such as Simmel, Coser and

Dahrendorf: family violence researchers see the family as a social group in conflict (Straus, 1979; Gelles, 1993). The Conflict Tactics Scale has been adopted by many researchers who have replicated their findings (see Straus and Gelles, 1988). Kersti Yllo describes the Conflict Tactics Scale as dominating the area of domestic violence 'to an extent rarely matched by other scales in other fields' (1993: 52). The 1985 Family Violence survey consisted of a sample of just over 6,000 households; the interviews were conducted by telephone and selected by 'random digit' dialling. It is these surveys that have resulted in the highly contentious finding that men are as much at risk of violence from their wives as women are from their husbands. Indeed the 1985 survey showed men to be slightly *more* likely to be the victims than women: 12.1 per cent as compared to 11.3 per cent (Straus and Gelles, 1986). On the basis of these results Steinmetz (1977–8) concluded that there was a 'battered husband syndrome' which had not previously been acknowledged. This has had serious policy implications – it has been used against battered women in court cases, cited by men's rights groups lobbying for child custody and child support, and to argue against funding for women's refuges (Pagelow, 1984; Dobash and Dobash, 1992; Brush, 1993; Currie 1998; Kurz, 1998).

Straus's work, and that of the family violence researchers generally, has been subjected to much criticism on theoretical and, particularly, methodological levels. Theoretically, it has been argued that the family violence position fails to identify the *precise* relationship between the violence and the various factors seen as contributory (Freeman, 1979; Smith, 1989). Multi-factorial research notoriously provides a list of correlated factors, but is unable to put them into a causal sequence. It frequently confuses factors which have a genuine causal relationship with those which correlate because they have the same cause or are merely coincidental. To this extent such studies should be seen as exploratory rather than explanatory (see Sutherland and Cressey, 1966). Furthermore, some of the factors are well-nigh tautological, for example, 'above-average marital conflict', 'husband or wife verbally aggressive'. And where explanatory theory is attempted all we have is a mish-mash of factors brought together into a 'system' without any prioritization of causes. Straus's General System Theory has also been regarded as too complex and given to abstraction to be of much practical value. Okun (1986) comments that it is difficult to include all the major variables affecting a system product, due to the multitude of factors involved and their myriad relationships. For reasons of comprehensibility and convenience Straus is seen as falling back on a continued partial approach.

Methodologically, as Schwartz and DeKeseredy have put it, with the proclamation of the 'battered husband syndrome', Steinmetz 'was immediately attacked for having invented instead the "battered data syndrome" (1993: 250). The conflict between the family violence researchers and feminists over this finding has been well documented (see, for example, Kelly, 1988a; Saunders, 1988; DeKeseredy and Hinch, 1991; Dobash *et al.*, 1992; Yllo, 1993; Kurz, 1993; 1998; Currie, 1998). The Conflict Tactics Scale has been criticized for not distinguishing between offensive and defensive acts, as research has shown that when women use violence it is largely in self-defence; between the different forms of violence; the intensity of the violence; and the nature and extent of the injuries inflicted (Okun, 1986; Kelly, 1988a; Saunders, 1988; DeKeseredy and Hinch, 1991; Dobash *et al.*, 1992; Walklate, 1992a and 1992b; Kurz, 1993; Yllo, 1993; Currie, 1998). Further, as Yllo (1993) points out, it is not explained why violence is conceptualized as a conflict tactic. Moreover, the use of self-report studies has long been regarded as a problematic method in social science research (Currie, 1985; Jupp, 1989). The results may well be due to the selective reporting of respondents, rather than being a true indication of what is really going on. In particular, Straus *et al.* do not take account of self-reporting differences between men and women; it has been suggested that men are more likely to under-report their violent acts than women (Kurz, 1993). Their results are clearly in opposition to feminist analyses, what is known from the 'real-world experiences of police, judges who issue restraining orders, emergency rooms and shelters' (Yllo, 1993: 52) and 'men's virtual monopoly on the use of violence in other social contexts' (Dobash *et al.*, 1992: 72). It is for this reason that the present study compares women's and men's experiences of violence from their partners in order to test the sexual symmetry hypothesis of the family violence researchers (see Chapter 8).

Finally, as a result of the attention given to the arguments of Straus, Gelles and Steinmetz, many feminists have expressed disquiet that this theoretical approach and its research has resulted in policy-makers adopting terms such as 'family violence'or 'spouse abuse', 'partner violence', 'domestic violence', which mask the gendered nature of such experiences (Kelly, 1988a; Walklate, 1992a and 1992b; Kurz, 1998).

3
Violence and the Three Feminisms

In this chapter I examine the way in which our notion of domestic violence as a problem emerged with the rise of feminism: although domestic violence has always been a problem, it was feminism that recognized it as such, pointed to its presence, conceptualized it and indicated its causes. But if domestic violence was so labelled by feminism, then feminism has been influenced markedly by the problem of male violence. I shall, therefore, start with an historical account of the construction of domestic violence as a problem, briefly describe three main strands of feminism and then turn to focus on radical feminism. I do this, however, critically, because it is radical feminism which has taken male violence as its central motif and which has made the most significant innovations in the field. Nevertheless, it should be noted that a concern about domestic violence has been present throughout the history of feminism: it was a key issue for first-wave feminists in the nineteenth century.

An historical perspective on domestic violence: women's resistance and action in first- and second-wave feminism

As noted in the Introduction, there is much documentary evidence to indicate that women have always suffered violence from their husbands or partners (see Martin, 1976; Tomes, 1978; Dobash and Dobash, 1979; Freeman, 1979; Gordon, 1988; Taves, 1989; Clarke, 1992; Doggett, 1992). On an individual level, throughout the centuries, women of all classes have developed, where possible, strategies of resistance to counter this particular form of abuse. Ann Clarke (1992), for example, shows how battered women have consistently tried to utilize the law to prosecute their husbands whether they legally had the right to do so or not:[1]

> since the early eighteenth century, women brought their husbands before magistrates and charged them with assault. By the 1780s and 90s, at least one woman a week appeared before the Middlesex Justices to prosecute her husband (or common-law spouse) for assault.
>
> (1992: 192)

Maeve Doggett, in her comprehensive and excellent book *Marriage, Wife-Beating and the Law in Victorian England*, relates the story of Caroline Norton, a nineteenth-century 'society beauty' and a writer, the granddaughter of Richard Sheridan, who suffered physical violence from her husband:

> When she left him he accused the prime minister, Lord Melbourne, of being her lover and sued him for criminal conversation. He exercised his legal rights to deny her access to her children and to deprive her of the money she earned through her writing.
>
> (1992: 87)[2]

In response, Norton documented her experiences in a number of publications and although no feminist (she spurned the 'wild and stupid theories advanced by a few women of "equal rights" and "equal intelligence"' [1854, reprinted, 1982: 165]) her presentation of domestic violence was included in an influential *Letter to the Queen on Lord Cranworth's Marriage and Divorce Bill* (1854; Doggett, 1992).

In the United States, Linda Gordon's study of social work case records in Boston for the period 1880–1960 shows how many of the 'family violence victims...did not stop strategising and agitating to make a better existence for themselves and their children' (1988: vi), despite little agency or legal assistance. These strategies included reporting the violence and seeking help from social work agencies, relatives, neighbours and friends; attempting to get the man arrested; obtaining work to support the family and relieve economic hardship; and even physically fighting back: women's violence 'was a matter of holding their own and/or hurting a hated partner they were not free to leave' (*ibid*.: 275). As Gordon puts it, 'in the process of protecting themselves battered women helped to formulate and promulgate the view that women have the right not to be beaten' (*ibid*.: 252).

However, despite women's individual efforts to counter men's violence, the construction of domestic violence as a *social problem* did not progress in a linear way. As various commentators have pointed out (Freeman, 1979; Brokowski *et al.*, 1983; Wilson, 1983), its recognition and definition as a social problem has only occurred at times when there is an active feminist movement, enabling the collective organisation against its occurrence. Thus, 'wife-beating' first emerged in this country as a concern of the women's suffrage movement in the mid-nineteenth century[3] and, as Doggett comments, for some of these first-wave feminists wife-beating was a central issue:[4]

> Chief among these were Frances Power Cobbe, Matilda Blake and Mabel Sharman Crawford. All of these women wrote articles dealing specifically with wife-abuse. In addition, there were numerous feminist writers who commented on wife-beating in the context of general surveys of the laws relating to women.
>
> (1992: 126)

John Stuart Mill also proved to be an important ally. In 'The Subjection of Women' he protested that 'the vilest malefactor has some wretched woman tied to him, against whom he can commit any atrocity except killing her, and, if tolerably cautious, can do that without much danger of the legal penalty' (1869; rpr. 1992: 151).

Frances Power Cobbe, the outstanding British campaigner for women's rights, and her colleagues highlighted the extent and severity of wife abuse. In her influential article 'Wife-Torture in England', Cobbe uses the phrase 'wife torture' to 'impress my readers with the fact that the familiar term "wife-beating" conveys about as remote a notion of the extremity of the cruelty indicated as when candid and ingenuous vivisectors talk of "scratching a newt's tail" when they refer to burning alive, or dissecting out the nerves of living dogs or torturing ninety cats in one series of experiments'[5] (1878: 72) and to indicate that without intervention, 'Wife-*beating* is the mere preliminary canter before the race ... Wife-*beating* in process of time, and in numberless cases, advances to Wife-*torture*, and the Wife-torture usually ends in Wife-maiming, Wife-blinding, or Wife-murder' (*ibid.*: 72, original emphasis). In this article Cobbe cites numerous reports of particularly horrific cases, for example:

> James Mills cut his wife's throat as she lay in bed. He was quite sober at the time. On a previous occasion he had nearly torn away her left breast.
>
> J. Coleman returned home early in the morning, and, finding his wife asleep, took up a heavy piece of wood and struck her on

the head and arm bruising her arm. On a previous occasion he fractured her ribs.

James Lawrence, who had been frequently bound over to keep the peace and who had been supported by his wife's industry for years, struck her on the face with a poker, leaving traces of the most dreadful kind when she appeared in court.

Fredrick Knight jumped on the face of his wife (who had only been confined a month) with a pair of boots studded with hobnails.

(*ibid.*: 74)

Further, Cobbe pointed out many cases went unreported: 'there are, for every one of these *published* horrors, at least three or four which *never are reported at all,* and where the poor victim dies quietly of her injuries like a wounded animal, without seeking the mockery of redress offered her by the law' (*ibid.*: 73–4). Nineteenth-century feminists also questioned the image of the battered woman as 'nagging' and 'provocative', which was frequently presented in mitigation to the courts:

I have no doubt that every husband who comes home with empty pockets and from whom his wife needs to beg repeatedly for money to feed herself and her children, considers that she 'nags' him. I have no doubt that when a wife reproaches such a husband with squandering his wages in the public-house, or on some wretched rival, while she and her children are starving, he accuses her to all his friends of intolerable 'nagging,' and that, not seldom having acquired from him the reputation of this kind of thing, the verdict of 'Serve her Right' is generally passed upon her by public opinion when her 'nagging' is capitally punished by a broken head.

(Cobbe, 1878: 68)

Indeed, their main concern was to emphasize the inadequacy of the law in its response to cases of wife-beating, a view supported by a number of prominent members of the legal profession. Cobbe reported: 'there was a large consensus of opinion that the law as it now stands is insufficient for its purpose. Lord Chief Justice Cockburn, Mr Justice Lush, Mr Justice Mellor, Chief Baron Kelly, Barons Bramwell, Piggott and Pollock, all expressed the same judgement' (1904: 593). Furthermore, there was widespread public disquiet about domestic violence. In 1875 the Parliamentary 'Blue Book' entitled *Reports on the State of the Law Relating to Brutal Assaults* was published, together with frequent press reports. It was these that motivated Cobbe to do something. In her autobiography she writes:

> One day in 1878 I was by chance reading a newspaper in which a whole series of frightful cases were recorded, here and there, among the ordinary news of the time. I got up out of my armchair, half dazed, and said to myself: 'I will never rest till I have tried what I can do to stop this.'
>
> (1904: 592–3)

She was particularly concerned about the so-called 'kicking district' of Liverpool, citing a Mr Serjeant Pulling who remarked: 'Nowhere is the ill-usage of women so systematic as in Liverpool, and so little hindered by the strong arm of the law; making the lot of a married woman, whose locality is the "kicking district" of Liverpool, simply a duration of suffering and subjection to injury and savage treatment, far worse than that to which the wives of mere savages are used' (Cobbe, 1878: 59). In June 1853, stiffer penalties were introduced in the form of 'An Act for the Better Prevention and Punishment of Aggravated Assaults upon Women and Children'. This Act had been proposed by Mr. Fitzroy, Member of Parliament for Lewes, who argued that women should be awarded the same protection as 'poodle dogs and donkeys'. The Act provided that assaults leading to actual bodily harm should be punished by up to six months' imprisonment with or without hard labour, or a fine not exceeding £20. The offender could also be bound over to keep the peace (Cobbe, 1878: 77). The merits of flogging as a punishment for wife abuse were also widely debated in Parliament (Cobbe, 1904; Freeman, 1979; Doggett, 1992).

However, maximum penalties were rarely enforced: Matilda Blake (1892), for example, pointed out that the killing of a wife was more likely to result in a manslaughter rather than a murder charge (this is still an issue for feminist campaigners today). Moreover, nineteenth-century feminists took very seriously the difficulties of punishing a wife-beater effectively without making his wife and children suffer too; thus Mabel Sharman Crawford argued that both fines and prison sentences affected the woman as much as her violent husband:

> For though it might be unquestionably fit and just to fine and imprison Ned Jones for assaulting Dick Smith, it was neither fit nor just to condemn Bill Sykes' ill used wife to share through either penalty the punishment inflicted on her brutal husband. Because

whilst the fine imposed taxed the means required for the support of the offender's family, the sentence of imprisonment entailed on her the penalty of hard labour to keep herself and children from starvation.

(1893: 293)

Much of this has great resonance today. Crawford also pointed out that women were deterred from reporting their husbands because of the likelihood of increased hardship as well as of reprisals:

Under present circumstances, therefore, the truth embodied in the common vulgar adage about the folly of injuring the nose to spite the face, must deter many a hapless wife from an appeal to law for protection against the habitual blows of a brutal husband. For not only would the sentence of imprisonment to which he might probably be condemned entail the pangs of want on herself and children, but she well may shrink with dread from the thought of being subjected in a few months' time to the vengeful fury of the punished tyrant on his release from prison.

(*ibid.*: 294)

She referred to cases of husbands who had killed their wives after serving prison sentences for assaulting them. Likewise, Frances Power Cobbe did not see tougher penalties as a solution for, following imprisonment 'the husband will return to them full of fresh and more vindictive cruelty' (1894: 80). She also commented that the gap between the incident and court appearance could lead the woman to withdraw her complaint or change her story, and cited the case, raised by Colonel Leigh in the House of Commons, of the woman who appeared without a nose and told the magistrate she had bitten it off herself. On the subject of flogging, Cobbe argued, it is, 'not expedient on the women's behalf that they should be so punished, since after they had undergone such chastisement, however well merited, the ruffians would inevitably return more brutalised and infuriated than ever; and again have their wives at their mercy' (*ibid.*: 594). Cobbe's answer to the dilemma over what to do to assist women was to offer them an exit from their violent marriages:

The only thing really effective, I considered, was to give the wife the power of separating herself and her children from her tyrant. Of course in the upper ranks, where people could afford to pay for a suit in the Divorce Court, the law had for some years opened to the assaulted wife this door of escape. But among the working classes … no legal means whatever existed of escaping from the husband returning after punishment to beat and torture his wife again. I thought the thing to be desired was the extension of the privilege of rich women to their poorer sisters, to be effected by an Act of Parliament which should give a wife whose husband had been convicted of an aggravated assault on her, the power to obtain a Separation Order under Summary Jurisdiction.

(1904: 594–5)

Cobbe subsequently led a campaign for the introduction of separation orders. With the assistance of Alfred Hill, a Birmingham magistrate and the son of an old friend, she drafted a Bill 'for the Protection of Wives whose Husbands have been convicted of assaults upon them'. Her proposals became part of the Matrimonial Causes Act which was passed in 1878. She described this as 'the part of my work for women … to which I look back on with most satisfaction' (*ibid.*: 592). This Act gave magistrates and judges the power to grant a separation order to a wife whose husband had been convicted of aggravated assault upon her, 'if satisfied that the future safety of the wife is in peril'. That proviso – which Cobbe did not support – was removed in 1895. The Act also allowed the woman to be awarded custody of any children under the age of ten years, and maintenance.

However, Cobbe did not believe that the Act would resolve the problem of wife-beating, although it would engender 'some alleviation of their wretched condition' (1878: 82). In her autobiography, she stated: 'I hope that at least a hundred poor souls each year thus obtain release from their tormentors, and probably the deterrent effect of witnessing such manumission of ill-treated slaves may have still more largely served to protect women from the violence of brutal husbands' (1904: 598). For although Cobbe often cited the orthodox explanations for wife-beating put forward at the time – alcohol, prostitution, overcrowding and the degradation of working-class life – the major cause resided in the unequal status of women, in particular that of wives. Thus, 'the notion that a man's wife is his PROPERTY, in the sense in which a horse is his property, is the fatal root of incalculable evil and misery' (1878: 62; original emphasis). And like many other nineteenth-century feminists, she argued that change would not occur whilst

the position of a woman before the law as wife, mother and citizen, remains so much below that of a man as husband, father and citizen, that it is a matter of course that she must be regarded by him as inferior and fail to obtain from him such a modicum of respect as her mental and moral qualities might win did he see her placed by the State on an equal footing.

(1878: 61)

There was a strong belief in the educational value of being granted formal equality with men. Thus it was hoped that if husbands saw their wives being granted equality by the state, they would be less inclined to regard them as their property and this would reduce women's susceptibility to abuse and also encourage women's resistance.

Thus in the first wave of feminism there was widespread concern about wife abuse and, as in the second wave, domestic violence was a pivotal issue. The explanation for it and remedies suggested were, of course, embedded in liberal feminism where equality with men was seen both to reduce the incidence of assault and facilitate the ability of women to remove themselves from the violent partner.

The period after the First World War

In the period after the First World War until 1970 domestic violence largely faded from the social problems agenda and, as indicated above, this has been attributed to the absence of a strong women's movement during this period (Freeman, 1979; Brokowski *et al.*, 1983; Wilson, 1983), for feminism is extremely influential in defining male violence against women as a major social problem. Thus, as Julie Blackman remarks, it is feminism that provides 'the impetus and the philosophical base for the naming of these injustices that accrue disproportionately to women and children within sexist societies' and 'as feminist activists moved the problem from the "taboo" to the "talked about", new notions of justice were advocated, and the inalienable rights of women and children were emphasized' (1989: 10). As Maynard points out:

It should not be imagined ... that in the intervening years [between first and second wave feminism] the abuse of women disappeared or abated. Research has shown that it is not so much the incidence of violence which has changed during the last century, as its perceived significance and visibility.

(1993: 111)

After 1970 the women's liberation movement grew rapidly and feminists began to examine and speak of their experiences of violence and provide support for other women who had been subject to abuse by men (Weir 1977; Wilson, 1983; Maynard, 1993). It was from this that the refuge movement began: 'women's liberation consciousness raising groups ... decided it was time to move from thought to action' (Dobash and Dobash, 1992: 25). In Britain the first refuge for battered women opened at Chiswick in 1971 – Chiswick Women's Aid. As Dobash and Dobash comment:

> It emerged in a rather unexpected manner, beginning with a campaign to protest against the elimination of free school milk and ending with a refuge for battered women ... Five hundred women and children and one cow marched through an English town in support of their claim. The cow aptly served as a symbol of their cause and the amiable spectacle brought considerable attention.
>
> While not a direct success, the march did bring solidarity among the women and initiated a successful attempt to set up a community meeting place for local women. It was here that women began to tell one another horrific stories of the violence they had received at the hands of their male partners. Here, that the doors were first opened for them to find refuge. Here, that violence against women began to be defined as a problem of epic proportions.
>
> (*ibid.*: 25–6)

One of the women who helped to found the Chiswick refuge, Erin Pizzey, emerged as its spokeswoman and generated national and international publicity for battered women through gaining widespread coverage on television, radio and in newspapers (see Martin, 1976). Pizzey's book, *Scream Quietly or the Neighbours Will Hear* (1974), which details the experiences of battered women, also had a considerable impact. However, as noted in the previous chapter, Pizzey subsequently caused considerable outrage amongst her early supporters by arguing that the violence was the result of individual pathologies residing within the man and also the woman victim, and more recently has argued (1998) that men are as likely to be victimized as women.

Following the opening of Chiswick refuge, women's rights groups began to found a network of refuges; some were allocated local authority housing, others squatted in unoccupied property. The National Women's Aid Federation[6] was established in 1974 as a co-ordinating body. As Brokowski *et al.* note, women 'flocked' to the refuges, 'indicating something of an unmet need' (1983: 4). For Dobash and Dobash, 'refuges vividly illustrate women's continued dependence in marriage and economic disadvantage whereby they must rely on a man for the basic necessity of accommodation' (1992: 60). In the United States, the first refuges are believed to be Women's Advocates in Minnesota and Transition House in Boston, opened in 1973 and 1974, respectively. These are described by Schechter as 'real and symbolic victories in the struggle of women to free themselves from male violence and domination' (1982: 62), although, in general, public recognition of the 'battered woman's movement' came later in the United States than Britain (see Pagelow, 1984; Dobash and Dobash, 1992). In Britain, by the mid-1970s, domestic violence had become a much more visible social problem and in response, a House of Commons Select Committee on Violence in Marriage was established to investigate it further. Since that time refuges and support groups have been set up in many countries and feminists continue to campaign on the issue, for example, to raise public and agency awareness and to challenge police and legal practice. Furthermore, as we shall see, male violence is an important topic for feminist theory, particularly that of radical feminism, which actively seeks to ground itself in women's experiences.

The three feminisms

Turning to contemporary feminist social theory, first, it should be noted that amongst second-wave feminists there has been considerable discussion (Evans, 1977; Bouchier, 1978 and 1983; Oakley, 1981; Mitchell and Oakley, 1986; hooks, 1984; Kourany *et al.*, 1993) over the meaning of 'feminism' and whether any unity can be assumed between what Bryson describes as the 'maze' of theories and perspectives which exist within feminism (1992: 4),[7] some of which I have already touched upon. Indeed, instead of 'feminism', it has been suggested we should be speaking of 'feminisms' (Maynard, 1989; Humm, 1992; Kemp and Squires, 1997).

However, on a more general level, feminism as a movement may be identified as 'any form of opposition to any form of social, political or economic discrimination which women suffer because of their sex' (Bouchier, 1983: 2). For as Michèlle Barrett has pointed out:

> however, you choose to define feminism, it is impossible not to centre its political project on some idea of a better position for women in the future. Feminism is very hard to conceive without the experiential dimensions of women's sense of oppression and without a vision of change.
>
> (1988: v)

With respect to feminist social theory, this has been described as that which 'addresses the broad question of how and why women come to be subordinated, and offers analyses of the social and cultural processes through which that subordination is perpetuated' (Jackson, 1993: 3). For many feminists, particularly radical feminists, a key concept for exploring the principles and structures which underpin women's subordination is that of patriarchy. As previously noted, patriarchy was originally used in its literal sense to mean 'rule by fathers' to justify the absolute authority of monarchs in pre-capitalist society. In contemporary feminism the concept of 'patriarchy' has been 're-discovered ... as a "struggle concept", because the movement needed a term by which the totality of oppressive and exploitative relations which affect women, could be expressed, as well as their systematic character' (Mies, 1986: 37). Patriarchy is usually taken 'to refer to the systematic organisation of male supremacy and female subordination' (Stacey, 1993: 53).[8] In criminology Frances Heidensohn (1998) points out that patriarchy can be used in two key ways: to explain women's experiences in the criminal justice system and the gendered nature of a large amount of criminal victimisation, particularly with respect to violence in the domestic sphere.

Let us turn now to the three main strands of feminist social theory: liberal feminism, socialist feminism and radical feminism.[9] Radical feminism, as it offers the most detailed analysis of the function of male violence in terms of women's oppression, will then be examined in detail in terms of those questions which, as it has been argued, an adequate theory of domestic violence should be able to answer.

Liberal feminism

In Britain and the rest of Europe the classic debates within contemporary feminist theory have typically been between radical and socialist feminism, whereas in the United States they have been between radical and liberal feminism (Walby, 1990; Dobash and Dobash, 1992).

Liberal feminism, as previously indicated, is an extension of the liberal project of the Enlightenment to include women. It involves the claim that as women are rational beings like men, they should have the same legal and political rights. Liberal feminists have, therefore, campaigned for the last three centuries for women's rights to enfranchisement, education, employment and property (see Sachs and Hoff Wilson, 1978; Naffine 1990). As we have seen above, in the nineteenth century many feminists were also actively involved in campaigning against wife-beating. But liberal feminism, unlike socialist and radical feminism, does not question or even analyse the existing social structure; it is therefore often referred to as 'bourgeois feminism' for 'its goal is to obtain sexual equality within the economic and political framework of capitalism' (Gregory, 1986: 65).

One of the central problems inherent in liberal theory identified in Chapter 1 is that of the classicist contradiction – that is, the contradiction between formal and substantive equality. As Bryson points out, the liberal feminist

demand for equality raises the question of 'equality with whom?' Here liberal feminists are often accused of reflecting only the concerns of middle-class white women who are privileged in every way other than their sex, and of ignoring the inequalities amongst men and the realities of class and race oppression. The liberal approach is also said to accept the necessity of hierarchical competitive society in which most men and women can only be losers; such a view is decisively rejected by radical and marxist feminists.

(1992: 168)

Liberal feminism, in its emphasis on the public sphere, has also historically overlooked the inequalities that exist between men and women in the private sphere. Thus, the argument of Frances Power Cobbe and her colleagues in the nineteenth century, that if women had formal equality – that is, if wives were granted the same political and legal rights as their husbands – this would result in a change in social attitude and the transformation of marriage from a relationship of dominance and subordination into one of equality and intimate friendship, is described by Maeve Doggett as 'overly optimistic', for

It is not enough for women to possess the same formal, legal rights as men: they also needed the same opportunity to exercise them. In particular, women needed *actual* economic power if their social status was to improve. However, very few (nineteenth century) feminists challenged the traditional division of labour between the sexes. They accepted that housekeeping and child-rearing were naturally and exclusively women's work and, in doing so, they consigned the vast majority of married women to continued financial dependence on their husbands. Such women could not compete with men in the outside world on equal terms, particularly if they had children.

(1992: 140, original emphasis)

As Bryson comments, 'the liberal idea of equality and of "sex blind" legislation ... ignores biological differences and the social realities of a gendered society' (1992: 167). Furthermore, Alison Jaggar (1983) has questioned the liberal conception of human nature: she considers it to be 'androcentric' in its emphasis on rational, independent, competitive and autonomous human beings. It ignores human interdependence, especially the long dependence of the young, the importance of co-operation and mutual support with others; in short, the values and commitment which are an essential basis for human society and that have, in fact, been central to women's lives throughout history. Finally, in terms of the political campaigns of liberal feminism, Jeanne Gregory forcefully highlights the dangers of arguing for equal rights in a capitalist society:

> Gains secured under the equal rights banner are inherently fragile as individuals or groups with competing rights claim equal legitimacy. A woman's right to choose an abortion is challenged in terms of the rights of the unborn foetus. Fathers compete with mothers for an extension of rights in relation to their children. Such divisions cannot be resolved within the framework of competitive individualism that capitalism breeds.
>
> (1986: 65)

Socialist feminism

There are many Marxist and non-Marxist socialist positions to be found under the heading of 'socialist feminism'. Socialist feminism was particularly prominent in the early 1970s. At this time, as Lynne Segal has noted, 'radical socialist politics of some sort were integral to a feminist outlook in Britain' (1987: 44). What unites the various socialist 'feminisms' is the belief that women's situation is influenced by its socio-economic context and that this context needs to be changed if we are to see an improvement in women's lives and social positions. As is apparent from our overview of liberal theory and liberal feminism, the kinds of social change the woman's movement demands and works for are difficult to secure within a capitalist society.

Early debates were centred on the application of Marxist theory to feminism. Marxism examines society in terms of the material conditions of production; that is, the circumstances under which labour is organized and goods are produced. In capitalist society, the fundamental social divide is that of class, analysed in terms of the exploitation of working-class (proletarian) labour by the bourgeoisie (those who own the means of production). Class struggle is presented as the principal driving force of history, and is seen as eventually resulting in an egalitarian (socialist) society in which oppression is eradicated. Marxist feminists have attempted either to assimilate feminism into a Marxist critique of capitalism or to develop Marxist theory to encompass the politics of the women's liberation movement (see Jackson, 1993). Indeed the latter group have been described by some commentators as feminist Marxists (Maynard, 1989).

Thus the various contributors to what has become known as the domestic labour debate, much of which was conducted in the journal *New Left Review* in the 1970s, focused on the relation between capitalism and housework, and engendered widespread commentaries (see, for example, Seccombe, 1973; Coulson *et al.*, 1975; Gardiner, 1975; Seccombe, 1975; Foreman, 1978; Kaluzynska, 1980; Walby, 1990; Bryson, 1993; Coole, 1993; Donovan, 1997). As Coole comments: 'the debate demonstrated the utility of a marxist approach very well and for the first time offered serious analysis of women's work in the home' (1993: 181). For work at home is seen as vital to capitalism and, what is more, a potential location for anti-capitalist struggle. For, as Mariarosa Dalla Costa and Selma James (1973) contend, the unpaid work women do at home enables the workers, their husbands, to work for capitalism in the factories and the offices. If the workers had to pay someone to do their housework, this would necessitate a huge increase in wages. Housework is presented as work in Marx's sense; it is seen as benefiting capitalism, and, as such, considered to be fundamental to women's oppression. As Walby puts it, the overall argument is that

Capitalism could not function without women cooking, cleaning and keeping house. Hence domestic labour must create value, women must be central to capitalism, and feminism must be central to socialist strategy.

(1993: 72)

Women also rear the labour force of the future. The international 'Wages for Housework' campaign has, therefore, pressed governments to quantify and value women's unwaged work and include it in their country's gross national product. However, Marxist feminist theories of this nature have met with heavy criticism (for example, Wilson and Weir, 1986). It was claimed that they misunderstood Marxist concepts: James and Dalla Costa, for example, were described as getting 'themselves into the singularly un-marxist position of encouraging women not to work (which they argue benefits only capitalism), of opposing the trade unions, of advocating withholding household labour from the family as a central tactic – all this and more as a consequence of basing their strategy on women as housekeepers' (Guettel, 1974: 48). Supporters of the domestic labour debate were also seen as perpetuating the view that housework is women's responsibility and for underplaying the extent to which the 'housewife' is often a wage-labourer too, and thus not addressing the contradictions that exist between these two spheres of work (Barrett, 1980). Moreover, as Bryson points out:

> What it notably failed to do...was to ask why it is that domestic labour is overwhelmingly performed by *women* or to explore the pre-existing structures or patriarchal attitudes that produced the present gender division of labour; any idea that men as well as capitalism benefit from present arrangements therefore tended to disappear.
>
> (1992: 239, original emphasis)

In the 1990s, however, 'Wages for Housework' claimed a partial victory for its ideas when the European Parliament adopted a report on 25 June 1993, which called for 'women's unwaged work – in the home, on the land and in the community – to be counted and included in the gross national products of its member states' (Wages for Housework Campaign, 1993).

Other Marxist feminists have focused their attention on the position of women in the labour market. It has been argued that women are concentrated in badly paid, low-status, often part-time positions because they are regarded as financially dependent on husbands, even though this may not reflect the reality of their situation (see Maynard, 1989; Donovan, 1997). The Marxist concept of a reserve army of labour has been applied to women, thus locating the specificity of women's paid labour within the general Marxist model of capital accumulation (Beechey, 1977; Bruegel, 1979). Women are seen as being brought in to, and out of, paid work as the interests of capital dictate (that is, in terms of economic expansion and recession). Married women are particularly susceptible to this as they are seen as having somewhere to go and something to do, in other words the home and housework, when employers dispense with their services:

> they provide a flexible working population which can be brought into production and dispensed with as the conditions of production

change ... married women have a world of their very own, the family, into which they can disappear when discarded from production.
(Beechey, 1977: 57)

As Phillips and Taylor comment, women are presented as the 'super-exploitables' (1980: 80) in capitalist society. Societal perception of men as the major 'breadwinners' and women as primarily housewives who may be working for a little extra 'pin-money' to supplement their housekeeping, can be seen as reinforcing women's economic dependence on men and necessitating the securing of a husband. Guettel, a Canadian Marxist feminist, has highlighted the wider implications of this, 'since she lacks access to subsistence jobs for herself ... she must defer to her mate and males in general ... where [women] must live, with whom, and by means of what, these are determined by economic factors, and they in turn determine the parameters of male–female relationships' (1974: 49–50).

For some Marxist feminists, arguments such as these have proved to be too economically deterministic. Michèlle Barrett, for example, in her highly influential book *Women's Oppression Today* (1980), whilst stressing the significance of the capitalist economic system, also considers ideology as important in terms of constructing and reproducing women's oppression. Central to Barrett's arguments is the role of the family, which is presented as having 'underwritten much of women's oppression' (*ibid.*: 187). She believes that it is only through an analysis of ideology that we can understand why women continue to marry and live in conventional relationships (in other words, heterosexual 'nuclear' families) which are oppressive to them. Ideology is a powerful factor in encouraging women to accept family life as it is structured today; it enables us to 'grasp the oppressive myth of an idealized natural "family" to which all women must conform' (*ibid.*: 251). This is not to suggest that Barrett rejects the human need for intimacy, sexual relations, emotional fulfilment and parenthood; rather, what she considers to be oppressive is the ideological assumption that such needs can only be met through the conventional family system. The family system is presented as encouraging women's dependence on men and serving to restrict women's lives, with respect to what they can and cannot do; as Barrett puts it, highlighting the links between ideology and women's material situation,

it is difficult to argue that the present structure of the family-household is anything other than oppressive for women. Feminists have consistently, and rightly, seen the family as a central site of women's oppression in contemporary society. The reasons for this lie both in the material structure of the household, by which women are by and large financially dependent on men, and in the ideology of the family, through which women are confined to a primary concern with domesticity and motherhood. This situation underwrites the disadvantages women experience at work, and lies at the root of the exploitation of female sexuality endemic in our society. The concept of 'dependence' is perhaps, the link between the material organisation of the household, and the ideology of femininity: an assumption of women's dependence on men structures both of these areas … it seems to be the case that even in households where women contribute considerably to the budget (whether professional 'dual-career families' or lower-paid workers) the ideology of women's dependence remains strong.

(*ibid*.: 214–15)

Thus, to improve the position of women, change will have to occur on both economic and ideological levels.

Barrett's perspective has been strongly criticized by black feminists for its lack of relevance to black women's lives. For black feminists the family has been seen as a site of refuge and resistance to racism. Black feminists have argued that it is the violence and coercion of a racist state, in terms of immigration laws and police practices, that is oppressive to black women, rather than the family (see, for example, Carby, 1982; Bhavani and Coulson, 1986). Barrett, in the introduction to the 1988 edition of *Women's Oppression Today*, acknowledges the criticisms and concedes that some of the theoretical principles on which the book is based are ethnocentric, 'perhaps the strongest example of this would be the analysis of the "male breadwinner–dependent wife system" which does not in fact apply to the black British population of West Indian origin to the same extent as it does to the dominant white ethnic group' (*ibid*.: vii).[10] However, she points out that we must be aware that, whereas some families provide an ideal environment for people, others do not and this has been found to be true over a variety of ethnically distinct family forms.[11] Further, in supporting the family, radicals risk finding themselves aligned with the Right; as Barrett comments:

The Thatcherite respect for traditional family values acquires, as the years go by, a closer and closer similarity to the religious 'moral majority' attitude in the United States. This puts radicals in rather a difficult position, not unlike those who had to stop attacking the welfare state as a reformist obstacle to socialism and start defending it when it was savagely cut back from the right.

(*ibid.*: xxi)

Eisenstein (1979) and Hartmann (1976; 1979) share Barrett's view that women's oppression cannot be reduced solely to an effect of capitalism. They argue that women's oppression must be understood through an analysis of both capitalism and patriarchy – men's domination of women. Capitalism and patriarchy are presented as 'dual systems' of oppression; hence we find such approaches frequently discussed under the heading of 'dual-systems theory' (for example, Walby, 1990). History, it is argued, must be seen as a struggle that has occurred along the dimensions of class *and* gender. Eisenstein considers patriarchy and capitalism to be so entwined that they have fused to become one inter-locking system of oppression: 'capitalist-patriarchy'. Capitalism and patriarchy are so dependent on each other that one needs the other in order to survive, and changes in one part of the capitalist-patriarchal system will result in changes in another part.

Heidi Hartmann, in the title of her classic article, uses the phrase, 'the unhappy marriage of marxism and feminism' to highlight the tendency of Marxist debates to subsume the feminist struggle into the struggle against capitalism; thus she writes, 'the marriage of marxism and feminism has been like the marriage of husband and wife depicted in English common law: marxism and feminism are one, and that one is marxism' (1979: 1). An appropriate comment given the subject matter of this book. For Hartmann, however, it is necessary to achieve a more 'progressive union' between Marxism and feminism:

> Both marxist analysis, particularly its historical and materialist method, and feminist analysis, especially the identification of patri-archy as a social and historical structure, must be drawn upon if we are to understand the development of western capitalist societies and the predicament of women within them.

(*ibid.*: 2)

Patriarchy is presented by Hartmann as pre-dating capitalism (as it does in its traditional sense) and she defines it as

> a set of social relations between men, which have a material base, and which, though hierarchical, establish or create interdependence and solidarity among men and enable them to dominate women.

> Though patriarchy is hierarchical and men of different classes,
> races or ethnic groups have different places in the patriarchy,
> they are also united in their shared relationship of dominance over
> their women; they are dependent on each other to maintain that
> domination.
>
> *(ibid.*: 11)

Capitalism and patriarchy are considered, in contrast to Eisenstein's
analysis, to be two distinct and autonomous systems although they
interact at certain points in time. This interaction is sometimes mutually reinforcing, on other occasions there is conflict between the two
systems, for instance,

> the vast majority of men might want their women at home to per-
> sonally service them. A smaller number of men, who are capitalists,
> might want most women (not their own) to work in the wage
> labour market.
>
> *(ibid.*: 14)

The major sites of women's oppression are considered by Hartmann
to be the home and paid employment. Unlike the more traditional
Marxist approaches, she stresses that men, as well as capitalism, gain
from the way in which society is ordered along gendered lines. Thus it
is pointed out that because men enjoy 'a higher standard of living than
women in terms of luxury consumption, leisure time and personalized
services'(*ibid.*: 6), men of all classes have a vested material interest in
the continuation of women's subordination. Hence, 'a society could
undergo transition from capitalism to socialism ... and remain patriarchal' (*ibid.*: 13). In the area of paid work, men are presented as organizing or being compliant in occupational segregation by gender in order
to retain their access to the best paid jobs. Women's low pay and lack
of opportunities mean, for example, that for many women separation
or divorce is not an option and women will frequently remarry: few
women are able to support their children independently and adequately. Within the household women bear the brunt of housework,
even if they are also in paid work. Women do the cooking, cleaning
and rearing of children which, as we have seen, benefits men and capitalism by providing the labour force. As Walby puts it, exploitation in
work and in the home 'act[s] to reinforce each other, since women's
disadvantaged position in paid work makes them vulnerable in making
marriage arrangements, and their position in the family disadvantages

them in paid work' (1990: 6). Further, Hartmann notes, the patriarchal system reproduces itself, for children learn their roles in the gender hierarchy by being primarily reared in the home by women who are socially defined and recognized as inferior: 'central to this process ... are the areas outside the home where patriarchal behaviours are taught and the inferior position of women enforced and reinforced: churches, schools, sports, clubs, unions, armies, factories, offices, heath centres, the media, etc.' (1979: 12). If women are to be free they must, therefore, fight against the capitalist economic system and patriarchy.

For Walby (1990), however, dual-systems theories, as presented in the work of Eisenstein and Hartmann, are limited in that they do not deal with the full range of patriarchal structures, particularly with respect to sexuality and violence.[12] Although Hartmann (1979) does refer to men's appropriation of women's bodies for sexual services in the home and to sexual harassment at work, this is not dealt with in any great detail. In radical feminist theory we find sexuality and violence are considered central to the oppression of women.

Before discussing radical feminist theory it must be emphasized that many of the concepts derived from socialist feminism will prove important in terms of our overall discussion of domestic violence. An analysis of the capitalist system can help to explain why men are able to get away with violence against women in the home as well as the factors that prevent women from leaving violent men. As noted in the chapter on classicism, capitalism has resulted in the increased privatization of the home and, as Schechter notes, 'privatization is dangerous because it allows violence to accelerate while everyone says "Mind your own business. This is a family problem"' (1982: 225). Further, factors such as women's lack of work opportunities, low pay and resulting economic dependence on men are likely to influence their decision to leave or return to violent partners, particularly if they have children. The prevailing ideology concerning the conventional family structure may also play a part in ensuring such relationships are maintained.

Radical feminism

Radical feminism developed towards the end of the 1960s and, as Jaggar (1983) notes, in contrast to liberal and traditional Marxist conceptions of feminism which are based in philosophical traditions that are 300 and 100 years old, respectively, is much more of a contemporary phenomenon. The theoretical impetus for radical feminism came, in part, from women's experiences of sexual domination in the New Left organizations which had sprung up during this decade. Jeanne Gregory comments that the neglect of women's issues by the male Left in the United States directly led to a 'mushrooming' of feminist organisations: Thus,

> The Chicago group was ... conceived in anger, following a political convention at which a women's resolution was considered too insignificant to merit discussion. The chairman patted one of the women on the head and told her: 'Cool down little girl. We have more important things to talk about than women's problems'. The 'little girl' did not cool down. Instead, she [Shulamith Firestone] became a radical feminist and wrote *The Dialectic of Sex*. You could not ask for a more vivid demonstration of the interrelationship between the political and the theoretical than this!
>
> (1986: 64)

Radical feminism is rooted in the experiences of women and, as such, is considered to be a theory that is *of* and *for* women (Bryson, 1992). Indeed Catherine MacKinnon argues that it is the only true feminist theory:

> Feminism has been widely thought to contain tendencies of liberal feminism, radical feminism, and socialist feminism. But just as socialist feminism has often amounted to traditional marxism ... applied to women – liberal feminism has been liberalism applied to women. Radical Feminism is feminism.
>
> (1989: 117)

For radical feminists it is the male oppression of women that is the most fundamental form of domination. Patriarchy is, therefore, central to their analysis of women's position in society. It is patriarchy not capitalism that is held responsible for women's oppression, and patriarchy is seen by radical feminists as having pre-dated capitalism. Men as a group are seen to dominate women as a group and are the beneficiaries of women's continued subjugation. Indeed, radical feminists often describe women as one class, men as another class; for all women are bound together in the same class position because of male supremacy. As Millett comments in *Sexual Politics*,[13] 'sex is a status category with political implications' (1977: 24). Men are presented as oppressing women in all areas of life. Important to this is the idea that 'the personal is political', which serves to highlight women's oppression in their private lives and personal relationships. 'The personal is political' clearly presents a challenge to conventional political theory, including that of liberal and traditional forms of Marxist feminism, which consider political power to be connected with the state or paid employment; in other words, the public sphere. For radical feminists, women are dominated not only in the public sphere but also in their private lives. Furthermore, such domination is intimate and bodily. Thus, for the majority of radical feminists patriarchal domination is considered to involve the male appropriation of women's sexuality and bodies and acts of violence.

The social construction of sexuality

Sexuality is not presented as a natural or unchangeable feature of human existence, but rather as socially constructed around male sexual desire. Radical feminists react against the male construction of sexuality in which, as Maynard puts it:

> women are regarded as sexual objects, penetration is seen as the major source of sexual pleasure, and men are expected to take the initiative in relationships. Women, on the other hand, are simply expected to be passive and pretty and be the playthings of men.
>
> (1989: 67)

Thus in 'The Myth of the Vaginal Orgasm' Anne Koedt argues,

> Women have been ... defined sexually in terms of what pleases men; our own biology has not been properly analysed. Instead, we are fed the myth of the liberated woman and her vaginal orgasm – an orgasm which in fact does not exist. ... New techniques must be used or devised which transform this particular aspect of our current sexual exploitation.
>
> (1970; rpr. 1992: 263)

Adrienne Rich takes this argument further, stressing that the problem is that women have been forced into 'compulsory heterosexuality', which involves a narrow form of sexual behaviour in which the emphasis is placed on penetration by the male sexual organ, and this is seen as fundamental to women's oppression. Lesbianism has been rendered invisible 'or catalogued under disease; partly because it has been treated as exceptional rather than intrinsic' (1980; rpr. 1992: 177). Such a critique of heterosexuality, as Jackson comments, 'raises the possibility of lesbianism as a positive alternative' (1993: 226). Indeed, for some radical feminists, lesbianism has been a personal choice, whereas for others it is a political choice (see Jeffreys, 1990, 1994; Wittig, 1992). For example, the Leeds Revolutionary Feminist Group argued that 'political-lesbianism' or sexual separatism should be adopted as an oppositional strategy to patriarchy. It suggested that political-lesbianism was neces-sary for feminists because 'the heterosexual couple is the basic unit of the political structure of male supremacy ... Any woman who takes part in the heterosexual couple helps to shore up male supremacy by making its foundations stronger' (1981: 6).

This presentation of sexuality has, however, been strongly criticized, particularly in terms of the search for new sexual relationships and 'techniques' to 'transform this particular aspect of our current sexual exploitation' (Koedt, 1992: 263). Further 'political-lesbianism' has proved highly controversial because of its implicit criticism of heterosexual women. As Stevie Jackson notes: 'if feminism is to address all women, then the critique of heterosexuality should be kept distinct from per-sonal criticism of heterosexual women' (Jackson, 1993: 227).

The centrality of sexuality

Catherine MacKinnon has written that 'sexuality is to feminism what work is to marxism: that which is one's own, yet most taken away' (1982a: 515). She contends that although Marxism and feminism are both concerned with power, given that their starting points are so different they cannot easily be brought together and 'attempts to create a synthesis between marxism and feminism, termed socialist-feminism, have not recognised the depth of the antagonism or the separate integrity of each theory' (*ibid.*: 523, 524). Furthermore, it is suggested that male-dominated forms of sexuality have permeated many areas, including that of work (Walby, 1990).

Catherine MacKinnon (1979), for instance, discusses sexual harass-ment at work. Indeed, she suggests that the concept of sexuality is coterminous with that of gender: the sexualisation of dominance and subordination. Thus the inequalities between men and women are presented as constructing what we understand to be gender:

> Sexuality is gendered as gender is sexualized. Male and female are created through the eroticization of dominance and submission. The man/woman difference and the dominance/submission dynamic

define each other. This is the social meaning of sex and distinctively feminist account for gender inequality.

(1993: 201)

For MacKinnon an analysis of rape should not, therefore, be separated from a critique of heterosexuality and she rejects the conception of rape as an expression of violence rather than sexuality, for it is impossible to divide the two:

> The male point of view defines them by distinction. What women experience does not so clearly distinguish the normal, everyday things from which those abuses have been defined by distinction...What we are saying is that sexuality in exactly these normal forms often does violate us. So long as we say those things are abuses or violent, not sex, we fail to criticize what has been made of sex.

(1982b: 52)

Many radical feminists have suggested that there is a continuum between 'normal' male sexual practice and sexual violence against women (see Kelly, 1988a). Indeed, Edwards (1987) points out that the notion of violence as interwoven with heterosexuality and both being fundamental to male power is a common theme in recent radical feminist writings. This will become evident in the application of radical feminist views on violence to the grid of questions.

Male violence against women

Radical feminist work has focused on a number of specific areas of male violence against women, as well as also seeing it as a 'unitary phenomenon' (Edwards, 1987), in order to explore the connections between sexuality, violence and the social control of women. Many radical feminists have considered male violence to be the basis of men's control over women. Early analyses, particularly those of American radical feminists, tended to focus on the subject of rape (Griffin, 1971; Medea and Thompson, 1974; Reynolds, 1974; Brownmiller, 1975).[14] They argued against the positivistic theories of rape which suggest that rape is an exceptional occurrence carried out by a few abnormal men (that is, by those with an inadequate or asocial personality). Rape is described as the 'all-American crime' (Griffin, 1971) and the 'basic truth' of rape is emphasized: it is not, as Brownmiller puts it, a crime of irrational, impulsive, uncontrollable lust, but 'is a deliberate, hostile, violent act of degradation and possession on the part of a would-be conqueror' (Brownmiller, 1975: 391).[15] Thus Medea and Thompson suggest:

> It is time, then, for women to stop thinking of rapists as sick or crazy men. You might very easily have dated [one] or your daughter might or your elder sister. [He] might have been the man you married or [the men] egging him on might have been friends of yours. The rapist is the man next door.
>
> (1974: 36)

Rape, and the threat of rape, is presented as enabling men to control women. It is seen as keeping all women in a state of fear because it is impossible for a woman to tell which men are safe and which are rapists. As Griffin argues, 'rape is a kind of terrorism which severely limits the freedom of women and makes women dependent on men' (1971: 7). It leads women to seek the protection of one man against all others. Reynolds further develops the social control thesis by suggesting that societal distinctions, as discussed in the preceding chapter, between what is 'appropriate' and 'inappropriate' female behaviour mean that certain women are targeted, that is those who violate the traditional female role expectations: 'rape is a punitive action directed toward females who usurp or appear to usurp the culturally defined prerogatives of the dominant male role' (1974: 66). Thus,

> It is that rape and the threat of rape operates in our society to maintain the dominant position of males. It does this by restricting the mobility and the freedom of movement of women, by limiting their casual interaction with the opposite sex, and in particular by maintaining the males' prerogatives in the erotic sphere. When there is evidence that the victim was or gave the appearance of being out of her place, she can be raped and the rapist will be supported by the cultural values, by the institutions that embody these, and by the people shaped by these values ...
>
> (*ibid.*: 67)

Radical feminists see all forms of male violence against women, including the threat and fear of violence, as functioning as a social control mechanism forcing women to modify their behaviour by, for instance, not going out at night alone for fear of being attacked. In doing this men are able to control women's activities and, therefore, to oppress them: male violence serves to keep women in their place.

As Bart and Moran comment, violence against women runs 'the gamut from pornographic phone calls to femicide' but 'all forms of violence are interrelated, coalescing like a girdle to keep women in our place, which is subordinate to men' (1993: 1). Pornography in particular is seen by writers such as Andrea Dworkin as a cornerstone of the structure which oppresses women, being both a symptom of male denigration of women and an institution that actively denigrates.[16]

I shall now apply the major principles of radical feminism to the grid of questions developed in Chapter 1; it is these which an adequate theory of domestic violence should be able to answer.

Human nature

For radical feminists human nature is presented as socially constructed. The positivistic assumption of the violent man as 'sick, ill, under stress, out of control' is dismissed as a myth which serves 'to remove the responsibility from men for their actions' (Kelly, 1988a: 34–5). To understand domestic violence we must, therefore, examine the construction of masculinity in sexist society. As Hanmer, Radford and Stanko argue, 'male supremacist societies ... have constructed and continue to celebrate forms of chauvinistic masculinity which not only tolerates men's use of violence, but upholds it as a virtue, whether in the promotion of war, in the defence of pornography, or in the nightly television struggles between fictional good and evil' (1989: 4).

Social order

Society is patriarchal in structure embodying male oppression of women.[17] Male violence is functional to the maintaining of male supremacy and female subordination. As Bograd has put it:

Our society is structured along the dimension of gender: Men as a class wield power over women. As the dominant class, men have differential access to important material and symbolic resources, while women are devalued as secondary and inferior. Although important social class and race differences exist among men, all men can potentially use violence as a powerful means of subordinating women ... violence is the most overt and effective means of social control. Even if individual men refrain from employing physical force against their partners, men as a class benefit from how women's lives are restricted and limited because of their fear of violence by husbands and lovers as well as by strangers. Wife abuse or battering reinforces women's passivity and dependence as men exert their rights to authority and control. The reality of domination at the social level is the most crucial factor contributing to and maintaining wife abuse at the personal level.

(1988: 14)

The family, and the institution of heterosexuality that forms its basis, is seen as 'a central institution in patriarchal society, one in which private struggles around patriarchal power relations are enacted, and hence one in which violence frequently features as a form of control of the powerless by the powerful' (Radford and Stanko, 1991: 200). For this reason, radical feminists are extremely critical of the division of society into public and private spheres, as if the abuse that occurs in private were of no general concern nor a key part in maintaining the structure of dominance in society in general. Furthermore, women's fear of violence by male strangers in public places – fuelled by public discourse, including that of the media, and women's actual experiences – is seen as leading to a lessening of public participation by women and a greater dependency on known men for protection. This is considered to create the conditions for individual men to assault 'their women'; the lack of intervention in cases of private violence by the criminal justice system and medical and social work agencies further reinforces this.

Definition

Radical feminists have challenged conventional definitions of violence and legal categories: these are seen to 'reflect men's ideas and limit the range of male behaviour that is deemed unacceptable to the most extreme, gross and public forms' (Kelly, 1988a: 138). They point out that when conventional definitions are utilized, women find themselves caught between their own experiences, which they regard as abusive, and the dominant male discourse which defines such behaviour as normal or to be expected. Indeed Kelly argues:

It is men's interest, as a class and as the perpetrators of sexual violence, to ensure the definitions of sexual violence are as limited as possible. Language is a further means of controlling women.

(*ibid.*: 130)

Radical feminist definitions, in contrast, have developed from understanding and documenting women's experiences and, as such, shift 'attention from only those forms of violence where physical harm and injury are obvious such as rape or battering, to more "taken for granted" forms such as sexual harassment' (*ibid.*: 27). These definitions have expanded, and indeed are seen as continuing to develop, 'as women named previously unnamed forms of abuse' (Radford and Stanko, 1991: 186). An example they give is Ruth Hall and Women Against Rape's (1985) introduction of the term 'racist sexual abuse', which spans both racial and sexual assault rather than suggesting that for black women these are separate issues. In terms of domestic violence it is noted how experience at the refuges made it obvious that this included not only physical violence but forced sex and a whole range of mental abuse (Kelly and Radford, 1987: 244).

Radical feminists are, therefore, concerned with how *women* themselves define violence: 'domestic violence' is that which women define as 'domestic violence'. As Kelly argues: 'if we are to reflect in our definition ... the range and complexity of what women and girls experience as abusive we must listen to what they have to say' (1988a: 71). In line with this, Radford comments, throughout the *Wandsworth Violence Against Women – Women Speak Out Survey*:

> during interviewing, analysis and writing-up we have made no attempt to define the terms 'violence', 'harassment' or 'threat'. Rather than engage with competing malestream experts' views on the subject, we considered it important for the women interviewed to interpret these terms according to their own experiences.
>
> (1987: 32)

The continuum of sexual violence

Radical feminists have moved from seeing the various forms of violence against women – domestic violence, rape, sexual assault, sexual harassment, incest, child sexual abuse and pornography – as separate phenomena to viewing them as part of a more general or 'unitary' phenomenon, that of 'sexual violence'. Sexual violence is defined by Kelly as 'any physical, visual or sexual act that is experienced by the woman or girl, at the time or later, as a threat, invasion or assault, that has the effect of hurting her or degrading her and/or takes away her ability to control intimate contact' (1988a: 41). As Maynard puts it, the various forms of violence are seen as 'acts directed at women because their bodies are socially regarded as sexual'; they are all linked, 'by virtue of the fact that they are overwhelmingly male acts of aggression against women and girls, often use sex as a means of exercising power and domination, and their effect is to intrude upon and curtail women's activities' (1989: 106–7).

Liz Kelly utilizes the term 'continuum' to describe the extent and range of sexual violence in women's lives: the concept of continuum is based on two of its *Oxford English Dictionary* meanings: 'a basic common character that underlies many different events' and 'a continuous series of elements or events that pass into one another and which cannot be readily distinguished'. Kelly argues:

> The first meaning enables us to discuss sexual violence in a generic sense. The basic common character underlying the many different forms of violence is the *abuse, intimidation, coercion, intrusion, threat and force men use to control women.* The second meaning enables us to document and name the range of abuse, intimidation, coercion, intrusion, threat and force whilst acknowledging there are no clearly defined and discrete analytic categories into which men's behaviour can be placed.
>
> (1988a: 76; original emphasis)

The concept of continuum enables the linking of the more common everyday experiences of abuse that women experience with the less common experiences which are defined as crimes: it shows how 'typical' and 'aberrant' male behaviour blend into each other. Thus,

> There is no clear distinction, therefore, between consensual sex and rape, but a continuum of pressure, threat, coercion and force. The concept of a continuum validates the sense of abuse women feel when they do not freely consent to sex and takes account of the fact that women may not define their experience at the time or over time as rape.
>
> (1987: 58)

Further it is stressed that we must not see the continuum as implying that one form of sexual violence is more serious than another: it is considered as 'inappropriate to create a hierarchy of abuse within a feminist analysis' (1988a: 76). For as Kelly points out:

> women's reactions to incidents of sexual violence at the time, and the impact on them over time, are complex matters. With the important exception of sexual violence which results in death, the degree of impact cannot be simplistically inferred from the form of sexual violence or its place within a continuum.
>
> (*ibid.*: 76)

Extent and distribution

Official statistics are regarded by radical feminists as vastly under-reporting all forms of violence against women. As we have seen, it is argued that for the official agencies many aspects of sexual violence are not seen as warranting the label of 'crime'. Furthermore, to take domestic violence as an example, it is repeatedly pointed out that women do not report for a wide variety of reasons, for example, because of fear of reprisals from the man, or his friends and family; embarrassment; that the police will consider it too trivial, and so on. Feminists have also pointed out that even when domestic violence is reported, the police are often reluctant to intervene and will frequently 'no-crime' such cases even when they clearly fit into the legal categorizations of assault (Kelly and Radford, 1987; Hanmer *et al.*, 1989).

Conventional victimization surveys, such as the national British Crime Surveys, are also seen as inadequate in measuring the extent of violence against women: they likewise focus on a narrow range of violent behaviours (see Radford, 1987) and women will frequently not inform interviewers of their experiences for this will invoke the pain of the original attack. The perpetrator may also be near to the interview situation and the interviewee too frightened to report accurately.

Radical feminist surveys, in contrast, point to a widespread problem of male violence: for example, McGibbon, Cooper and Kelly's (1989) study on domestic violence in Hammersmith and Fulham revealed 39 per cent of women had experienced 'verbal or physical threats', 35 per cent 'punched/shoved', 18 per cent 'beaten up' and 10 per cent 'attacked with a weapon' from a male partner at some time in their lives.[18] And Hanmer and Saunders' (1984) survey in Leeds and Radford's (1987) in Wandsworth found 59 per cent and 76 per cent of women, respectively, had at least one experience of sexual violence in the previous year. Indeed, Liz Kelly, using the concept of a continuum of sexual violence, emphasises 'that all women experience sexual violence at some point in their lives' (1987: 59). As such,

> a clear distinction cannot be made between 'victims' and other women. The fact that some women only experience violence at the more common, everyday end of the continuum is a difference in degree and not in kind. The use of the term 'victim' in order to separate one group of women from other women's lives and experiences must be questioned. The same logic applies to the definition of offenders.
>
> (*ibid.*: 59)

In terms of the distribution of male violence, radical feminists argue that it cuts across class and race divisions. Thus, they are highly critical of discussions which consider such variables as relevant: for as Radford and Stanko comment:

> When familial violence is recognised, the old stereotypes around race and class surface. Violence is assumed to be a characteristic of black and working class families, which were then pathologised. If the violence is deemed the norm in 'pathological' families, then either no intervention is called for or alternatively black families are targeted for therapy to bring them into the white, nuclear family 'norm'. Conversely, in white middle-class families, the prevailing myth is that 'nice' professional men don't do it. The strength of this myth is such that some middle class women find it hard to convince police and other state professionals that they need support.
>
> (1991: 198)

Furthermore, it is pointed out that 'historical evidence and evidence from a range of cultures and societies suggests that sexual violence occurs in most societies and that certain forms of sexual violence occur in the majority of human societies, particularly rape and violence to wives' (Kelly and Radford, 1987: 238). In examining the distribution of violence overall by relationship to the male perpetrator, it is, however, suggested by many radical feminists that he is more likely to be a known man than an unknown man: women's attackers 'are most likely to be those near and dear rather than the shadowy stranger' (Radford and Stanko, 1991: 198). It is domestic rather than stranger violence that presents the greatest problem for women. Indeed, Hanmer and Saunders (1984) point out that violence against women in public may actually be 'private' domestic violence: violence from male partners is not necessarily confined to the home.

Causes

For radical feminists the causes of men's violence lie in patriarchy and the construction of masculinity within this social order. Male violence, whether in the home or in public space, is a reflection of the unequal power relations between men and women in society, and also serves to maintain those unequal power relations. Violence is essential to a system of gender subordination (MacKinnon, 1989;

Radford and Stanko, 1991; Hester *et al.*, 1996). As Kelly and Radford comment:

> We see patriarchy as a systematic set of social relations through which men maintain power over women and children. One of the forms of control common to patriarchal societies is the use of sexual violence. The presence of sexual violence is ... one of the defining features of a patriarchal society. It is used by men, and often condoned by the state, for a number of specific purposes: to punish women who are seen to be resisting male control; to police women, make them behave in particular ways; to claim rights of sexual, emotional and domestic servicing; and through all of these maintain the relations of patriarchy, male dominance and female subordination. Patriarchal oppression like all forms of imperialism/ oppression/ exploitation is ultimately based on violence.
>
> (1987: 238–9)

Anne Edwards notes that violence is a 'socially produced' and frequently also a 'socially legitimated' cultural phenomenon: 'masculinity and femininity, "man" and "woman", male and female sexuality are all socially constructed' (1987: 26). Thus 'masculinity as it is currently constructed in western culture, draws on notions of virility, conquest, power and domination and these themes are reflected in gender relations and heterosexual practices' (Kelly, 1988a: 30). As we have seen, such ideology is often presented by radical feminists as taking the form of pornography which directly represents and contributes to the patriarchal social order and the construction of male and female relationships. Andrea Dworkin suggests that 'at the heart of the female condition is pornography; it is the ideology that is the source of all the rest' (1983: 223).

Impact

Through focusing on women's experiences, radical feminists have highlighted the impact of men's violence on women. With respect to domestic violence, McGibbon, Cooper and Kelly have pointed out:

> Living with the threat and reality of violence has profound impacts on the lives of women and children. It is not only the physical and emotional consequences of violence which undermine women's sense of self, but also the isolation, shame and persistent criticism and humiliation that often accompanies assaults ... Women and children's

lives are also diminished by the constant energy they have to put into coping with fear, and trying to 'manage' family relationships in order to minimize the violence.

(1989: 6–7)

Furthermore, societal attitudes which blame women for the violence and the lack of support from the police and other agencies is seen to compound the impact of women's experiences. Andrea Dworkin has documented her own experiences in 'Living in Terror, Pain: Being a Battered Wife' showing the effects as long-lasting: 'there isn't a day when I feel fear that I will see him and he will hurt me' (1993b: 239).

As I have stressed throughout this section, male violence is presented as functioning as a form of social control of women serving to keep women in their place, which is subordinate to men. Betsy Stanko, for example, demonstrates how women's lives are structured around concerns for personal safety:

Wherever women are, their peripheral vision monitors the landscape and those around them for potential danger. On the street, we listen for footsteps approaching and avoid looking men in the eyes. At home, women are more likely than men to ask callers to identify themselves before opening the front door and to search for ways to minimize conflict with potentially violent partners... Women's lives rest upon a continuum of unsafety... For the most part, women find they must constantly negotiate their safety with men – those with whom they live, work or socialise, as well as those they have never met.

(1990: 85)

Male violence denies women their freedom and autonomy. And the myriad forms of violence that women experience are described as having a cumulative effect. Thus it is not surprising, from this perspective, that conventional victimization surveys, such as the British Crime Surveys, have shown women to have a high fear of crime. For radical feminists this fear is based in reality. Moreover, it is emphasized that women's fear of crime is quite simply women's fear of *men*.

In discussing the impact of men's violence radical feminists have also stressed the many resisting, coping and survival strategies women adopt: indeed, it is argued that we must think of women as 'survivors' rather than as 'victims' of men's violence. For the term 'victim' is seen as implying a passive response to violent incidents and their aftermath, whereas Kelly's research revealed that:

Despite being in fear of their lives, or that incidents might escalate, many women chose to resist sexual violence. Resistance included physical struggle, verbal challenge and refusal to be controlled by abusive men. Some women's resistance resulted in the avoidance of rape or a particular incident of abuse. Other women altered the course of the assaults. For some women, particularly battered women, continued resistance often meant they experienced more severe violence.

(1988a: 183–4)

Kelly also found women were distrustful of men and experienced conflicts about heterosexuality. She argues that these are not to be seen as

dysfunctional reactions but part of women's active and adaptive attempts to cope with the reality of sexual violence. They can only be defined as 'dysfunctional' if men's interests are the starting point for analysis. Whilst so much of women's experience of heterosexual sex is neither pleasurable nor freely chosen, it is in women's interests to refuse to enter, or stay in, heterosexual relationships in which they feel pressured or coerced.

(*ibid.*: 216)

Methods

There are, as I indicate throughout this book, many valuable criticisms made by feminists of the research methods used in mainstream social science. It has been said, for example, of conventional positivistic research that 'it appears to some critics that social scientists are suffering from "physics envy", and therefore try to be as methodologically hard as their brothers in the natural sciences in an attempt to prove that they, too, are objective scientists' (Yllo, 1988: 34). Main stream (or 'malestream') social science, despite its claims to objectivity, is presented as the world perceived from the perspective of men (see Harding, 1986; 1987). Work on domestic violence is considered necessarily limited because it does not take into account gender and power, which are central factors for feminist researchers (Bograd 1988; Yllo, 1988; Kurz, 1998).

The concern of radical feminists is with women's experiences and the validating of those experiences: thus, their approach is to take an explicitly 'feminist standpoint' in their work. Indeed, as we have noted, theory is seen as arising out of experience. Further, instead of objectivity, or 'value-free' research, radical feminists argue for 'conscious partiality'. As Bograd comments, it is 'crucial that researchers make explicit the values that guide their work' (1988: 21). Thus Liz Kelly is 'explicit about her identity as a woman, a researcher, and a political activist' (*ibid.*: 22). From the work of radical feminists, to para-phrase Howard Becker (1967), it is clear whose side they are on: their political commitment to the ending of the oppression of women is made obvious.

With respect to violence, 'instead of trying to fit women's experi-ences into predefined "commonsensical" categories, feminist researchers began to explore what violence means to the participants themselves' (Bograd, 1988: 22). Again, and as we have noted above, this feature is particularly evident in the work of Liz Kelly (1987; 1988a; 1988c; Kelly and Radford, 1996). Feminist researchers also examine what violence means to them; that is, they locate themselves within the research experience. Kelly describes the impact that researching sexual violence had on her – it made her more aware of sexual violence, led to feelings of vulnerability and also brought back memories of assaults that had occurred in childhood and adolescence which she had psychologically blocked. As she points out:

> Moving between the interviews and my own experiences and reac-tions was an integral part of the research methodology. Had I 'tuned out' these responses I would probably not have noticed or fully understood the importance of aspects of women's experience of sexual violence.
>
> (1988a: 19)

Other core research principles for radical feminists have included a concern to break down hierarchical relationships between researcher and researched. As Stanley and Wise have argued, the conventional relationship in which personal involvement is minimized and objectivity is emphasized

> is obscene because it treats people as mere objects, there for the researcher to do research 'on'. Treating people as objects – sex objects or research objects – is morally unjustifiable.
>
> (1983: 168)

Thus a more collaborative approach has been advocated in which the research is seen as a two-way process. This is achieved by engaging with the interviewees on a personal level and, in some cases, involving them in the interpretation of the data in order to build up what is meaningful to them (see Reinharz, 1979; Hoff, 1988; Kelly, 1988a).

On the choice of method, the emphasis on women's experiences originally led to a preference for the qualitative method, that is in-depth interviewing. In-depth interviews are seen as more likely to capture the reality of women's experiences. Quantitative methods, in contrast, are described as 'having a special capacity for dehumanizing the people we study' (Yllo, 1988: 44); they are 'inherently patriarchal', 'hard' and 'masculinist' (see *ibid*.).[19] Thus Loraine Gelsthorpe comments:

> Some writers suggest that quantitative methods are inconsistent with feminist values, have an objective appearance and, therefore, have no place in feminist methodologies ... they argue that quantitative methods cannot convey an in depth understanding of, or feeling for, those being researched ...
>
> (1990: 90)

But, as she points out, 'the problem is perhaps not quantification itself but insensitive quantification' (*ibid*.: 91) and there has in the last decade been more of an acceptance of quantitative methods, in particular the social survey (see Kelly *et al.*, 1994; Maynard, 1994; Hester *et al.*, 1997). As Kelly puts it, 'certain research questions, important to feminists, can only be answered where relatively large numbers, and a cross-section of the population, participate in the study', for instance, 'answering the question "how common is child sexual abuse" has implications for social policy' (1990: 113). In the area of violence, there have been several radical feminist surveys in this country (see Hanmer and Saunders, 1984; Radford, 1987; McGibbon *et al.*, 1989; Kelly and Radford, 1997). These have been characterized by an extremely sensitive approach, such as the careful wording of questionnaires, providing help-line cards, referrals to support groups, setting up self-help groups and organising community meetings (Kelly and Radford, 1987; Radford, 1987). Furthermore (as noted above in referring to the Wandsworth survey; Radford, 1987), radical feminists have generally retained an emphasis on subjective experience by using women's definitions of violence. Thus Hanmer and Saunders comment:

> In our study we did not want to pre-determine the meaning of the term violence. We wanted women to define violence for themselves.

We wanted to know about the experiences of women and the lines that they drew around their experiences.

(1984: 30)

Policy

The ultimate goal of radical feminism is to overthrow the patriarchal social order: 'a future free of the threat and reality of sexual violence requires nothing less than the total transformation of patriarchal relations' (Kelly and Radford, 1987: 247). In the short term, however, they argue for men's violence to be treated seriously. For men this involves the

> questioning and challenging [of] the patriarchal construction of masculinity... [This] requires men to take responsibility for their sexual practice: to, for example, critically examine the use of force, coercion or pressure in heterosexual relations and how pornography affects their attitudes to, and behaviour in relationships with, women.
>
> (*ibid.*: 239)

For women this can amount to a separatist position. Indeed, according to Jill Radford and Elizabeth Stanko, we must question 'whether heterosexuality is the natural, normal and only possibility for women, whether it is indeed voluntary or compulsory for women living under the conditions of patriarchy and whether it is in our best interests' (1991: 200). The implication of this is that as men are the major perpetrators of violence, women should try to have as little as possible to do with them. This can be seen as including the present legal system, for this is frequently seen as having failed to respond to the problem of male violence. Catherine MacKinnon argues this is because

> the state is male in the feminist sense. The law sees and treats women the way men see and treat women. The liberal state coercively and authoritatively constitutes the social order in the interest of men as gender, through its legitimizing norms, relation to society, and substantive policies. It achieves this through the embodying and ensuring male control over women's sexuality at every level, occasionally cushioning, qualifying, or de jure prohibiting its excesses when necessary to its normalisation.
>
> (1993: 207)

Many radical feminists have, however, campaigned for changes in legal and police practice, and argue for the government and public agencies to improve their response to women and to make men account-able for their behaviour. In terms of governmental crime prevention advice, the Home Office's emphasis on 'stranger danger' and reducing fear of crime has been strongly criticized (see, for example, Stanko, 1990; 1992; Radford and Stanko, 1991; Hester *et al.*, 1996). But, as Susan Edwards notes, this is not without some ambivalence, for some radical feminists, whom she calls 'feminist idealists', 'have argued that the state and the law, the legal mechanism and the police are part of a patriar-chal structure, under which attempts at legal reform are only tinkerings within the overall system of control and regulation – so legal change serves only to perpetuate the basic conditions of patriarchy' (1989: 15).[20] MacKinnon proposes instead of changes to man-made law, the introduction of a feminist jurisprudence grounded in women's experi-ences, which is, as Smart comments, an attempt 'to provide a way out of the engulfing embrace of liberalism which, in the form of law reform, has done so little to emancipate women' (1989: 76). Radical feminists have also acknowledged the limitations of the criminal justice system. As Radford and Stanko point out, removing the married man's exemp-tion in terms of marital rape 'will not automatically protect women from sexual abuse by their husbands' (1991: 195).

On the police, radical feminists, whilst stressing the need for improve-ment and generally welcoming improved policies, are cautious of giv-ing the police too much power. It is noted, for example, how the first Domestic Violence Units in London were located in Tottenham and Brixton, the location of poor black–police relations (Mama, 1989; Radford and Stanko, 1991). Mama suggests that 'such units have a hidden agenda, concerned with convicting more black men' (1989: 304–5). Likewise Hanmer and Saunders (1984) argue that too much police power will lead the police to harass women, just as they harass members of the black and Irish communities. They base this assump-tion in their own personal experience. Thus they comment:

we were, co-incidently, being harassed by the West Yorkshire Police. The first call was about arson attacks on sex/video shops in a suburb of Leeds and the second and third were about the attempted bomb-ing of the Leeds Conservative Party head-quarters. The last visit involved a thorough search of our home. The papers taken were cor-respondence from well-known women academics and publishers in Britain regarding a French feminist theoretical journal, *Nouvelles Questions Feministes*, whose editor-in-chief is Simone de Beauvoir, one copy of a British feminist women-only magazine, and a graduate student's essay on menstruation ... Our only 'crimes' are to help individual women who have been abused, and to write about violence from men to women, including how little the police do to protect women from attack by men ... We conclude that to dare to speak out is to have a police file made on you; to be 'lifted' without evidence.

(ibid.: 111–12)

With respect to other professional agencies, for example, social work, Victim Support and the various counselling services that have sprung up in the last few years, radical feminists frequently argue that they fail to 'offer a gendered analysis about violence against women' (Radford and Stanko, 1991: 198). It is pointed out, particularly with respect to 'the newly arrived caring professionals', that they frequently present

Physical battering ... [as] either a reflection of bad marital relations, personality disputes, or intoxicating substances, not the manifestation of unequal power and a need for control. Sexual abuse, following the same line, arises because of men's uncontrollable lust or miscommunication with women and children, not as an exercise of patriarchal power.

(ibid.: 198–9)

Further, 'instead of forwarding women's and children's best interests, we see too many of these professionals containing women within the structures of heterosexuality and the family and building lucrative careers for themselves on the backs of male violence' (*ibid.*: 191). Thus the need for radical feminists to monitor all agencies and policy development is stressed.

In contrast to state and professional agencies, feminists have provided women-centred support services, such as Women's Aid and Rape Crisis. Unlike the more mainstream agencies these organizations offer 'unconditional support for women and children in whatever strategies they elect' (*ibid.*: 191). These organizations have arisen directly out of women's experiences and 'because of the inadequacies in the responses of statutory agencies and the extent to which myths and stereotypes are reflected in their practice' (Kelly, 1988a: 380). Moreover, the need for women's collective support and action is constantly stressed throughout the radical feminist literature. As Hanmer and Saunders argue,

Our strength must be in our women's groups and organisations. We have to organise to protect ourselves and our children from all forms of male violence and control.

(1984: 112)

While Liz Kelly maintains:

> It was never the intention of those of us who chose work in this area in the 1970s that our work become limited to 'band aid' solutions: as Maria Zavala puts it, 'a MASH unit, patching up the wounded and sending them back to the front line' ... No matter how effective our services and support networks, no matter how much change in policy and practice is achieved, without a mass movement of women committed to resisting sexual violence in all its forms there will continue to be casualties in the 'shadow war' and women's and girl's lives will continue to be circumscribed by the reality of sexual violence.
>
> (1988a: 238)

In the next chapter many of the insights of radical feminism will be used to contribute to the theoretical and methodological backcloth of this book. Of particular note are its conception of human nature as socially constructed; of male violence as widespread and central to the maintaining of the patriarchal social order, serving as a key mechanism for the social control of women, and its advocacy of sensitive research methods. However, there are some crucial difficulties with its analysis which need to be addressed.

Criticisms of radical feminism

Essentialism

Although radical feminism quite correctly stresses the social construction of masculinity and criticizes the essentialist notion of the use of 'the instinctive man' as an excuse for violence, it tends to lapse itself into essentialism. Thus there is a tendency in radical feminism to hold an essentialist notion of masculinity and of patriarchal institutions. That is, male behaviour is seen in some ahistorical way to be the same whatever place and whatever time one is talking about: 'Boys will be boys', 'Men: they are all the same'. But there is obviously variation across time in the extent of violence against women and the gross variation in international patterns of homicide against women clearly indicates that place is also of great significance. Furthermore, the specific forms of violence (for example, changes in the number and nature of serial killing) must be explained: why they emerge or change at certain times (see Messerschmidt, 1993). Anthony Giddens, for example, argues that violence in general (whether in politics or in the home) occurs when hegemony, rule by consent, breaks down. Domestic violence, then, would occur when male hegemony is threatened (see Giddens, 1992); it would not be a universal constant. Such essentialism is rooted in the literature. Thus Brownmiller's arguments in *Against Our Will: Men, Women and Rape* (1975), whilst having considerable influence, have been criticized, as have those of other radical feminists, for biological essentialism (see Wilson, 1983; Edwards, 1987; Lovenduski and Randall, 1993; Walklate, 1995). Brownmiller, for example, suggests that men rape because they have the biological capacity to do so; thus 'men's structural capacity to rape and women's corresponding structural vulnerability are as basic to the physiology of both sexes as the primal act of sex itself...when men discovered they could rape, they proceeded to do it' (1975: 13–14). However, in more recent radical feminist writing, especially in Britain, there has been a concern to stress that the criticism of biological essentialism is a misrepresentation of radical feminist analyses: violence is seen a product of the social construction of masculinity (Hanmer *et al.*, 1989; see also Walby, 1990, on Brownmiller). It is pointed out that 'demands that men examine and reject their misogynistic construction of masculinity, and their oppressive practices would be meaningless if they came from biologistic arguments about the inherent and therefore unchangeable nature of man' (*ibid.*).

Masculinities

Closely related to the problem of essentialism is the manner in which radical feminism tends to obscure differences between men. Important here is the current debate over masculinities: the plural form in which masculinity is expressed in different ethnic, class and age situations. As James Messerschmidt puts it:

> The radical feminist focus on alleged differences between men and women acted to obscure differences among men. For example, the social experiences of African-American men differ from those of white men due to racist and classist structures that systematically disadvantage African-American men. Moreover, radical feminism obscures the fact that men exercise unequal amounts of control over their own lives as well as over the lives of women. By concentrating on alleged differences between men and women, radical feminists fail to consider the variations among men in terms of race, class, age and sexual preference, focusing instead on an alleged 'typical male,' as if he represents all men. Radical feminist theory disregards how

social differences between men create, for example, varying forms of masculinity and, for example, different types and degrees of violence against women. This theoretical focus on the 'typical male' leads to a 'model of male agency which is at best one-dimensional' (Liddle, 1989: 762). Such an analysis regards 'masculinity as more or less unrelieved villainy and all men as agents of the patriarchy in more or less the same degree' (Carrigan, Connell and Lee, 1987: 140).

(1993: 45)

This problem relates to the tendency to prioritize gender over the main axes of social structure (that is, class, ethnicity and age) or, indeed, ignore all else but gender. This is, of course, a parallel problem to that of socialist feminism which, as we have seen, tended to ignore ethnicity and stress class. Obviously, masculinity, as it is enacted, occurs in particular sites in the social structure and is shaped and dictated by class, age and ethnicity, just as women in these sites are affected by the particular masculinity which they encounter in the context of their own class, age and ethnic positions.

The overemphasis on sexuality

As we have seen in the discussion of socialist feminism, there are many facets to women's oppression that cannot be reduced to sexuality alone. For instance, there is the question of the position of women in the labour market. With respect to violence, although an examination of the construction of heterosexual relationships is fundamental to the understanding of male violence against women in the home, an emphasis on male sexuality cannot account for other forms of violence such as lesbian battering (Lobel, 1986; Renzetti, 1992; 1998).

Furthermore, as Bryson notes, the classifying together of all heterosexual acts – as in Kelly's concept of the continuum of sexual violence – may have the effect of concealing 'the horror of actual rape' (1992: 215). Many feminists (for example, Segal, 1987; Lovenduski and Randall, 1993) have protested against the hostility expressed by some radical feminists towards male sexuality. To imply that male violence leads women to question their heterosexuality and that separatism may be a preferred option in patriarchal society is out of touch with the wishes of the majority of women and the reality of their lives.

A problem of method

As we have seen, radical feminists argue for broad, all-encompassing definitions which aim to reflect women's subjective experience. However, it can be argued that an over-reliance on such an approach masks the very real definitional differences that exist amongst different groups of the population arising from factors such as gender, age, ethnicity, class and education. Categorizing all forms of violence together prevents the examination of the differential impact of violence as experienced by different groups of women and the assessment of their specific needs.

Moreover, some of the principles identified as constituting a 'feminist method' are difficult to put into practice when interviewing men or in large-scale survey work. For example, the breaking down of hierarchical relationships may be hard to achieve, if not impossible, if the interviewee is a man. Moreover, if we are to examine the construction of masculinity, the research process must at some point involve men. A 'collaborative approach' is, in addition, likely to prove impractical if 1,000 people are participating in the study. And the democratization of the research process will be hampered if some of those being interviewed do not like the interviewer or express attitudes and politics that are abhorrent to the research team, as is likely to occur in survey work where a cross-section of the population is participating in the research.

Finally, radical feminist surveys have been criticized for using either too small or biased samples which prevent their results from being generalized to the population as a whole (see MacLean, 1985). In part, such a criticism can be met by pointing to the problems of underfunding and arguing that with sufficient funds sizeable and reliable samples would be possible. But there is a tendency in radical feminism which would argue that 'small is good' and perhaps believe that women's opinions and consciousness are so similar that the differentiation of sub-populations is relatively unimportant. The position argued in this book is that both small- *and* large-scale research work is necessary, preferably in conjunction, and that the level of consensus between different parts of the population is necessarily problematic.

4
Feminist Realism: a Synthesis

Left realism

Left realism[1] emerged in the mid-1980s as a criminological theory of the Left. Its genesis was in the political conjuncture of neoliberalism and the New Left. In this period, throughout the developed world, conservative governments emerged, committed to *laisser-faire* economics and law and order politics, to incentives for work and punishment for crime. On the Left a libertarian current, inherited from the 1960s, took a diametrically opposite viewpoint on crime and policing. Realism sets itself up against both these positions. Its intellectual and political influence has been greatest in Britain (Matthews and Young, 1992; Lea and Young, 1993; Young, 1997) but parallel work is evident in the United States (see Currie, 1985; DeKeseredy and Schwartz, 1996) and in Canada (see Lowman and Maclean, 1992). This chapter will begin with a brief introduction to left realism and then turn to analyse its main principles in relation to our grid of questions. It will conclude by exploring the possibility of some synthesis between radical and left realism. That is a feminist realism which will take from the more positive insights of both theories and learn from the problems encountered by both.

The starting point of left realism is to take on board people's concerns about crime, showing these to be more rational and realistic than either the new administrative (see Chapter 1) or the Marxist-influenced critical criminologies make out. Left realists describe much of critical criminology – sometimes termed 'left idealism' – as typically minimizing the importance of working-class crime by emphasizing the crimes of the powerful (that is, those of the ruling class: the police, corporations and state agencies) and seeing 'the war against crime as a side-track from the class struggle, at best an illusion invented to sell news, at worst an attempt to make the poor scapegoats by blaming their brutalizing circumstances on themselves' (Lea and Young, 1984: 1). As John Lowman has put it, realists have faulted critical criminology 'for treating crime as an epiphenomenon, with the criminal – conceived as a sort of socialist homunculus or proto-revolutionary – being viewed as determined and blameless, punishment as unwarranted or amplificatory' (1992: 141). Thus John Lea and Jock Young point out there was a

> belief that property offences are directed solely against the bourgeoisie and that violence against the person is carried out by amateur Robin Hoods in the course of their righteous attempt to redistribute wealth. All of this is, alas, untrue.
>
> (1984: 262)

Left realism starts with the problems as people experience them: it therefore treats 'seriously the complaints of women with regards the dangers of being in public places at night, it takes note of the fears of the elderly with regard to burglary, it acknowledges the widespread occurrence of domestic violence and racist attacks' (Young, 1986: 24). And it is feminist research, such as that documented in the last chapter, that is credited with influencing left realism's perspective on the victim of crime. For feminist work on rape, domestic violence and sexual harassment is described as having brought home 'the limits of the romantic conception of crime and the criminal' as conveyed by critical criminology (Matthews and Young, 1986: 2; see also, Jones *et al.*, 1986). Thus left realism is committed to the construction of a more accurate victimology in criminology, one that takes into account the extent of victimisation and also its social and geographical focus.

However, the concern of left realism is not just with 'taking crime seriously' and the victims of crime; crucially, it argues that criminology must embrace the totality of the criminal process if it is to reflect the *reality* of crime. That is, it must take into account the fact that crime must involve formal and informal control systems (the reaction to crime), as well as offenders and victims (the criminal action). This is described by realists as the 'square of crime' (Figure 4.1).

Left realists seek to explain crime in relation to the four corners of the square, and as such they describe previous criminological theories as suffering from the problem of 'partiality' in that they focus on just one part of the square: formal control (as in classicism), informal social

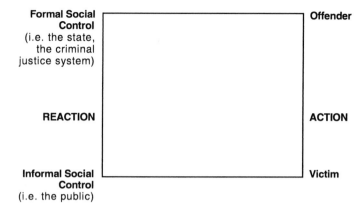

Formal Social
Control
(i.e. the state,
the criminal
justice system)

Offender

REACTION

ACTION

Informal Social
Control
(i.e. the public)

Victim

Figure 4.1　The square of crime

control (as in new administrative criminology/control theory), the offender (as in positivism) or the victim (as in victimology). Realism's approach, therefore, 'emphasises synthesis rather than a simple dismissal of opposing theories' (Young, 1988b: 158) and attempts to develop a coherent analysis which encompasses these diverse positions.

Human nature

> As an activity, crime involves a moral choice at a certain point in time in changing determinant circumstances. It has neither the totally determined quality beloved by positivism, nor the wilful display of rationality enshrined in classicist legal doctrine. It is a moral act, but one which must be constantly assessed within a determined social context. It is neither an act of determined pathology, nor an obvious response to desperate situations.
>
> (Young, 1997: 487)

For left realists the human situation involves freedom of choice in a world of determined circumstances. Human behaviour is presented as a problem-solving activity; individuals choose to act in a certain way in response to the structural problems that face them. Left realism is, therefore, similar to subcultural theory (see, for example, Cohen, 1965; Willis, 1977). Using this framework, a man who is violent to his wife or girlfriend will be seen as exercising moral choice (free will) in reaction to certain restricting circumstances. These circumstances are typically considered to be determined by his particular position in the social structure. In general, crime is 'one form of subcultural adaption which occurs where material circumstances block cultural aspirations and where non-criminal alternatives are absent or less attractive' (Young, 1994: 111). However, as the offender is exercising a moral choice – that is, has purposively chosen violence as a problem-solving activity – he is seen as fully responsible for his actions. For, as Jock Young comments:

> mugging, wife-battering, burglary and child abuse are actions which cannot be morally absolved in the flux of determinacy. The offender should be ashamed, he/she should feel morally responsible within the limits of circumstance and rehabilitation is truly *impossible* without this moral dimension.
>
> (1986: 28–9, original emphasis)

Social order

Left realists are critical of the existing social order based on capitalism and leading to massive inequalities in the social structure. Echoing Merton, they point to the fundamental contradiction within capitalist societies between the widespread cultural belief in a meritocracy and the actual, grossly unequal class structure. For the meritocratic system on which capitalism is legitimated gives rise to a widespread contradiction between people's aspirations and their actual opportunities. As Corrigan, Jones, Lloyd and Young put it:

> On the metaphor of the race track: some people start half way along the track, while others are forced to run with a stone about their necks while other still are not allowed on the track at all. The result feeds alienation and discontent. Many of the well-off succeed through the right connections rather than genuine effort: they started at the finishing post. The unsuccessful are rejected from a society which has little respect for them economically or politically.
>
> (1988a: 8)

Thus capitalism is presented as a system which creates disorder and for left realists crime is a clear indicator of a disordered society. For social order to be achieved, society must be seen to be fair: 'society is held together to the extent that it is seen by its members as just' (Young, 1994: 116). It is a just politics that is important and left realists are committed to the social democratic reform of the capitalist system.

Definition

The definitional issue has always been a stumbling block within criminology. Often criminologists have relied on simplistic definitions of crime and seen it as an 'act', or alternatively they have denied the significance of the act and claimed that it is a function of the 'reaction'.

(Matthews and Young, 1992a: 17)

For left realists definition is central to the analysis of crime, thus the difficulties in defining what is 'domestic violence' are acknowledged, but seen as part of the necessary structure of what constitutes violence. Realism, with its focus on the square of crime, attempts to understand this 'construction' of crime as a constant interaction between changes in behaviour ('action') and definition ('reaction'). For crime is not inherent in any action as the positivists believe, nor is it a simple construction as labelling theorists suggest, but both components come into play. Thus realists argue that they 'do not and cannot take or accept official definitions of crime unquestioningly... [nor do they] accept public or commonsense definitions of crime uncritically or adopt essentialist conceptions' (*ibid.*: 10).

Realism is critical of legalistic definitions of domestic violence (see Chapter 1) and it is pointed out that this form of violence 'can involve a variety of sub-species, each with its own life-cycle' (Young, 1992a: 41). Thus we must be specific about the 'type' of violence involved. Furthermore, as previously noted, there are certain modes of domestic violence (for example, mental cruelty) that fall *outside* the legal categories of 'violence'. This, according to left realists, 'suggests the necessity of typologies which cut across legal or formal definitions' (*ibid.*: 41). Further, these typologies must correspond to people's 'lived realities': the problem with conventional surveys such as the British Crime Surveys is that they utilize objective/legalistic definitions without taking into account subjective definitions and, in doing so, 'commonly trivialize that which is important and makes important that which is trivial' (Young, 1988a: 173).

Public definitions of domestic violence are seen as varying according to the values and perceptions of the person doing the defining: what is 'violence' to one person may not necessarily be 'violence' to another, although all crimes are seen as involving definitional variation – the subjective component is presented as being greater for violence than property crimes. Moreover, a person's definition of what constitutes violence is likely to be affected by such social factors as gender, age, ethnicity, class and education. For instance, educated women have been found to report more violence in general against them than those with less education (Sparks, 1981). Furthermore, the context in which the violence takes place may also be important, and definitions of what is intolerable behaviour will change over time.

Thus, subjective definitions are deemed important, for they are necessarily part of what constitutes violence. Furthermore, in line with left realism's democratic approach to understanding crime, it is considered 'the privilege of various publics to make their own appraisal' (Young, 1988a: 176). However, such a position does not lead to a position of relativism: for left realists note that within and between all social groups there is a wide consensus about what is serious violence and this 'unity of interest allows us the possibility, both of a common measuring rod, and a political base for taking crime seriously' (Young, 1992a: 59). It is seen to be not 'beyond the capabilities of researchers to ask questions of not only reported violent behaviour but to construct tolerance scales towards violence' (*ibid*.: 58).

Extent and distribution

The construction of crime rates

For left realists, crime rates 'are a product ... of changes in the number of possible offenders, the number of potential victims, and the changing levels of control exercised by the official agencies of control and the public' (Young, 1992a: 27–8). Thus, in accordance with the emphasis on the construction of crime rates as a process, the rate of crime is presented as resulting from the interaction of the four points of the square of crime. And changes in the crime rate over time may well be a product of an increased sensitivity to violence or a rise in violent behaviour, or indeed both. Rates of domestic violence would, likewise, be calculated in this way. Thus, if domestic violence is found to have risen, this would by necessity be due to changes in definition over time with respect to what is tolerable behaviour within a relationship or to changes in the frequency of domestically violent acts or to some combination of both. This is not seen as making 'it any the less "real"': for this is exactly what crime rates *really* are' (Young, 1988a: 161, original emphasis).

Extent

All forms of violence against women, including that of domestic violence, are presented by left realists as widespread. Indeed, as Young comments, 'a typical category of violence in Britain is a man battering his wife' (1986: 22). Official statistics are seen as severely underestimating the scale as domestic violence is frequently not reported to the police by the public. In the first Islington Crime Survey, conducted by left realists, of all the categories of assault, domestic violence was found to be the least likely to be reported to the police (Jones *et al.*, 1986). Moreover, when it is reported, domestic violence, along with sexual offences, is particularly susceptible to 'no-criming'. No-criming, the nullifying of a crime report, can occur when 'the police do not consider an act to be criminal within the legal definitions set out by the criminal code, and sometimes [when] the police recognise the event to be criminal but can see no resolution to it' (*ibid.*: 37).

Indeed, the general problem of the hidden figure of crime unknown to the police has led realists to argue that 'to base criminological theory, or social policy for that matter, on the majority of official figures is an exercise in "guesstimates" and tealeaf gazing' (Young, 1988a: 164). Crime surveys, particularly those based on local areas, are seen as presenting us with a much clearer picture of the extent of crime than that available from official statistics. In the first Islington Crime Survey, respondents were asked in detail, using sensitive interviewing techniques (see below), about their experiences of domestic violence: an 'alarming proportion of assault' – 22 per cent – was found to be 'domestic in nature' (Jones *et al.*, 1986: 63). However, it is readily admitted by left realists, that, like police figures and for similar reasons, crime surveys are more likely to underestimate domestic violence and sexual offences than all other forms of crime (Crawford *et al.*, 1986). As Young notes, 'domestic crimes are not only less likely to be reported to interviewers, but have in all probability a greater frequency amongst those who refuse interview' (1988a: 169). The chief advantage, then, of the crime survey is that the hidden figure is smaller; not that it is by any means eliminated.

Distribution

Left realists argue that crime is focused both geographically in certain areas, particularly the inner city, and socially in certain groups. Indeed statistics that conflate low and high crime areas tend to obscure the fashion in which crime is pinpointed within the population. For there is no such thing as an 'average' victim, and local surveys have shown that it is those who are the most 'vulnerable' in society – that is, the working class, women and ethnic minorities – who tend to have the highest rates of crime overall against them. Further, most crime is seen as perpetrated by persons from within the victim's own social ranks, for instance,

> the vast majority of working class crime is directed within the working class. Similarly, despite the mass media predilection for focusing on inter-racial crime it is overwhelmingly intra-racial.
>
> (Young, 1986: 23)

Most conventional crime is, therefore, seen as being intra-class and intra-racial. It occurs within groups, not between groups. However, with respect to domestic violence and indeed all forms of violence against women, this is considered to be largely inter-gender. Specifically, it is committed predominantly by men against women: domestic violence and sexual offences, 'are almost exclusively ... "female prerogative[s]"' (Young, 1988a: 170).

In terms of social structural distribution, domestic violence is not thought to be evenly or randomly distributed throughout the population. Thus it is considered more prevalent in the lower socio-economic groups: 'crimes of violence, for example, are by and large one poor person hitting another poor person – and in almost half of these instances it is a man hitting his wife or lover' (Young, 1986: 23). Furthermore, the first Islington Crime Survey found younger women to have higher rates of domestic violence against them than those in the older age groups.

Causes

The present period in criminology is characterized by a retreat from a discussion of wider social causes of offending. With a few notable exceptions (Currie, 1985; Braithwaite, 1979), the social democratic tradition of making the link between social structure and offending is severed. In part, this is a response of establishment criminology to new right governments, which, quite clearly, wish to embrace theories which disconnect their policies from rises in the crime rates ... The British school of administrative criminology was doubtful about the validity of causes of 'dispositions' altogether. The realists of the right, such as James Q. Wilson, did not deny that there were causes of crime. Indeed, they outlined a plethora of causes (Wilson and Herrnstein, 1985). Rather, they point to the few 'causes' which can be altered without making social changes which would be politically unacceptable, which stresses the individual rather than the social causes of crime. Travis Hirschi (1969), in his influential 'control theory', abandons causation to the extent that it is identified with motivation. Cause metamorphoses from active desire into absence of restraint.

(Young, 1992a: 30–1)

Left realism, in contrast, is concerned with the *social causes* of crime. A significant influence on the theory has been the work of Merton (1938) and Cloward and Ohlin (1960) on anomie and relative deprivation (see Lea, 1992). Although left realists do not advocate monocausality, relative deprivation is presented as a major cause of crime. As Jock Young comments, it occurs

> when people experience a level of unfairness in their allocation of resources and utilize individualistic means to attempt to right this condition. It is a reaction to the experience of injustice.
>
> (1997: 488)

Crime can, therefore, occur anywhere within the social structure. It is not the monopoly of the poor; for relative deprivation is experienced throughout the classes. John Lea (1992), for example, relates the concept of relative deprivation to white-collar and corporate crime. It is not dependent on absolute levels of deprivation: indeed, realists stress that the crime rate was low in the 1930s despite extreme levels of poverty. On the whole, however, Left realists emphasize the importance of working-class crime and, as such, it is pointed out that 'it is among the poor, particularly the lower working class and certain ethnic minorities who are marginalised from the "glittering prizes" of the wider society, that the push towards crime is greater than elsewhere in the social structure' (*ibid.*: 487–8).

Violence against women

Left realists have written little about the specific causes of domestic violence. On violence against women in general, it is acknowledged that the core problem is patriarchy (see Young, 1988a; Painter *et al.*, 1990b), that the definition is a social construction and that violence is socially activated in given situations. However, the role of biological difference is not rejected out of hand; it is merely relegated to the role of an intervening variable. As Young puts it:

> [left] realism does not reject the fact of correlations between biology and crime, whether that involves body shape, hormone systems,

size, or age. In rejecting biological reduction, [various] theories throw the baby out with the bathwater and reject biology itself. It is a fact that larger, more powerful people commit more violence than smaller people, that male hormones correlate strongly with violence, that the well muscled are more of a threat than the plump and unfit. People do not, after all, cross the street at night to avoid old ladies. Thus realism argues that the causes of patriarchal violence against women or the machismo of lower-working-class youth are rooted in social situations, not biology, and that the physical capacity to commit crime is merely an intervening variable.

(1997: 489)

With respect to the 'social forces' that activate violence, the focus remains on relative deprivation. The experience of relative deprivation is seen as having an important role in the construction of masculinity: 'men frequently react to adversity by creating a culture of *machismo* which is insensitive to violence and, indeed, in some groups glorifies it' (Young, 1988a: 175; 1999, Chapter 1). John Lea argues that 'interpersonal "expressive" violence' should be seen as a way of 'establishing status in the absence of conventional means and symbols' (1992: 74). Hence, '"crimes of passion" such as homicide, and inter-personal violence such as sexual assault and rape, have a concentration among the poor and deprived and can be seen as arising from the dynamics of relative deprivation' (*ibid.*: 74–5). To explain this further, Lea makes use of a quotation from Steve Box on the dynamics of rape by men from poor backgrounds:

When men from this latter group rape they rely primarily on physical violence because this is the resource they command. Being relatively unable to 'wine and dine' females or place them in a position of social debt, and being less able to induce in women a sense of physical and emotional overcomeness these 'socially' powerless men are left with a sense of resentment and bitterness which is fanned and inflamed by cultural sex-role stereotypes of 'successful' men being sexually potent (Box, 1983: 152).

(*ibid.*: 75)[2]

For left realists it is the inequalities in capitalist society, together with the competitive individualism that capitalism breeds, that results in relative deprivation and the subsequent utilization of violence.

A note on the parallel with socialist feminism

The main arguments presented by left realists on violence are similar to those of socialist feminists. Thus Elizabeth Wilson (1983), Lynne Segal (1989; 1990) and James Messerschmidt (1993; 1997) present violence as a result of the frustrations generated by class and racial inequalities. Wilson comments: 'the working-class youth's aggression – "bovver" – becomes a front to conceal his inner desperation and to protect him against a hostile world that condemns him, essentially, to failure' (*ibid.*: 231). While Lynne Segal argues, with reference to domestic violence, 'what we are confronting here is the barbarism of private life reflecting back to the increased barbarism of public life as contemporary capitalism continues to chisel out its hierarchies along the familiar grooves of class, race and gender' (1990: 271). For socialist feminists,

> It is social cooperation, not excessive individualism, that would form a better basis for social life and for relations between the sexes, and would best meet the needs of most of us, women and men together.
> None of this will happen so long as our society is run on the profit motive, which is the elevation of greed as the basic social principle.
>
> (Wilson, 1983: 242)

Impact

> The myth of the equal victim underscores much of conventional victimology with the notion that victims are, as it were, equal billiard balls, and the risk rate involves merely the calculation of the chances of an offending billiard ball impacting upon them. People are, of course, not equal; they are, more or less, vulnerable, depending on their place in society ... It is high time, therefore, that we substituted *impact* statistics for *risk* statistics.
>
> (Young, 1992a: 51–2; original emphasis)

Overall crime is seen as having a substantial impact on people's lives. For example, fear of being victimized shapes people's lives; thus in the first Islington Crime Survey a quarter of all respondents avoided going out after dark, specifically because of fear of crime, and 28 per cent felt unsafe in their own homes. There was a virtual curfew on a substantial section of the female population, with over a half of women 'often or always' not going out at dark because of fear of crime. These fears are presented by left realists as basically rational: those who fear crime most tend to have the highest risk rates. Moreover, those who are most likely to experience crime – women, ethnic minorities and the working class – suffer a greater degree of impact because of their relatively 'vulnerable' position in the social structure. They tend to have less access to money and resources and suffer from other social problems. Indeed, it is pointed out:

> If we were to draw a map of the city outlining areas of high infant mortality, bad housing, unemployment, poor nutrition, etc, we would find that all these maps would coincide and that further, the outline traced would correspond to those areas of high criminal victimisation.
>
> (Young, 1992a: 52)

The effect of crime is, therefore, seen as compounding other social problems. With respect to the specific difficulties experienced by women, the Ladywood Crime Survey, conducted by left realists, indicates that:

> Women on poorer council estates and deprived inner city areas bear the brunt of all social problems. This occurs because of gender inequalities in the division of labour within the home and structural inequalities in society. In urban areas, these fundamental inequalities have increased significantly throughout the 1980s. Cuts in public sector expenditure, changes in the structure and organisation of the housing market and the social benefit system, have increased women's unemployment and dependence. These changes also reinforce women's restricted access to community facilities such as child care, transport, education and health.
>
> (Painter *et al.*, 1990b: 27–8)

In this context, domestic violence would be considered by realists to have a considerable impact on women's lives in terms of the actual violence experienced and in compounding the specific problems encountered by women. As Young comments, 'crime in the home occurs within a relationship of economic dependency: the woman – particularly if she has children – cannot walk away' (1988a: 175). A poor or inappropriate response from the police or other help-seeking agencies is also considered to add to the impact of the violence. Furthermore, domestic violence is seen as occurring 'within an emotional bond, which gives it all the more hurtful poignancy' (*ibid.*: 175).

Empirical data on the impact of domestic violence

The first Islington Crime Survey (Jones *et al.*, 1986) asked women in detail about the impact that domestic violence had on them. Ninety-six per cent of those with experience of domestic violence reported that it had a 'very big effect' on them and their households. Table 4.1 shows the type of violent behaviours reported, the degree of injuries, weapons used and the help sought from general practitioners. These results provide an insight into the scale and effects of domestic violence.

Table 4.1 Findings from the first Islington Crime Survey: % of those experiencing domestic violence

	%
Type of violence	
Grabbed/pushed	75
Punched/slapped	92
Kicked	57
Weapon used	20
Raped	–
Attempted rape	0.7
Sexually assaulted	2
Other	6
Injury sustained	
Bruises/black eyes	97
Scratches	62
Cuts	45
Broken bones	10
Other	15
Type of weapon	
Bottle or glass	33
Knife or scissors	21
Stick, club or blunt object	28
Firearm	–
Other	17
Reasons for attending doctor	
Physical injuries	94
Difficulty sleeping	35
Worried, anxious, nervous	46
Felt depressed	40
Shock	41
Headaches	37
Nausea	24
Other	5

Source: ibid.: 172–4.

Methods

The method most commonly associated with left realists is the local crime survey. Left realists have been responsible for a number of local surveys.[3] Many of these surveys have been commissioned and funded by socialist local authorities.[4] The local crime survey is seen by left realists as

> a democratic instrument: it provides a reasonably accurate portrayal of people's fears and of their experience of victimization ... Social surveys ... allow us to give voice to the experience of people, and they enable us to differentiate the safety needs of different sectors of the community.
>
> (Young, 1992a: 50)

In terms of structure, local crime surveys, like the national British Crime Surveys conducted by new administrative criminologists (see Chapter 1), make use of face-to-face interviews and structured questionnaires to obtain information from a sample of the population about crimes that have been committed against them. However, unlike national surveys, the local survey is focused on specific areas – usually inner-city locations. Left realists, as we have seen, argue that national surveys are unable to deal adequately with the fact that crime is focused geographically in certain areas and socially amongst particular groups of people. The use of large samples in the local crime surveys enables the experience and impact of crime to be broken down in terms of its social focus. That is on social groups based on the combination of age, gender, social class and ethnicity. Such a high level of focusing is considered to correspond 'more closely to the lived realities of different groups and sub-cultures of the population' (Young, 1992a: 38). Indeed it is pointed out:

> just as it is inaccurate to generalise about crime and policing from gross figures based on large geographical areas, it is incorrect, even within particular areas, to talk in terms of, for example, 'all' young people, 'all' women, 'all' blacks, 'all' working-class people, etc. Generalizations which remain on such global levels frequently obfuscate quite contradictory experiences, generating statistics which often conceal vital differences of impact.
>
> (*ibid.*: 39)

Thus, in the Second Islington Crime Survey, it was found that:

> the introduction of age into the analysis of fear of crime by gender changes the usual generality of men having a low fear of crime and

women high. In fact, older women have a fear of crime rather like men in the middle age group, and younger women have a fear rather like old men. And, in the case of footstops by the police, it becomes evident that differentials based on race are much more complicated than the abstraction that blacks are more likely to be stopped than whites. No older black women in our sample were stopped. Young, white, women were over three times more likely to be stopped than older black men. And even the differential between young black men and young white men becomes remarkably narrowed when class is introduced into the equation.

(Young, 1992a: 39)

In their endeavour to explore the total process of crime – the four points of the square of crime – left realists have also widened the usual scope of the crime survey. They incorporate a wide range of questions on victimization, including racial and sexual harassment, domestic violence (first Islington Crime Survey), child abuse (second Islington Crime Survey) and commercial crimes (second Islington Crime Survey); self-report questions on offences committed; public evaluation of the police and other agencies (for example, local council, victim support schemes), belief about police illegalities, attitudes to the punishment appropriate to various crimes, avoidance behaviours, and so on. Indeed, it is suggested that the range of the local survey could be extended further: 'it would be quite easy to add to a criminal victimisation survey, a medical epidemiological questionnaire in order to measure the prevalence of illness caused by chemical pollution' (Young and Matthews, 1992a: 14).

Researching violence against women

In the very difficult area of violence against women, left realists, influenced by the work of feminists (in particular Russell, 1982; Hanmer and Saunders, 1984; Hall, 1985), stress the necessity of using committed, sympathetic interviewers to gain more reliable results. Indeed, the first Islington Crime Survey utilized a number of the methodological innovations outlined by Russell in *Rape in Marriage* (1982) for interviewing respondents in the crime survey situation. These included:

- an interview schedule designed to encourage good rapport
- selection of interviewers based on interviewing skills
- extensive training of interviewers in relation to sexual assault (and also domestic violence) and its investigation in the field

- utilization of an indirect questioning procedure which would help to reduce embarrassment or difficulty of relating the incident directly to the interviewer (Jones *et al.*, 1986: 69)

Young further emphasizes the importance of carefully worded questions: for 'there is a world of difference between simply asking the interviewee if she has been raped (as do most conventional surveys), and defining rape as 'sexual intercourse without consent' (1988a: 168).[5]

Overall, crime surveys are presented by realists as a major advance in the techniques available to both criminology and policy studies. Local crime surveys are particularly useful in terms of providing an input into where crime control policy should be directed. However, whilst conducting local surveys is an essential aspect of Left realism, realists are aware that this method of research has certain limitations. Thus it is pointed out:

> although questionnaire schedules appear objective they display the subjective values of the social scientist and are differently interpreted according to the subjective values of each subgroup. To take the values of the social scientist first: the menu of possible answers allowed the interviewee is determined by the questionnaire. In the most obvious instances, they tend to view the modal victimization as akin to burglary. That is a clear, distinct event – the sort of crime that would occur against a middle-aged, middle-class, male researcher. Incessant crime, such as many aspects of domestic violence, is scarcely grasped by this method. Similarly, the schedules are obsessed with fear of crime when, perhaps, a truer reflection of many subgroups might be anger.
>
> (Young and Matthews, 1992a: 15)

An additional difficulty is that surveys, like official statistics although to a lesser extent, have a hidden figure of crime in terms of non-response from the sample member. Most surveys – national and local – have a non-response rate of 20 per cent or above resulting from refusals or failure to contact the sample member. There is, therefore, 20–25 per cent of the sample whose victimization is unknown. Young acknowledges that such a large unknown population could easily skew the findings of the survey: 'at the most obvious level, it probably includes a disproportionate number of transients, of lower working class people hostile to officials with clipboards attempting to ask them about their lives, and of those who are most frightened to answer the door because of fear of crime' (1988a: 169). Indeed, a subsidiary study for the second Islington Crime Survey showed that refusers were more likely to have been the victims of crime in the last 12 months than those who agreed to take part (Crawford *et al.*, 1990).

Amongst those interviewed it is also suggested that a hidden figure exists with respect to those crimes that are not revealed to the interviewer out of fear or embarrassment. As we have seen, this is considered to be a particular problem with respect to domestic violence. Further, most of the surveys tend to focus on the last 12 months mainly to enable results to be compared to official statistics. However, as Young notes:

> people's attitudes to crime are built up during their life, and without 'have ever' questions – like those used by Ruth Hall in her 1985 study – this aspect is lost. Many victimization studies, therefore, have a hidden figure, not only partially in terms of the present, but also totally in terms of the past.
>
> (1988a: 168)

Finally, and most critically, realism argues that

> the [hidden] figure is not only quantitatively high … but that it is flexible – it expands or contracts with the values one brings to it. None of this is insurmountable but only within a paradigm capable of analysing crime, both as a product of behaviour and value.
>
> (Young, 1988c: 180)

Policy

Realism argues that in order to control crime, interventions should occur at all points of the square of crime. Coercive legal action is necessary, as are structural interventions directed at the causes of crime, mobilization of public opinion and support of the victim. Thus left realists are critical of those approaches that focus on just one part of the process: it is argued that whilst more effective policing or more jobs or public mobilization through Neighbourhood Watch Schemes or the target-hardening of buildings may make some gains, 'intervention on one level alone – even if effective – will inevitably have declining marginal gains' (Young, 1992a: 41). A multi-pronged strategy is necessary, although it is pointed out that interventions at the level of the social structure have priority over the others and are most effective. For domestic violence to be combatted, intervention needs to be made on all levels, although in the last analyses, the deep structural relationships of patriarchy have to be tackled if a substantial lessening of the problem is to be achieved.

Realists are, therefore, committed to multi-agency crime control policy, the 'planned, coordinated response of the major social agencies to problems of crime and incivilities' (Young, 1992b: 64). Social control in industrial societies is seen to be a multi-agency task, the various agencies are mutually dependent, and each agency is dependent on public support, whether it is an agency dealing with domestic violence, child abuse or juvenile delinquency. However, the particular configuration of agencies involved will differ according to the crime and the stage in which it is being tackled. This is demonstrated in Table 4.2.

Thus, with respect to domestic violence, left realists would ask what agencies should be involved against what type of domestic violence and at what point of its development (Young and Matthews, 1992a: 6). Furthermore, such a multi-agency format must be democratic in

Table 4.2 Agencies involved in crime control

Stages in the development of crime	Factors	Agencies
Causes of crime	Unemployment Housing Leisure	Local authority Central government Business
The moral context	Peer group values Community cohesion	Schools Family Public Mass media
The situation of commission	Physical environment Lighting Home security	Local authority Public Police
The detection of crime	Public reporting Detective work	Public Police
The response to offenders	Punishment Rehabilitation	Courts Police Social services Probation
The response to the victim	Insurance Public support	Local authority Victim support groups Public Social services

Source: ibid.: 65.

nature: 'we must establish a structure in which different agencies, and the victims themselves, have an equal voice in deciding the outcome' (Lea, 1987: 367).

Left realists have written specifically on the treatment of domestic violence by the criminal justice system and its representation in the mass media. On the criminal justice system, left realists have pointed out that its response to domestic violence is inadequate (see Kinsey *et al.*, 1986) and have argued that the net should be widened in this area (as well as for child abuse, racial attacks, and so on), whilst being reduced for other crimes, such as minor drugs offences. Legal intervention in domestic violence may well prove an effective means of social control, and may help protect the victim. However, it needs to be backed up by support from other agencies, for, as Lea notes:

> In some situations the ability or willingness of victims to utilize the resources of the Criminal Justice System is dependent on assistance from other agencies. A woman, for example, who prosecutes her husband for violence carries an enormous emotional burden combined with the risk of losing economic support. Therefore, even when an issue is one of serious crime there is a need for the presence of non-criminal justice agencies of an advisory and supportive role to also have an interest in the situation.
>
> (1987: 367)

In terms of the mass media – the moral context of the crime (see Table 4.2) – the 'barrage of misinformation' about crime generated by the mass media is considered to have an impact, for whilst

> a typical category of violence in Britain is a man battering his wife ... this is rarely represented in the mass media – instead we have numerous examples of professional criminals engaged in violent crime – a quantitatively minor problem when compared to domestic violence. So presumably the husband can watch criminal violence on television and not see himself there. His offence does not exist as a category of media censure.
>
> (Young, 1986: 22)

Realists would argue for an accurate portrayal of domestic violence in the mass media to underscore the fact that it is both widespread and a 'criminal' offence; this might have an impact on offenders and also encourage family and community support for victims, and public condemnation of offenders.

However, for left realists in the last analyses, it is *politics* that is of foremost importance in the control of all forms of crime:

> Crime involves politics: it does so because it is politics which determines the social conditions which cause crime, the degree to which the justice system is egalitarian, and the definition of what are crimes in the first place.
>
> (Young, 1994: 117)

In the latter part of this chapter I shall indicate how many of the theoretical and methodological principles of left realism have informed the approach taken in this book. For example, in terms of the problematic nature of the social construction of definition, the endemic nature of violence against women and its differential and compounding impact. There are, however, certain problems with realism which must first be examined.

Criticisms of left realism[6]

Problems of theory

Gelsthorpe and Morris point out that whilst left realists acknowledge the influence of feminist work and

> examine gender differences in perceptions of risk, fears for personal safety, avoidance behaviours and victimisation and show not only that women are more fearful than men, but that they have good reason for this... There is a startling omission: they ignore the significance of gender relations as a central factor in understanding most crimes against women and make no reference to a key concept for a feminist understanding of these crimes: male power. It is never made explicit that women's fear of crime is women's fear of men.
>
> (1998: 103)

Thus left realism is described as 'gender-blind' (Edwards, 1989; Scraton, 1990) and 'tokenistic' (Radford and Kelly, 1987) in its approach to women, paying 'at times... extensive lip service only' (DeKeseredy and Schwartz, 1991: 158) to feminism. Documenting the extent of violence against women does not adequately address feminist concerns. As Brown and Hogg comment:

> what much feminist research and analysis has demonstrated is that an adequate understanding and response to violence against women

is not to be found in the exposure of one more 'crime problem' and the connection between work in this area and the study of crime in general or the traditional methods of criminology, but in locating it in an analysis of the family and gender relations.

(1992: 159)

Left realism, as we have seen, does not fully explore the influence of either societal or familial patriarchy. Indeed, left realism generally lacks an analysis of power – whether in terms of male power, as experienced in interpersonal relationships, or structural power in the hands of the state (see Sim *et al.*, 1987; Jefferson *et al.*, 1991; Taylor, 1992; Walklate, 1992d).[7] Although the state forms one corner of the square of crime, it is the role of the criminal justice system that is mostly discussed in a taken-for-granted fashion.

Further, left realism's early focus was largely on 'mugging', thefts and other types of street crime (see Lea and Young, 1984), which has led to an overwhelming emphasis on working-class experience and the development of an economically-based theory of crime causation. As Ian Taylor notes, such a class-based analysis has resulted in female victims being viewed as 'honorary members of the core working-class'. In concentrating on the lower socio-economic groups and intra-class crime, realism 'does not deal "seriously", we may say – to appropriate a left realist use of terms – with the independent importance of patriarchy and sexual inequality across the social formation as a whole' (1992: 106). Violence against women is not class-specific: domestic violence occurs throughout the class structure; and relative deprivation – whilst being a useful explanatory concept for street crime – does not, as DeKeseredy puts it, 'adequately answer an important question: why do *men* victimize *women* in patriarchal, capitalist societies?' (1992: 267; my emphasis). Thus, although emphasizing the importance of specificity, realism tends to fall back on general, all-encompassing concepts to explain crime – the underlying assumption is that all crimes, whether they be street crime, burglary, pub fights or domestic violence, are essentially the same. Moreover, with respect to its long-term policy goals, changes in the economic structure of society may not necessarily lead to changes in the patriarchal social order.

Nor does left realism adequately cover the 'lived realities' of women's experiences. DeKeseredy comments that the theory fails to analyse 'variations in woman abuse across marital status categories', which is 'surprising since Young contends that "a realist criminology must start from the actual subgroups in which people live their lives, rather than

the broad categories which conceal wide variations within them"
(1988a: 171)' (1992: 267). Further, the coping and resisting strategies
adopted by victims are largely ignored (see Walklate, 1992c and 1992d;
Ruggiero, 1992) – strategies which, as we have seen, are well documented in the radical feminist literature. As Walklate argues:

> [the realist] view of the individual [victim] varies somewhat; one
> passively adapting, the other consciously aware and to be taken seri-
> ously. Both images have been constructed within a structurally
> defined framework, but one is descriptive and the other more
> explanatory. Neither of these understandings of structure, however,
> facilitates an understanding of how individuals actively resist or
> campaign against their structural conditions... There is a good deal
> of evidence to support the argument that individuals do actively
> resist or campaign against their structural powerlessness. Much of
> the in-depth work produced by the feminist movement with and
> for women illustrates this and has seen the parallel emergence of
> support networks for survivors of domestic violence, incest and
> rape. These responses to structural powerlessness are defined collec-
> tively and challenge patriarchy.
>
> (1992d: 113–14)

Problems of essentialism

A frequent criticism of realism, particularly in feminist circles is the
accusation of essentialism. This is made clear in Pat Carlen's accusation
that left realism attributes 'to the commonsense phenomenon "crime" –
a phenomenon that consists of many different types of law-breaking
and many different modes of criminalization – a unitary existence
known to all people of good will and commonsense' (1992: 59; see also
Smart, 1990: 77). She suggests that the populist tendency in realist
politics, the tendency to appeal to the common sense of all people and
to see the crime problem as a 'unifier', contributes to this essentialism.
Alison Young and Peter Rush suggest that such populism is facilitated by invoking the notion of universal victim. Whereas as 'a *soi-
distant* new criminology once put it, we are all deviants [now] we are
all victims... To be a victim is to be a citizen... [thus] class, age, race,
gender are, for realism, only secondary characteristics of the victim'
(1994: 159).
   There has undoubtedly been a tendency within realism to appeal to
popular opinion by stressing the widescale impact of crime across the

population and this is coupled with a 'realism' which suggests that popular fears are more rational than is often suggested by traditional criminology. The concept of rationality is, of course, a good deal more complicated than such political rhetoric implies (see Sparks, 1992), but the role of left realism in arguing that public fears must be addressed by liberals is an important one and an advance on the frequent rejection by those on the Left of the political spectrum of fear of crime as a moral panic or an illusion. Ironically, of course, this is precisely the critical path that radical feminism took, which, in turn, manifestly influenced realism. Such popular appeal to common sense does, of course, carry with it the danger of seeing crime as unproblematic and of ignoring the definitional question. But against this, realism has its roots and subsequent development in a position which is fundamentally anti-essentialist. That is, it stresses at its analytical core the square of crime where the police and public *variously* define what is criminal and what is its demarcation. Thus, for example, what is violent crime and what are the limits of permissible and non-permissible violence are seen as a constantly contested arena over time and between different agencies and sections of the public. Great stress is made on the non-unitary nature of crime, of its different varieties and indeed how legal categories often conceal great variations of behaviour under their rubric. Further, the emphasis on specificity: on the lived realities based on the particular intersection of age, class, race and gender that actors find themselves in does not remotely suggest a unitary notion of social groups, for example, where all young people or all working-class people or all blacks or all women are seen as having a common identity. Indeed the reverse is true. The conceptual direction of realism is anti-essentialist, although its political rhetoric might suggest otherwise.

It is perhaps the very fact that feminism itself has engaged in a long, and largely fruitful, struggle with essentialism in its scholarship that it should be so aware of essentialist tendencies in criminology. But often such criticisms go badly awry. Thus Ngaire Naffine, in her recent book *Feminism and Criminology*: 'Realists say they are sympathetic to feminist accounts of crime, but their approach is oddly naive. They suggest, for example, that although there might be some quibbling about the precise definition of crime' (and here she quotes Jock Young), 'all groups...abhor violence against women.' She comments, 'violence against women is therefore used to demonstrate that there is a basic consensus about the meaning of crime: that crime is therefore a generally agreed-upon thing in the world which is susceptible to scientific measurement and explanation' (1997: 64). The full quote from Young's 'Ten Points of Realism' reads:

> Crime is, by its very nature, a product of action and reaction. It involves behaviour and the variable legal response to that behaviour: an infraction and an evaluation. Criminal statistics, whether official, self-report, or victim report are, therefore, neither an objective fact of behaviour, nor merely a social construction dependent on the evaluation of the powerful. Different groups within society and different societies at various parts of historical time vary in their definitions of what is tolerable behaviour. The statistics of violence, as we have seen, depend on the extent of violent behaviour and the tolerance level to violence. There is no objective yardstick for crime, but a series of measuring rods dependent on the social group in which they are based. All societies and social groups, however, stigmatize a wide range of usurpation of the person and of property. At any point in time, various social groups will agree up to a point, then differ from that point onward. The measuring rod is not – and cannot be – consensual in an absolute sense, but it has a considerable overlap of agreement. All groups, for example, abhor violence against women, but they will vary in their definition of what constitutes abhorrent violence.
>
> (Young, 1992: 57)

Surely, this is pretty clear. Yet the constructed nature of crime and the intentional contradiction of the phrase 'all groups abhor violence against women, but they will vary in their definition of what constitutes abhorrent violence' is lost in Naffine's book by the simple artifice of quoting only the latter part of an ironic passage.

Problems of method

Left realists have favoured local crime surveys. However, as we have seen, they acknowledge that the use of face-to-face, doorstep interviews, even with sensitive interviewing techniques and a concern with the whole panoply of crime, is likely to lead to an underestimation of domestic and sexual violence against women, more than all other forms of crime (Crawford *et al.*, 1990). Thus, whilst they claim that the first Islington Crime Survey 'discovered that an alarming proportion of assault – 22% – is domestic in nature' (Jones *et al.*, 1986: 63), this translates to an incidence rate (the number of incidents uncovered) of just 8 per cent. The prevalence rate (the number of women affected) would be even lower because of multiple victimization. Although this is a higher percentage than that generated by the national British Crime Surveys (see Chapter 1), the hidden figure of domestic violence is still likely to be considerable. As such, conclusions drawn with respect to its distribution must be treated with caution. As Walklate points out: 'the private domain is much more difficult to penetrate by formal interview means, not only because of the nature and dynamics of the interview procedure but also because this involves penetrating the everyday realities of women's experience' (1989: 33).

Moreover, an approach which mainly focuses on the collection of quantitative data cannot fully explore the nature of women's experiences: surveys do not 'necessarily offer a "real" picture, a totality of that individual's response to the incidents ... she is reporting' (Walklate, 1992c: 290). This is not to suggest that realists are unaware of the importance of qualitative methods (see Young and Matthews, 1992a). However, such an invocation as to the necessity of such research is rarely put into practice. There is a need to collect qualitative data, through in-depth interviews: this would enable, for example, the examination of the coping and resistance strategies employed by women in response to male violence. As Sayer argues:

> with a less formal, less standardized and more interactive kind of interview, the researcher has a much better chance of learning from the respondents what the different significances of the circumstances are for them. The respondents are not forced into an artificial one-way mode of communication in which they can only answer in terms of the conceptual grid given to them by the researcher.
>
> (1984: 223)

Qualitative research must, therefore, be incorporated within the realist method, if it is truly to reflect the reality of crime and correspond to people's 'lived realities'. Qualitative data also help with the interpretation of quantitative data (see Jupp, 1988) and 'to move from the discovery of correlations to the imputation of social causality' (Young and Matthews, 1992a: 15). For to understand causality one must comprehend the meanings and decisions of the actors involved. Correlation merely tells one about the juxtaposition and the possibility of social causality. It does not prove causality; it merely insinuates it. Such an insinuation may be off the mark; high correlation, for example, may be fortuitous and of no causal significance; low correlation may occlude actual causation, which occurs in a few instances where the right combination of circumstances occur. Qualitative methods can allow us to put the causal flesh on the bones of the empirical findings which the mass survey provides us with.

Finally, left realism has been criticized for an absence of reflexivity in the research process (Ruggiero, 1992; Currie, 1992). As Ruggiero argues:

> Their square of crime should ... evolve into a *pentagon*, the fifth vertex being occupied by the *observers* ... The realists lack the kind of reflexivity which would be necessary to explain the social condition of the existence of their own discipline and its role in constructing and shaping social problems. They do not consider how their own subjectivity and their own role may influence their 'realistic' depiction of social phenomena.
>
> (1992: 136, 138; original emphasis)

Building on feminism and left realism

The first task of this book was to examine systematically each of the theoretical traditions in terms of their ability to explain and tackle domestic violence. We have seen that the work of radical feminists and left realists has the greatest purchase on the phenomenon. Both strands have much to contribute and my immediate task is to suggest what can be gleaned from each tradition as a prelude to the empirical sections of the book and in order to move towards the creation of a synthesis – a feminist realism – within criminology. For, as several commentators have pointed out, realism has much to gain from a closer consideration of feminist arguments (see Edwards, 1989; Currie, 1991, 1992; Walklate, 1992c and 1992d; Aluwalia, 1992). Indeed, Aluwalia regards the left realist and feminist positions on fear of crime to be of such a similar nature that 'the way forward would surely be to cultivate cooperation rather than to proceed in isolation from each other' (1992: 259). While Sandra Walklate (1992c) suggests that both feminism and realism may prove relevant in the construction of a critical victimology.

Let us briefly look at the major insights from each position following the framework I have used throughout:

Human nature and social order

Both positions are constructionist in that they see human beings as being constructed by capitalism and by patriarchy, respectively.

However, as James Messerschmidt (1993) has argued, there is always a tendency for radical feminism to fall into essentialism and to suggest that all men and all women at different times and places display a constancy of behaviour. In particular that all men are oppressors and all women victims (or survivors). The realist stress on *specificity*, the fact that human behaviour always differs by time, space and sub-group, counters this and, whilst reasserting the predominant role of men as aggressors, acknowledges a greater variability of behavioural patterns. It has been the task of socialist feminists to attempt to bring together these macro-structures of power. The extent to which realism stresses the dual systems of capitalism and patriarchy widens out the singular focus on patriarchy of radical feminism. Thus of great relevance to our thesis is the radical feminist contention that violence is central to the maintaining of patriarchal order, a notion which can tentatively be melded with the realist stress on capitalism as creating differential levels of vulnerability within society. For if radical feminism points to the causes of domestic violence within the social order, realism can perhaps help to explain why men are able to get away with such violence and the factors that prevent women from leaving violent men.[8]

Definition

If radical feminism alerts us to the fact that what constitutes 'domestic violence' is not a given, taken-for-granted construct, but one that is subject to male-oriented definitions, realism generalizes this and stresses the problematic nature of *all* social problems. Definition is always up for grabs: for the central contention in realism is the dyadic nature of crime and deviance. Furthermore, there are no monolithic definitions of what constitutes a problem whatever base one takes as defining domestic violence, whether it be that of men, women or any sub-group therein. An initial task of our study, therefore, is to establish to what *extent* there is a consensus of definition amongst women and what are the limits of this consensus.

Extent and distribution

Although both radical feminism and left realism agree on the widespread nature of violence against women, there is a lack of clarity as to how such violence is distributed by class, age and ethnicity. For example, there is a tendency in radical feminism to view domestic violence as evenly spread throughout the social structure, whereas realists point to a differential distribution, particularly in relation to class. The precise contours of the problem are, however, by no means clear: relative deprivation can in a realist analysis occur throughout the class structure – although it will of necessity vary – whilst the length of time a woman remains in a violent relationship or moves out before violence ensues may well be class-related. The distribution and extent of domestic violence is thus a key issue, which must be explored.

Impact

Both radical feminists and realists stress the considerable impact of violence on women's lives, but whereas radical feminists tend to see male violence as a central pillar in patriarchy and in the control and restriction of women, realists stress a greater differentiation of impact. With this in mind, the differential impact of domestic and non-domestic violence on women's lives by social group and public and private space are examined in this book. Of great interest here is the exploration of *the coping and resisting strategies* stressed by feminist researchers.

Methods

As we have seen, there has been a tendency for radical feminists to favour qualitative methods, and realists to emphasize the utility of the quantitative victimization study. There is, however, nothing inherent in either position to generate such a dichotomous approach and the emphasis in this research is on the use of both quantitative and qualitative approaches. As Jupp comments: 'the use of different methods ... maximizes the theoretical value of any research by revealing aspects of phenomena which the use of one method alone would miss' (1989: 74).

Both radical feminism and left realism stress the importance of using sensitive research methods. Radical feminists, in particular, emphasize the necessity of providing help-line cards and agency referrals when interviewing women about their experiences of violence.

Policy

Ultimately, for both radical feminists and left realists, change would have to occur at the level of the social structure (in terms of the ordering of society along patriarchial and capitalist lines, respectively) for there to be a considerable reduction, or even an end, to domestic violence, and both would argue that political commitment is necessary to bring about this change. However, there are various measures that can be adopted to alleviate the problem, for example, adroit use of the criminal justice system and the development of multi-agency approaches. Indeed, Susan Edwards notes that those 'left-wing feminists who turn to an improved police response, better laws and a more sympathetically trained police force, judiciary and magistracy as part of a wider set of demands for reform, may loosely be seen to identify with left realism' (1989: 15).[9]

Afterword

Carole Smart, in her famous polemic against realism, 'Feminist Approaches to Criminology: Postmodern Woman Meets Atavistic Man' (1990), poses realism as at core a paradigm which is essentialist and explicity casts doubts on any possible synthesis between feminism and realism. I have shown how, although essentialist tendencies are present in realism, they are also an ever-present problem in feminist writing on violence, and that the analytical direction of realism runs in a distinctly anti-essentialist direction. Smart writes:

> feminist realists ... are on quite a different trajectory from the left realists. It may be convenient to the left to support the work of feminists in this area but it is unclear to me where this unholy 'alliance' is going analytically. Like the protracted debate about the marriage of Marxism and feminism, we may find this alliance ends in annulment.
> (1990: 81)

She cites as proof that as radical feminism arose as a grassroots concern to protect women 'it has not been sympathetic to the study of maculinit[ies]' (*ibid.*: 81) which a realist approach would suggest in terms of dealing with the totality of a crime rather only a partial focus. Thus it has focused on women to the exclusion of men. In fact, subsequently, 'masculinity' has been a concern of feminist writers in the 1990s, Bea Campbell's *Goliath* (1993) being a key book in the last decade, whilst conferences, readers and colloquia have abounded on the relationship between masculinities and feminism.

Part II

5

Researching Violence

In 1993 I conducted a survey of 1,000 individuals – the North London Domestic Violence Survey – which is the largest survey of domestic violence so far conducted in Britain. This study made use of qualitative as well as quantitative methods, and its main focus was on women's experiences of violence from husbands or boyfriends, including ex-husbands and ex-boyfriends, although information was also collected on other forms of domestic and non-domestic violence experienced by both men and women. In this chapter I explore the conceptual and methodological problems of conducting research in such a sensitive area. In subsequent chapters I examine how these findings substantiate my critique of existing theories of violence and help develop the basis of a feminist realism.

Defining domestic violence

As we have seen in the discussion of the various theoretical traditions, one of the first issues that needs to be confronted in researching this subject is that of definition. There is a lack of consistency between researchers, policy-makers and members of the public on the relationships and types of behaviour that should be included under the rubric of 'domestic violence', and considerable debate over whether the term should be used at all (see, for example, Bograd, 1988; Smith, 1989; DeKeseredy and Hinch, 1991; Kashani and Allan, 1998).

With respect to relationships, 'domestic' can quite clearly refer to violence that occurs in the context of marriage or cohabitation, between siblings, between parent and child, in heterosexual and in gay and lesbian relationships. It can, in addition, be used to cover pre-domestic relationships, for example, dating relationships, and post-domestic relationships, as in the case of partners who are no longer living together. 'Domestic violence' has been the term most favoured in policy-making circles because it is seen as covering all domestic relationships (Smith, 1989; British Medical Association, 1998). Many commentators (for example, Brokowski *et al.*, 1983), however, argue for a more specific terminology. For, although 'domestic violence' may be useful as a contrast to 'stranger violence', serving to highlight the fact that considerable violence occurs in domestic relationships, its generality is not helpful with regards to theoretical or policy concerns. It is necessary to identify the specific relationships involved, as each type may involve different factors and have different needs, which will have to be matched by specific policies. More importantly, as feminist researchers point out, 'domestic violence' is a gender-neutral term and as such fails to clarify who is the victim and who the perpetrator, masking the fact that women are most frequently subjected to violence *by men*. It is for this reason that various researchers prefer to use terms such as 'wife battering', 'wife abuse' or 'woman abuse' in order to emphasize the target of violence (Bograd, 1988; DeKeseredy and Hinch, 1991).[1] Edwards (1989) and Walklate (1992a and 1992b) enclose 'domestic' in inverted commas to acknowledge its problematic character, particularly in the light of the controversial work of the family violence researchers, led by Murray Straus of the University of New Hampshire, which denies its gender dimension (see, for example, Straus and Gelles, 1986; 1988). In this project the gendered nature of much domestic violence is emphasized and I have tried to be as specific as possible in clarifying the relationships involved. The term 'domestic violence' has been retained for convenience only, as information was collected on violence in a wide range of relationships, including parent and child, siblings, and against women in dating relationships.

The second problem of definition relates to 'violence': what is it that constitutes 'violence'? This has two levels: how the different researchers define violence and the various definitions that women themselves make. It is clear that different rates of domestic violence will be calculated depending on the yardstick the researcher uses. Is a shove, for example, domestic violence or not? What is the status of threats of violence or mental cruelty? Some researchers have preferred to confine their attention to physical behaviours: Bograd, for example, in *Feminist Perspectives on Wife Abuse*, states:

> Wife abuse is defined in this volume as the use of *physical force* by a man against his intimate cohabiting partner ... Violence may qualitatively change the nature of intimate relationships, even if they

were characterised previously by the presence of severe psychological abuse. Violence threatens the physical safety and bodily integrity of the woman, and intensifies and changes the meanings of threats and humiliation.

(1988: 12; my emphasis)

Gelles and Cornell, although presenting a different theoretical position from Bograd (they are usually associated with the family violence approach), likewise restrict their definition, arguing that 'from a practical point of view, lumping all forms of malevolence and harm-doing together may muddy the waters so much that it might be impossible to determine what causes abuse' (1985: 23). The implication is that physical violence is worse than psychological abuse/mental cruelty. Walker (1979), however, reported in her study that most of the women described verbal humiliation as their worst experience of battering, irrespective of whether physical violence had been used. The North London Domestic Violence Survey started from the premise that mental cruelty, threats, sexual abuse, physical violence and any other form of controlling behaviour used against a woman by her husband or boyfriend are all domestic violence, are serious and merit individual investigation. This was reflected in the questions asked. It was also made clear throughout what definition was being used with respect to the various categories of domestic violence and the different rates which result from any given definition.

Furthermore, respondents, like the researcher, will vary in defining what constitutes 'real' violence (see Kelly, 1988a). Some respondents will define a push or shove as physical violence, whereas others will not. The values held by respondents are likely to be affected by gender, age, ethnicity, class and education. For this reason the very first question in the self-complete questionnaire (stage two of the research) established women's definitions of violence and the level of consensus that exists amongst women with respect to any given definition. Subsequent questions were based on separating out the prevalence and incidence of the various forms of domestic violence. Qualitative interviews were, in addition, incorporated into the project to examine in more depth how women define their experiences.

The method used

The method used was essentially a variation of the mass victimization survey, adapted to deal with the specific problems involved in researching domestic violence, for example, those of definition, fear of reprisals (that is, the perpetrator may be near to the interview situation), embarrassment, and so on (see Walklate, 1989). The intention was to combine and build on those aspects of left realist and radical feminist work that constitute the basis of a good research practice.

Before commencing the project, two pilot studies were conducted at separate locations involving 100 individuals. The purpose of the pilots was to test the use of supplementary self-complete questionnaires (see stage two, below). This resulted in revisions to the questionnaire and fieldwork strategies.

The research proper

The North London Domestic Violence Survey was conducted in three stages, but before the first stage could commence a sample had to be constructed, an interviewing team selected and a questionnaire designed.

In order to construct the sample, the Post Office Address File was employed as the sampling frame. This is considered to be superior to the Register of Electors, which has often been used as the sampling frame for victimization surveys, as it is updated every three months and does not suffer from the under-representation of minority groups. It has been established that the Register of Electors excludes about 4 per cent of private households, in particular those with young people, the unemployed, ethnic minorities and those in rented accommodation (Todd and Butcher, 1982). However, the Post Office Address File is not a list of households but of delivery points or letter boxes, and as a significant number of households in the survey area were known to share a single property (and thus a common letter box and entry on the Post Office File) to improve the accuracy of the sample these households were mapped and incorporated within the sampling frame.

From the final sampling frame 50 per cent of all households in the survey area were selected: a total of 1,205. At each household an alternate male/female respondent, aged 16 years or over, was identified for interview. A random selection within the household was made using the method detailed by Kish (1965).

Given the sensitive nature of this research, great care was taken over the selection of the interviewing team. Interviewers can determine the success or failure of a research project: poor interviewers make mistakes, misread questions, lead or mislead respondents, fail to probe when necessary, lose questionnaires and falsify responses (Walklate, 1989). In this survey, all the interviewers were chosen for their understanding of and commitment to the problem of domestic violence. The majority were highly experienced, having worked on previous surveys. Six interviewers were recruited from the minority groups represented in the study area. Of these, five could speak some of the relevant community languages. All interviewers received intensive training and information on the help available to those experiencing domestic violence. They were monitored in the field by a supervisor with counselling and social work experience.

A major feature of the interviewing brief was to interview respondents on their own; this was to try to ensure that respondents did not feel inhibited, and that neither their nor the interviewer's safety was compromised in any way. If the respondent was not alone when the interviewer called, an appointment was made for a later date. Where possible interviewers and respondents were matched by gender.

All respondents received Help-Line cards which featured the telephone numbers of a wide range of agencies. My intention was to avoid the 'interview and run' style that has characterized many surveys; I wanted to ensure that, should the need arise, support was available (see Radford, 1987). In a project of this nature it is essential that relevant support services are available locally and willing to take on any referrals from the survey. The importance of back-up support was highlighted in one of the pilot studies when a 65-year-old woman told an interviewer about her experience of being raped over 40 years ago by her husband's friend. The interviewer was the *first* person she had informed and she was clearly still affected by the experience, particularly as her husband had remained in frequent contact with the man concerned. As a result, the interviewer, at her request, put her in touch with a counselling service which she found beneficial. The interviewer also made several follow-up visits.

Questionnaire design and fieldwork

The questionnaires employed were carefully formulated, particularly in the light of the difficulties involved in defining and measuring violence. I tried to be as specific as possible in clarifying the relationships involved and used subjective and objective indices of violence. With respect to measurement, data were collected on prevalence (the number who have experienced violence at some time in their lives and in the last 12 months) and on the number of incidents of violence that have occurred in the last 12 months. The latter enabled the survey to generate a rate that facilitates comparison with police figures.

All the households in the sample received a letter informing them that a general crime survey was being conducted in their area – no mention was made of domestic violence. The interviews were carried out over a nine-month period, which is a much longer time-scale than that of previous local surveys, and this, together with the dedication and sensitivity of the interviewers, must account for the comparatively high response rates achieved by the survey. The length of the fieldwork period meant that at least ten attempts could be made to contact the sample members, at different times of the day, different days of the week, after holidays, and so on. And it allowed time to remind women – through follow-up visits – to return the supplementary questionnaires (see stage two).[2]

The stages of the research

Stage one

Stage one was conducted along the lines of the traditional victimization survey method. An interviewer-administered questionnaire was used and included questions on avoidance behaviour, victimization, policing and demographics. The funder had originally requested a general crime survey (see Funding below). Thus, the questionnaire was constructed so that the more general questions relating to crime were asked first; this provided a useful lead into asking about more sensitive issues. Where possible, open-ended questions were included to let respondents speak for themselves about their experiences. This general questionnaire was administered to 571 women and 429 men, representing a response rate of 83 per cent of the 1,205 households in the sample.

One of the aims of this stage of the study was to generate data on the attitudes of men to domestic violence, so a section of the questionnaire was directed at male respondents only. Vignettes were used detailing where in a 'conflict' situation men could see themselves as using violence. Dobash and Dobash have suggested that 'the four main sources of conflict leading to violent attacks are men's possessiveness and jealousy, men's expectations concerning women's domestic work, men's sense of the right to punish "their" women for perceived wrongdoing, and the importance to men of maintaining or exercising their position of authority' (1992: 4) and it was this that I tried to reflect in designing the 'conflict' situations. The 'conflict' situations, therefore, included quarrels over domestic arrangements, child care, infidelity, and so on. This was supplemented by male self-report questions on actual violence: men were asked if they had ever hit their partner in any of the 'conflict' situations. Obviously, if you ask men directly if they had hit their partner, they are likely to reply 'no', but if you present them with a 'conflict' situation it was conjectured that this might elicit a more honest and greater response rate.[3]

Whilst it is true that even by using such an approach some men will see their violence as not 'severe' enough to mention, feel it is not relevant having occurred outside the scope of the 'conflict' situation or will simply lie, such data give us a baseline. It enables us to say that *at least* this proportion of men would be liable to use violence against their partners. Various researchers have found vignettes to be a useful tool for the researching of sensitive subjects (Finch, 1987; Lee, 1993).[4] This section was included in the survey in order to move away from the conventional research emphasis on women alone; it is, after all, *men* not women who largely perpetrate violence on women and as such we should provide some focus on their behaviour.

The vignettes were also presented to 100 women respondents, They were asked if they could predict their partners likely response in any of these 'conflict' situations. This was to provide comparative data for the male responses and to discover whether women, in relationships where violence has not occurred, are still controlled by its possibility. That the violence has not occurred may well be due to avoidance of the 'conflict' situations.

Women and social class

As stated above, demographic information (that is, relating to the respondent's gender, age, ethnicity and social class) was also collected in this stage of the survey. With respect to assessing social class, the conventional view is

> that social class inheres not in individuals but in households. The household is the unit of analysis, and the class position of that unit is determined by the occupation of its head.
>
> (Abbott and Sapsford, 1987: 2)

This is seen in the majority of local crime surveys: questions are asked only of the head of household's class position. This approach is clearly problematic for women. In discussing the work of socialist feminists in Chapter 3 it was noted that women are frequently in low-paid or unpaid employment and their occupations are – or are perceived as – influenced by their child care and domestic responsibilities. Thus – and this is particularly true for married or cohabiting women – their class position is evaluated in terms of that of the main 'breadwinner' – usually their male partner. Indeed, Abbott and Sapsford comment that in many of the class stratification studies conducted in Britain and the United States,

> the instructions given to interviewers tend to be such that if an adult male is present in a household it is almost certain that his occupation will determine the coding of the class position of that household. This means in practice that some people (mainly adult males) have a class position determined by their own occupation, while other people (mainly, but not exclusively, married women) have their class position determined by the occupation of someone with whom they live.
>
> (1987: 2)

This form of class analysis clearly fails to consider gender inequalities and does not adequately incorporate women into the examination of class inequalities. In the North London Domestic Violence Survey it was regarded as essential to collect information on the individual respondent's class position. For we need to know the woman's class position in order to assess the impact. For it is hypothesized that economic dependence on men and lack of employment opportunities traps women in violent relationships. But the man's class position is also important if class is to be investigated as a causal factor in domestic violence. To obtain as full a picture as possible, respondents were, therefore, questioned on their class position, their partners (if married or cohabiting), their head of household (if this was not themselves or their partner) and, if under 25 years old and single, that of their head of household at the age of 12. The latter category was included, as the present class position of those under 25 years and single – whilst still of relevance in terms of assessing impact – is not regarded as a good indicator of their actual position, for this is likely still to be determined by that of their family of origin.

Stage two

This stage involved women respondents only; the method used has been termed the 'piggy-back' method. A sample of women interviewed for the first stage of the project were handed a supplementary self-complete questionnaire on domestic violence, together with a stamped addressed envelope. The interviewer was instructed to emphasize that the information recorded would be treated with confidence and that the respondent's identity would not be revealed to anyone. The personal contact made in the formal interview situation (stage one of this project) had been previously found to motivate the respondent to complete and return the questionnaire, thus helping to boost the response rate. Pilot work had shown that this method generates a better and more accurate response than that of the traditional victimization survey. This is likely to be because the method assures the respondent of her anonymity. Given the intrinsically private nature of domestic violence, it is easier for the respondent to record her experiences on paper than relate them verbally to a stranger, no matter how good an interviewer, standing on the doorstep. Postal surveys also allow time for the respondent to reflect on questions which result in more considered, precise answers. This stage included questions on: definitions of domestic violence, the different forms of domestic violence perpetrated by husbands and boyfriends, including ex-husbands and ex-boyfriends; their incidence and prevalence; the use of various agencies by women and their assessment of the various agencies' effectiveness. Questions were also included on physical violence and sexual assaults from other family members, and sexual assault and rape from men whom women have dated/gone out with on not more than five occasions. Despite such a wide scope, the questionnaire was kept as short and concise as possible to ensure that it would be filled in and returned. To avoid asking the same questions twice, particularly those designed to collect demographic data, each supplementary questionnaire was given a number allowing it to be matched with the main questionnaire. This also enabled us to keep track of those questionnaires which had been returned and to follow up on those still to come in. In addition to completing the questionnaire, many respondents wrote detailed accounts of their experiences, thus generating qualitative data around a quantitative survey.

A key aspect of the self-complete questionnaires was that they were only given to women whose partners were not in at the time of the interview. This strategy not only gave the respondent time to reflect in answering questions when compared to the interview situation, it also had the vital element of secrecy. Questionnaires were handed out to 535 women. They, therefore, *represent a second survey selected on this criterion* and the response rate is calculated in terms of the numbers handed out. It is important to stress that the sample was not selected in terms of the willingness of women to answer a supplementary questionnaire. This would have biased it perhaps towards those who had experienced domestic violence. Four hundred and thirty questionnaires were returned, a response rate of 80 per cent.

Stage three

This stage consisted of in-depth interviews with women who had experienced domestic violence. Women who had spoken to the interviewer about their experiences in stage one of the project were asked if they would agree to a further interview. Fifteen were interviewed in this way. To supplement the qualitative component further, another ten women were interviewed following referral by various agencies, including the police and women's refuges. In-depth interviews were included in response to the widespread recognition of the importance of a 'triangulation' of method (Denzin, 1970; Jupp, 1989). That is, the collection of both qualitative and quantitative data is essential if the experience of domestic violence is to be accurately portrayed. Qualitative data, such as that generated by in-depth interviewing, are necessary to interpret survey data fully. Likewise, quantitative data are necessary to interpret fully the typicality of case studies. The purpose of this stage was to provide information on the individual impact of domestic violence and its context, and to contribute to the understanding of the longitudinal development of domestic violence. Qualitative interviews further tackle the problem of 'incessant' violence, that is when violence occurs with such regularity it is simply not quantifiable in terms of the discrete, 'event orientation' implicit in victimization surveys (Genn, 1988; Walklate, 1989).

The problem of funding

To conduct such a large-scale survey necessitates considerable funding: it is impossible to do such research either part-time or on one's own. Obtaining the funding for this survey proved extremely difficult. The problems involved in financing research projects on violence against women, particularly by feminists, are well documented. Indeed, Hanmer and Saunders have argued that in not providing the necessary grants, 'the interests of existing power-holders, largely men, are being served by knowing as little as possible about violence to women' (1984: 11). Supported by the Centre for Criminology, Middlesex University, I applied to over 100 charities, companies and research bodies, with no success. Chris Nuttal, head of the Home Office Research and Planning Unit, said in reply to the application that he doubted that the survey could improve on the figures produced by the British Crime Surveys or the first Islington Crime Survey – this despite Lorna Smith's recommendation in the Home Office report on domestic violence that more local surveys should be carried out in order to provide a more accurate estimate of the scale of the problem and to 'aid local decision-making and policy planning' (1989: 103). The Economic and Social Research Council, the major social science research funder in Britain, rejected my application. One of the referees suggested that I was 'proposing to reinvent the wheel in certain respects', in particular the survey work of Murray Straus and his colleagues in the United States, the family violence researchers and recommended the use of the Conflict Tactic Scales. This assumes that the results of one piece of work can easily be transposed from one country to another and ignores the detailed criticisms of Straus *et al.* that exist in the United States and Britain (see Chapter 2). Further, this referee commented, with respect to my intention to examine class in the light of the debates in this area:

> When you say that 'the distribution of such violence by subgroup within the population is, at present, completely speculative' you are perhaps exaggerating. Several American studies have addressed this issue ... Spouse abuse is *clearly correlated* with low social status in its various manifestations.
>
> (my emphasis)

This is a very questionable assumption. Even more controversially the referee stated:

> Why restrict your study to female victims? Far more is known about them, and we know that women hit men as often as men hit women. Furthermore, you could gain by getting the point of view of both spouses.

Clearly, this referee unquestioningly accepted the family violence data alleging that men are as likely to be subjected to violence from their wives as women are from their husbands. Indeed, it was with this in mind that the North London Domestic Violence Survey included interviews with men to enable this hypothesis to be tested. Furthermore, with respect to the latter point, I believe that interviewing both spouses, a method which has been favoured by many North American researchers (Szinovacz, 1983; O'Leary and Arias, 1988), should not be advocated in researching such a sensitive area. It fails to take into account the power-control relations that exist between men and women, and are reflected in their personal relationships. These are likely not only to affect their responses, but clearly create a risk that such an approach could lead to repercussions on the victim. It was at this juncture, after many refusals with regards to funding, that the Centre for Criminology was approached by a local authority in London to conduct a general crime survey, funded by the Department of the Environment. Using the results from the pilot surveys I argued for the need to incorporate a domestic violence component into the survey. The local authority agreed and the domestic violence component subsequently became central to the method. Being commissioned to do a piece of research in this way does, however, result in certain restrictions, for example, with respect to the project's location, the time-scale, and so on. Further, local authorities almost always want some measure of control over the dissemination of the research findings. Lastly, funding is rarely sufficient to provide in-depth analysis of data and usually allows only a superficial perusal in order to produce a one-off report. Fortunately, Middlesex University provided a 0.5 Research Fellowship which allowed my work to continue for a 12-month period.

Responses to the survey

The responses to the survey were extremely positive; many women wrote to say how pleased they were that research was being conducted in this area and to have the opportunity to contribute their experiences. Much concern was expressed for women currently being subjected to domestic violence. Below are some of the comments made:

I think surveys like this are very useful for forming a basis on which to tackle the problem. Unfortunately, people in charge (i.e. police, politicians etc.) only seem to act when confronted with statistics. To ask people is the best source of information and the only indication of what is really going on in the community and behind people's front door.

Your interviewer was nice, friendly and very approachable and I am glad I did this. I hope something comes out of it. Thank you. Good luck.

I have known many women locked into violent relationships, both physical and mental. I do hope your survey will result in some practical and immediate help for them.

I am glad this survey is being done. I have never experienced violence of this sort, but I have nothing but contempt for those who perpetrate it, sympathy for those that suffer it, and admiration for those with the courage to change their situations by leaving. Domestic violence is, I believe, much more widespread than those in power would have us believe probably so that they do not have to invest resources into it.

Hopefully, if I can pass on anything I've gained from my own experiences, that someone else might be able to benefit from them at some point, it would be nice to think that is the case.

I do hope that this survey will help things get done. I do hope so. I have been lucky, but for those who aren't something has to be done for them.

Where the survey came in for specific criticism was from four women who pointed to the heterosexual bias of the self-complete questionnaire and argued that it should have included questions on 'lesbian battering'. In fact, I chose to restrict stage two to male violence for two reasons: first, I started from the position that male violence on women is a greater social problem and, at present, warrants the more detailed attention; and second, the areas covered by the questionnaire had to be limited to ensure a good response rate. The initial large-scale survey, stage one of the project, did, of course, allow for the recording of violence in other relationships and an in-depth interview was conducted with a woman who had experienced violence in a lesbian relationship.

6
Revealing the Hidden Figure

In this chapter I chart the hidden figure of domestic violence. I focus on women's definitions of 'violence', their experiences of different forms of violence from husbands and boyfriends (including ex-husbands and ex-boyfriends), the impact that these experiences have had and when and to whom violence was reported. I draw from the evidence uncovered in the North London Domestic Violence Survey and the in-depth interviews which followed it.

How women define domestic violence

In the chapters on theory and method I noted that there is a wide variation with respect to what might be defined as 'domestic violence'. Different theorists define domestic violence differently. In this survey I was intent in finding out how wide the variation is in women's definitions. Thus in stage two of the survey, women were asked what actions they would designate as 'violence' in a relationship between a husband or wife, or boyfriend and girlfriend. The results are presented in Table 6.1.

Thus, as would be expected, 92 per cent of women consider physical violence that results in actual bodily harm to be domestic violence, but mental cruelty is also seen by the vast majority of women as domestic violence (80 per cent). Indeed, more women would define this as domestic violence than threats of physical violence (68 per cent). Important also to note is that rape, defined on the questionnaire as 'made to have sex without giving consent' (whether or not actual physical violence is used or threatened), is seen as part of domestic violence. This indicates that most women do not support the myth

Table 6.1 Women's definitions of domestic violence

Behaviours	Agreed with statement %
Mental cruelty Domestic violence includes mental cruelty. Mental cruelty includes verbal abuse (e.g. calling of names, being ridiculed especially in front of other people), being deprived of money, clothes, sleep, prevented from going out, etc.	80
Threats Domestic violence includes being threatened with physical force or violence, even though no actual physical violence occurs.	68
Actual physical violence Domestic violence includes physical violence (e.g. grabbing, pushing, shaking) that does not result in actual bodily harm.	76
Physical injury Domestic violence includes physical violence that results in actual bodily harm (e.g. bruising, black eyes, broken bones).	92
Rape Domestic violence includes being made to have sex without giving consent.	76

n = 430.

that rape is only an offence if the woman is beaten (that is, if there is bruising, black eyes, and so on) and the man is a stranger. Indeed, the survey showed a clear majority of *all* women would define all of these five aspects (mental cruelty, threats, physical violence without actual bodily harm, physical violence with actual bodily harm and made to have sex without consent) as constituents of what makes up domestic violence.

When the data were broken down by age, ethnicity and class, it was found that whilst the majority still defined all the behaviours presented to them as domestic violence, some differences did emerge.

Table 6.2   Women's definitions of domestic violence, by age

Age	Behaviours*				
	Mental cruelty %	Threats %	Actual violence %	Physical injury %	Rape %
16–24	84	72	72	95	79
25–34	83	73	74	96	79
35–44	83	72	88	97	81
45–54	84	76	83	98	80
55–64	53	40	51	60	50

$n = 430$.
* See Table 6.1 for full definition.

Definitions by age

As Table 6.2 reveals, there is surprisingly little variation with respect to definition between any of the age groups below 54 years. Women who are 55 and over, however, are less likely than the other groups to define the behaviours listed as domestic violence, including physical violence resulting in actual bodily harm (for example, bruising, black eyes, broken bones). This variation indicates that there has been a change in attitude over the years with respect to what constitutes domestic violence and in levels of tolerance over what is 'acceptable' behaviour within a relationship. That younger women are more likely to define the behaviours as 'violence' is, of course, an extremely positive sign – there is clear indication from these data that women's tolerance of domestic violence has sharply declined between the generations.

Definitions by ethnicity

In Table 6.3 African-Caribbean women emerged as the group most likely to define *all* the behaviours presented to them as domestic violence: 97 per cent agreed that it included mental cruelty, 89 per cent threats of violence, 90 per cent physical violence that does not result in actual bodily harm, 98 per cent physical violence resulting in actual bodily harm and 85 per cent being 'made to have sex without giving consent'. African women, in contrast, were found to be the least liable to see mental cruelty (67 per cent and, more noticeably, 'made to have sex without consent' (55 per cent) as constituents of domestic violence. Irish women were also less likely to see the latter as domestic violence.

Table 6.3 Women's definitions of domestic violence, by ethnicity

Ethnicity	Behaviours*				
	Mental cruelty %	Threats %	Actual violence %	Physical injury %	Rape %
English/Scottish/ Welsh	83	70	77	97	82
Irish	76	71	84	94	76
African-Caribbean	97	89	90	98	85
African	67	73	81	93	55
Other Western European	80	80	79	94	80
Other**	82	69	76	90	77

$n = 430$.
* See Table 6.1 for full definition.
** 'Other' included those of Asian, Turkish, Greek, Turkish Cypriot and Greek Cypriot origin – the numbers were too small to be broken down by specific group.

Definitions by class

Professional women were more likely than lower-middle-class and working-class women to see mental cruelty, threats of violence, physical violence that did not result in actual bodily harm and rape all as constituents of domestic violence. With respect to the definition 'physical violence that results in actual bodily harm' there was absolute and high agreement between the classes.

Overall it is important to stress that the broad definition of domestic violence that is adopted by the majority of women interviewed reflects attitudes to what amounts to intolerable coercion in their lives. Each aspect, of course, may occur together and compound the problems which women face. Furthermore, it would be wrong to view such violence as a simple continuum of seriousness, ranging from mental cruelty through to threats and actual bodily violence. For example, prolonged mental cruelty was shown in some of the qualitative interviews to have a greater impact than the sporadic, isolated incident of actual bodily violence. Clearly, however, women's prioritization of this range of events under the rubric of domestic violence, would suggest a demand for a wide range of agency intervention, for example, not only the police and general practitioners, but also counsellors, social services, the housing department, informal support groups, and so on.

Table 6.4 Women's definitions of domestic violence, by class

Class	Behaviours*				
	Mental cruelty %	Threats %	Actual violence %	Physical violence %	Rape %
Professional	89	80	82	92	80
Lower-middle-class	79	71	74	91	75
Working-class	76	60	71	92	71

n = 430.
* See Table 6.1 for full definition.

To argue that such a multi-agency approach is necessary is not, of course, to suggest that any *one* agency has a magic wand which will simply 'solve' the problem. All agencies are important and the particular configuration of agencies involved, together with the decision about which are to take a leading role, will depend on the problems of specific groups of women and the stage at which a violent relationship is being confronted.

The changing parameters of definition

Despite the wide consensus amongst women with regards to what constitutes domestic violence, it is important to stress that this varies by age, class and ethnicity, and that such definitions change over time. This is clearly shown in the qualitative data. Women who had been subjected to domestic violence reported in the in-depth interviews that, at the time, they found it difficult to define their experiences as 'violence'. For example, many women felt they had 'deserved it' and, indeed, were frequently told by their partners that they had. This prevented them from seeing the behaviour as 'mental cruelty', 'domestic violence', and so on. The following extract reveals the difficulties that one woman had in classifying her experiences,

> He'd often say quite nasty things [called her a 'slag', 'tart', said she was ugly, lazy and dirty and made derogatory comments about her friends and family] and that had become customary. I had always thought that I'd asked for that because he'd always told me I had. He was always saying how dare you do this? how dare you show me up? and I used to think, Oh what sort of person am I? I was always taking responsibility for things that went wrong. So I didn't

consider that mental cruelty although it was very upsetting and has affected my confidence. If someone like you had come along then and asked me if I was experiencing mental cruelty I would have said 'no'. It took a long time to realise how unreasonable he was. The actual physical violence was not what I thought was bad, I wouldn't have called it domestic violence. I was being punched, kicked and slapped (also sexual abuse). But never broken bones and if I got bruised they were never that bad. It wasn't obvious and I didn't feel like it was obvious. My sister-in-law was experiencing extreme physical violence, I classed that as real domestic violence. I didn't ever class myself in the same category. I didn't think it was real domestic violence. She has experienced broken bones, been in hospital many, many times. One time he kicked her in the elbow so hard that he shattered it. She took an overdose and was in hospital. While there she decided to take out an injunction, but he persuaded her to have him back, as soon as she did, she spent another few days in hospital. He'll kill her or she'll kill herself in the end.

As she did not consider her experiences serious enough to justify the label 'domestic violence', it never occurred to her to make use of any of the specialist agencies: 'I thought refuges were for those like my sister-in-law ... if I'd realised I could have gone I would have got out a lot earlier and would have got better legal advice.'

Several women also spoke about the difficulties of defining rape, particularly with respect to the issue of consent. Rape was defined in the survey as 'made to have sex without consent':

My husband [now-ex] used to force me to have sex with him, but at first I didn't see it as a crime. I had had a sheltered life and thought that was what happened in marriage.

Incidence, prevalence and time-span

The structure of the questionnaire made it possible to separate out the incidence and prevalence of domestic violence. Incidence refers to the number of incidents of violence occurring; prevalence to the number of individuals affected. Obviously incidence rates will be higher than prevalence rates as the same individual may have several incidents within a given time-span. In terms of time, I asked both 'have ever' questions and whether the violence had occurred in the last 12 months. 'Have ever' questions are important in that they estimate the percentage of individuals who have been affected at some time in their lives and it should be stressed that women's fear and concern about domestic violence, indeed all forms of violence, will relate to such lifetime experiences. 'Have ever' questions clearly facilitate a more comprehensive examination of impact. This is indicated by the following comments of a woman who had been sexually assaulted by a boyfriend 30 years ago:

> When these things happened to me it was not as much out in the open as now, so it was not talked about. In fact it was nearly ten years later I told my husband after being married a year because it was causing problems and ten years after that I told my mother. It worries me sometimes my husband forgets or thinks that after 30 years I should be over it. But you never forget, just the little things said or done can make you remember.

The events in the last 12 months are also vital in order to know which individuals are affected in a year (prevalence per year) and what number of incidents occur per year (incidence per year). The *latter* figures represent the yearly potential demand on the agencies concerned. It should be stressed though that the figures throughout represent the number of women who have revealed their experiences to the survey team. However high they may seem, and however well the research method has facilitated response, the percentages presented here represent bottom-line figures. For many women will undoubtedly still have been too fearful, embarrassed or unwilling to reveal their experiences to strangers. It must also be made clear that these figures refer to *all* women; if I had used as the base only those women who are or were in relationships at the time – that is, those who are at greatest risk of domestic violence – the percentages would be considerably higher than those presented here.

The prevalence of domestic violence in a woman's lifetime

Women were presented with a range of different types of violence and questioned as to whether they had experienced any of these at some time in their lives. The results are recorded in Table 6.5.

Note that all these items have been defined by the majority of women as domestic violence. As Table 6.5 shows, violence from a partner is not a rare phenomenon. Whether it is defined as mental cruelty, threats, actual violence with injury or rape, it has occurred to at least a quarter to a third of all women in their lifetime. There is, of course, a

Table 6.5 The prevalence of domestic violence in a woman's
lifetime, by type of violence

Violent behaviours	%
Mental cruelty	
– including verbal abuse (e.g. the calling of names, being ridiculed in front of other people), being deprived of money, clothes, sleep, prevented from going out, etc.	37
Threats of violence or force	27
Actual physical violence	
– Grabbed or pushed or shaken	32
– Punched or slapped	25
– Kicked	14
– Head butted	6
– Attempted strangulation	9
– Hit with a weapon/object	8
Injuries	
– Injured	27
– Bruising or black eye	26
– Scratches	12
– Cuts	11
– Bones broken	6
Rape[1](def. = made to have sex without consent)	23
–Rape with threats of violence[2]	13
–Rape with physical violence	9
Composite violence	30

$n = 430$.

continuum in terms of frequency: mental cruelty is more common
than actual physical violence, actual physical violence more common
than violence which results in an injury. But *all* are common occurrences. Indeed, even if we were to take one of the more extreme definitions of domestic violence, bones have been broken, 1 in 16 have been
so inflicted. Furthermore, as has been stressed, all of these forms of
domestic violence may occur together, and have equal and compounding impact whether mental cruelty or broken bones. Indeed mental
cruelty was seen by many women to be particularly damaging, thus
confirming Walker (1979). One woman wrote, 'in my opinion mental
cruelty is equally as bad as physical violence except the scars do not
show and never heal'. Another reported, 'it is not the physical bashing

so much as what you are told constantly – the belittling really wears you down – it is the mental abuse that really does the damage.'

In terms of the mode of physical violence, as would be expected there is a continuum from being pushed or shaken to being hit with a weapon. But even attempted strangulation, which might be considered the more serious end of this continuum, has occurred to just under 1 in 10 women and assault with an object or a weapon to over 1 in 12. And it should be mentioned that the 1997 *Criminal Statistics* (Home Office, 1998) indicates that in homicide cases, strangulation is the second most common method, (after the use of a sharp instrument) of killing women, accounting for 25 per cent of deaths.

In this section it is also important to comment on how widespread rape is: just under a quarter of women had been raped by their partner. Furthermore, this had occurred with threats of violence to over 1 in 7 women and with actual physical violence to just under 1 in 10 women in the population surveyed.

The concept of composite domestic violence

In analysing the data my aim was to look first, at the prevalence and incidence of the various forms of domestic violence; second, the longitudinal development of domestic violence; and finally, to explore variations across sub-sections of the population with respect to its occurrence, impact and levels of reporting. To facilitate the latter it is necessary to choose one indicator of domestic violence with which to cross-tabulate by the different social groups. A single indicator was created of the general rate of violence by combining the categories punched or slapped, kicked, head-butted, attempted strangulation and hit with a weapon/object (that is, excluding mental cruelty, rape, threats of violence and 'grabbed, pushed or shaken'). I termed this general rate *composite domestic violence*. This is not, of course, to suggest that violence does not occur outside the composite or is less serious. Indeed this study starts from the premise that mental cruelty, threats, sexual violence, physical violence and any other form of controlling behaviour used against a woman are all to be seen as violence. However, I found in both the qualitative and quantitative work that the composite is a definition of domestic violence which virtually all women would agree on. There is a greater divergence of opinion with other forms of violence. The use of a consensus definition enables the argument that violence rates are simply a reflection of definitional variations between different parts of the population to be countered (see Hough, 1986). Composite domestic violence is incontestably domestic violence whoever's definition one utilizes. Despite the exclusion of the various aspects of violence detailed above, 30 per cent of women had had acts perpetrated against them by partners or ex-partners at some time in their lives which fell into the category of composite domestic violence.

The prevalence and incidence of domestic violence in the last twelve months

Women were asked whether the various forms of domestic violence (mental cruelty, threats, physical violence, violence with injury and rape) had occurred within the last 12 months and the number of times that such violence had been inflicted.[3]

Thus 12 per cent of women had experienced actual physical violence (including being grabbed or pushed or shaken, punched or slapped, kicked, head-butted, attempted strangulation, hit with a weapon/object) from their partners in the last 12 months, 8 per cent of all women had been injured and 6 per cent raped by their partner. These figures alone, over such a short period, illustrate the scale of the problem.

From Table 6.6 we are also able to ascertain the extent to which domestic violence is an infrequent occurrence or a repeated event. That is to translate these prevalence figures (number of individuals) into incidence figures.

As we can see from Table 6.7, domestic violence is often repeated in all categories even over a relatively short period of time such as 12 months. More than a quarter of all injuries, for example, have occurred more than six times a year.

Table 6.6 The prevalence of domestic violence in the last twelve months, by type of violence

	All %	No. of times %			
		1–5	6–10	11–20	20+
Mental cruelty	12	5.0	2.0	1.0	4.0
Threats of violence	8	5.0	2.0	0.2	1.0
Physical violence	12	8.0	2.0	0.5	1.0
Injuries	8	6.0	1.0	0.5	0.5
Rape	6	4.0	1.0	0	0.5
Composite Domestic Violence	10				

$n = 430$.

Table 6.7   Frequency of domestic violence incidents in the
last twelve months, by type of violence

	% of Incidents		
	5 and less	6–10	11 and over
Mental cruelty	42	17	42
Threats of violence	61	24	15
Physical violence	70	17	13
Injuries	75	13	13
Rape	73	18	9

$n = 430$.

In terms of estimating the amount of potential demand on agencies
with regards to domestic violence, it is important to distinguish the
number of incidents which have occurred per year (incidence rate) in
contrast to the number of individuals involved (prevalence rate).

Incidence rates are the usual way of expressing crime rates, that is,
the number of burglaries per 100 of the population. If we consider
domestic violence where injury has occurred and where legal action
would certainly be possible, we have an astonishingly high assault rate
of 17 per cent (that is, allowing for rate per *total* population of men
and women) due to domestic violence (see Table 6.8).

Average victimization rates are the average number of times a person
has been victimized: that is incidence divided by prevalence. As we can
see, the average rate of domestic violence committed against each
woman is high for every type of victimization. Domestic violence is far
from a one-off occurrence. Thus the average number of times a woman
has been physically injured in the last 12 months is four. Domestic
violence is thus not only widespread but frequently repeated over a
relatively short period of time.

It is important to be aware of the significance of the size of these figures when compared to previous national and local crime surveys. It
is not that the researchers do not understand the limitations of their
findings. Thus the authors of the 1988 *British Crime Survey* write: 'There
is little doubt that BCS counts of sexual offences and domestic or
non-stranger violence are underestimates' (Mayhew *et al.*, 1989: 5).
Indeed, as we have seen in Chapter 1, they have introduced the use of
Computer-Assisted Self-Interviewing (CASI) in order to tackle the low
figures. The problem remains that they do not realize the *degree* of

Table 6.8 Prevalence rate, incidence rate and rate of multiple victimization over a twelve-month period, by type of violence

	Prevalence rate by 100 women	Incidence rate by 100 women	Average victimization rate
Mental cruelty	12	123	10.3
Threats	8	73	9.1
Physical violence	12	85	7.1
Injuries	8	34	4.3
Rape	6	25	4.2

underestimation. Let us compare some of the findings of the 1996 British Crime Surveys with the present results (see Table 6.9).

The 1996 British Crime Survey used both conventional victim sheets and CASI, so the clear contrast in figures can be directly measured. The rate of physical assault found by CASI is over three times that revealed by victim reports and the rate of assault with injuries more than double. Understandably, the researchers are self-congratulatory and note that 'the balance of evidence suggests that the CASI estimates are reasonably accurate' (Mirrlees-Black, 1999: 61). Yet when one compares these figures with those of the present study it is obvious that, even allowing for the problems of different demographic composition of the samples, CASI only scratches the surface. I have detailed in Chapter 1 how this is a product of the method which, amongst other things, does not ensure anonymity.

A further problem in the 1996 British Crime Survey was the finding that the rate of violence was the same for men and women: 4.2 per cent of both sexes reporting assault in the last year. Mirrlees-Black quite rightly points to the seriousness of assault and its repetition being higher for women than for men, yet the equality of prevalence remains. Of course, this is completely contradicted in the present survey where women are seen to be by far the predominant victims. This British Crime Survey finding clearly underscores the problem of lack of anonymity. For women, violence is often seen as a failure, a relationship that has gone wrong in which they may see themselves as partly at fault. For men, it is much more an accepted part of everyday life – it is not as significant an event. In an interview situation with an outsider present and quite frequently a partner or friend, there can be little doubt that women will under-report when compared to men.

Table 6.9 Percentage incidence of domestic violence
against women in a twelve month period

	Physical assault %	With injuries %
1996 BCS Victim Reports	1.3	1.0
1996 CASI	4.2	2.2
North London Domestic Violence Survey	12.1	8.0

BCS: Conventional Interviewing Form.
CASI: Computer-Assisted Self-Interviewing.
NLDS: Anonymous Self-Complete Questionnaire, in respondents
own time.

The range of domestic violence experienced by women

Clearly asking about specific behaviours and presenting tables of figures can never solely convey the range and degree of violence experienced by women. The qualitative data obtained from the supplementary questionnaires and in-depth interviews indicated that, in addition to the violent behaviours already mentioned, women had been burned with cigarettes, bitten, scalded, pushed down stairs (illustrating that what might be construed as 'less severe' violence, 'pushing and shoving', can be objectively serious with respect to physical harm), knocked unconscious and had experienced miscarriages as a result of an assault. Indeed, it was not unusual for violence to begin or escalate during pregnancy, a time when a woman is physically and emotionally vulnerable. Some of the women described their experiences:

I have been abused verbally and physically which has resulted in bleeding, broken teeth, black eyes and severe, swollen joints. I have been threatened and prohibited from going out. I feel I have had my privacy taken away from me, my papers are read and phone calls listened to.

He stole my money, beat me, strangled me, threw a cup of hot tea at me.

He would always threaten me, e.g. he'd say, 'if you don't do as I say I'll kick your fucking head in'.

I was subjected to cruel taunts, threats of violence, stopped from seeing friends (even female) and going out, except to go shopping or to work; was 'persuaded' to participate in derisory sexual activities, denied access to my family; was shaken, pushed, pinched, punched and slapped, was criticized in public and had various household objects thrown at me including cups of coffee; had clothes torn off my body.

I've been kicked unconscious, beaten with cuts and bruises, had to go to hospital.

He didn't actually hit me, just shoving which he was very good at because it is quite easy to shove someone into something so you don't actually have to punch them. I was shoved almost on to a cooker. I ended up sticking my arm into a frying pan. I was pregnant at the time.

I have been beaten up, had black eyes and been told he would steal my baby.

I have had my head banged against the wall and hair pulled... beaten to a pulp.

I have been raped, punched, bruised, mainly because I didn't consent to sex.

In one incident I was hit around the head, he put his full weight behind the blow. He pulled my legs from underneath me. I had a bruised kidney, ear, side of face and injured lip. The kidney caused me a lot of pain. I had difficulty in sitting. Another time he threw a stool at me then got me on the floor and stuck his knees in me.

I was slapped around, kicked in the stomach while four months pregnant resulting in a miscarriage.

He used to rape me, one time in front of the kids.

The last time, he chased me with a machete saying he was going to kill me. I got it off him, cutting myself in the process. He then got an axe. Fortunately the police arrived.

The longitudinal development of domestic violence

In the in-depth interviews women were asked about the development of the violence over time. Whilst it must be made clear that there are many variations, certain patterns did emerge.

At the beginning of the relationship, not surprisingly, the majority of women recalled that there was little indication of the violent behaviour to come. One woman professed to have had no knowledge of her husband's previous convictions for violence – they came to light a couple of years after they were married, when he was prosecuted for being drunk and disorderly. Husbands and boyfriends were described as 'loving and gentle', 'one of those really nice fellows, considerate', 'the perfect man', 'nice, very affectionate, the sort of man who would have given you the moon', and so on. However, once the relationship was more established women reported that their partners gradually became more controlling in their behaviour towards them. That is, for example, by trying to organise the woman's life; dictating the type of paid work, if any, that she could undertake; controlling the amount of money she had, the way she made use of her leisure time and putting emotional pressure on her to spend all her time with him, rather than seeing friends and family. This controlling behaviour was typically accompanied by verbal abuse and irrational sexual jealousy. This was followed – sometimes months, sometimes a few years, later – by the onset of physical violence. Many women recalled that physical violence often occurred when they had become more dependent on their partner, for example, as a result of increased isolation from friends and family, and thus feeling the lack of an outside support system. And, as noted previously and completely contrary to the expectations of evolutionary psychology theory, it was not uncommon for violence to begin when the woman became pregnant. One woman said that she thought her partner had begun 'to feel so safe in the relationship, that he could do anything'.

The nature of the relationship

In this section more specific details of the nature of the relationship were sought, in particular whether they were living together when the last incident occurred or did not live together and whether it occurred before or after the relationship had ended. From this point onwards all figures presented, unless otherwise stated, refer to 'composite domestic violence'.

What is of interest here is that a significant proportion of incidents occurred with men whom the woman was not living with or indeed had never lived with – 12 per cent of life-time incidents and 22 per cent of incidents in the last 12 months. The absence of domestic circumstances clearly does not seem to guarantee non-violence, nor does not being in a relationship at the time the violence occurred: a quarter of violent incidents occurring in the last 12 months involved former partners. Overall, 37 per cent of women experiencing domestic violence were not living with their partner or were not in a relationship with him. If the man was a former husband or boyfriend, women were, in

Table 6.10 The nature of the relationship in which domestic violence occurred

Relationship	Violence	
	At any time[a] %	Last 12 months[b] %
Husband or live-in boyfriend	62	63
Current boyfriend (not living with)	4	11
Former husband or former live-in boyfriend	26	14
Former boyfriend never lived with	8	11
Former partner	34	25
Present partner	66	74
Lived with	88	77
Never lived with	12	22

[a] $n = 129$; [b] $n = 43$.

addition, asked if violence had occurred whilst they were together. In 6 per cent of the life-time cases and two per cent of those in the last 12 months it occurred only *after* the break-up of their relationship. It is clearly necessary for agencies to be aware that domestic violence does not always come from within the home.

Violence after the end of a relationship

In the following accounts four women describe the violence that occurred after the end of their marriages:

I was divorced in the 1970s. I was constantly threatened and harassed by my ex-husband. It resulted in many sleepless nights.

After the split he kept coming back. He was only violent after the divorce. I had a broken cheek bone, split lip, was knocked out, and so on. It escalated once I'd got a new partner. He made constant threats. It was a nightmare. I was afraid to leave the house. The police were involved, he was arrested on two occasions but he persisted. He would stand outside my door, shouting at me. No matter where I was he was there. It only ended when he died.

When my husband left, he'd often come back after a drink and try to get in the flat. Once he climbed through a window, he hit me and tried to strangle me. At other times he'd stand across the other side of the road and just stare at the flat.

While we were separated my ex-husband forced his way back into the house. He broke the lock. He threatened me with violence and also verbal abuse. I was terrified.

Domestic violence by class, age and ethnicity

The prevalence data were broken down by class, age and ethnicity to see if the experience of domestic violence varied according to social group.

Class and domestic violence

Whilst domestic violence is clearly experienced by women in all social classes, it would appear that professional women are less at risk than lower-middle-class and working-class women. The question that arises, therefore, is whether these different rates reflect differentials in class propensity to violence or whether they relate to different definitions of domestic violence by class or to class differences in ability to end the relationship before violence commences. First, it must be noted that the focus is on the individual's (in this case the woman's) class position, *not* the household's class position. If class is to be analysed as a possible causal factor, it is obviously the man's class position that is relevant. With this in mind analysis of the data obtained from the use of vignettes (see Chapter 7 below) found no evidence to support the assertion of many previous researchers that domestic violence is largely perpetrated by men from the lower socio-economic groups (McClintock, 1963; Straus, 1977; Gelles and Cornell, 1985; Young, 1986; Schwartz, 1988; DeKeseredy and Hinch, 1991). Second, in terms of definition, I have focused on composite domestic violence where there is a very high agreement between the classes, so differences in sensitivity to violence cannot explain the differences recorded above. What may be true, however, is that professional women, because of their greater

Table 6.11 Domestic violence by class

| Class | Violence | |
	At any time[a] %	Last 12 months[b] %
Professional	25	7
Lower-middle-class	29	11
Working-class	30	10

[a] $n = 129$; [b] $n = 43$.

access to resources, may be more able to get out of a relationship before it becomes *physically* violent. The qualitative work shows that physical violence is often preceded by a pattern of controlling behaviour, for example, organizing the woman's daily routine; what she wears; the amount of money she has; putting emotional pressure on her to spend all her time with him, rather than seeing family and friends; ridiculing her, and so on. Further, various commentators have suggested that it is the structural difficulties women face (their relative poverty in comparison to men; fewer employment possibilities, particularly if they have children; frequent financial dependence on men and as primary unpaid carers of children) that trap them in a violent relationship (Pahl, 1985; Tolmie, 1991; Victim Support, 1992). The argument against this is that lower-middle-class women have comparatively greater resources than working-class women yet their incidence of domestic violence is equal to that of working-class women. Here, however, it is significant to note that the lower-middle-class women interviewed were more likely to have children than professional women, which would serve to lock them in to the relationship. Also, they were less likely to define mental cruelty as domestic violence, which was found to be a feature of the controlling behaviours in the early stages of a violent relationship.

Age and domestic violence

Table 6.12 shows that the prevalence of domestic violence decreases after the age of 44 years. This is shown by the decline in the last 12 months and the fact that the 'have ever' (violence at any time) figures do not progressively increase. The difference between the younger and older age groups overall could, however, be explained in part by differences in defining what constitutes domestic violence. In our discussion

Table 6.12 Domestic violence by age

	Violence	
	At any time[a]	Last 12 months[b]
Age	%	%
16–24	24	13
25–34	34	12
35–44	35	10
45–54	25	7
55–64	31	6

[a] $n = 129$; [b] $n = 43$.

of definitions it was shown that significantly fewer women over 55 years regarded the behaviours presented to them as domestic violence than those in younger age groups. Thus, even where physical violence resulted in actual bodily harm, only 60 per cent of women in the older age group regarded this as domestic violence compared to almost 100 per cent of women in younger age groups. The results for the last 12 months are likely to be due to the greater number of women aged 45 years and over who are no longer in a relationship.

Ethnicity and domestic violence

Domestic violence clearly occurs throughout *all* the ethnic groups surveyed. There was no significant difference in the 'have ever' (violence at any time) figures although the rate for African-Caribbean women was higher in the 12-month period.

Impact of the violence

The serious nature of domestic violence is illustrated by the finding that 8 per cent of women, experiencing violence at some time in their lives, had stayed overnight in hospital as a result, 20 per cent had taken time off work, 46 per cent reported 'feeling depressed or losing self-confidence' and 51 per cent felt 'worried, anxious or nervous'. The qualitative data further supported the degree to which the experience of domestic violence affected women emotionally and psychologically, as the following comments confirm:

> Your own self-worth diminishes, even to the point of blaming yourself for the situation. You really begin to believe that you can't make a life on your own – after all you're not in control of your own life

Table 6.13 Domestic violence by ethnicity

	Violence	
Ethnicity	At any time[a] %	Last 12 months[b] %
English/Scottish/ Welsh	31	9
Irish	29	9
African–Caribbean	30	12
Other	28	11

[a] $n = 129$; [b] $n = 43$.

situation, are you? You've had your 'stuffing' – your sparkle, spirit and joy of life – knocked out of you.

It affects your confidence. Once your confidence has been destroyed and if it's been destroyed for a long time you do need an awful lot of confidence-building. You need someone constantly rationalizing the situation for you because you can't be objective and if you'd been made to feel responsible for it [the violence] all that goes on for a long, long time. I still can't speak to my ex-husband without my brain going to pieces. I can't speak to him rationally.

It's robbed me of my happiness. I went out with my friend the other day to the seaside and had such a nice time that I kept thinking something was wrong. I couldn't remember what a nice time, or being happy, felt like.

Several women also reported having had nervous breakdowns, suicidal thoughts and a few even attempted suicide. Not surprisingly, the effects of having experienced such violence were found to be long-lasting, as is indicated by the second comment. In addition to the types of impact detailed above, women whose relationship had ended said that it had made them fearful of *all* men, worried about getting involved with another man in case they found themselves in a similar situation ('I'm scared of men and it happening again'), that it had affected subsequent relationships ('I feel nervous with men who come too close to me…I just can't trust a man'). Many were scared of reprisals ('I feel constantly nervous that he will return…I am always looking over my shoulder', 'my husband threatened to kill me and I'm always worried he might find me'), and unfortunately, as the relationship data reveal, these fears are based in reality, given the number of women who are subjected to violence from ex-partners.

Coping and resisting strategies

In discussing the impact of domestic violence, it is important to stress the coping and resistance strategies adopted by women in response to such violence. As we have seen, radical feminists have argued that we must think of women as 'survivors' rather than as simply passive victims of men's violence (see Chapter 3). Indeed, one woman reported that the experience had made her 'feel more stronger, I dealt with it and survived and am determined that nothing like that will ever be done to me again'.

The types of strategies women utilized varied. Several women said they 'argued back' in terms of questioning their partner's behaviour and, in doing so, frequently risked more violence: 'if I'd kept my mouth shut it might not have been so bad, but I felt I couldn't let him get away with it'.[4] Liz Kelly notes that it is this refusal to be silenced that is described as 'nagging', 'asking for it' and 'provocation'. It is:

> This logic or reversal of responsibility [that is] used consistently by abusive men to justify their violence…The assumption is made that, if women did not behave in this way, the violence would cease. (1988a: 179).[5]

Some women tried to respond physically – although this also often led to further violence. Thoughts of killing the man were found to be not uncommon:

> When you're lying there in bed holding parts of you, thinking I feel I've been hit by a bus and they just go to sleep. You think, how could you after all that just go to sleep? And when they're asleep you think I could kill you now, that's how it gets to you. I know it must sound terrible, but you think go and get a knife or something, you could easily do it.'

However, for many women, particularly those who had experienced violence for a number of years and had children, the preferred approach was to try to limit the violence by either avoiding certain situations they thought might lead to violence or by trying to get away from the man, particularly if he was drunk, by either moving to another room or leaving their home temporarily ('I used to walk around the streets until I felt he was likely to have calmed down or be asleep'). Indeed, after the relationship ended, some women, in order to avoid further violence, moved from their home towns or cities, and in two cases to other countries.

The impact on the children

Many of the women with children reported that they were concerned about the effect that the violence had on the children. Several women said they were worried that their children would grow up believing violence to be an acceptable part of a relationship ('It bothers me that the children, especially the boys, think that all women put up with being treated horrible and that violence against women especially wives is OK'). One woman commented:

> I didn't think the children were affected as it usually happened while they were in bed, until my son said, aren't our neighbours strange, they hold hands, he takes her shopping, to work.…That

pulled me up, I had to explain to him that is what a partnership should be like – give and take. It made me realize that they weren't sleeping through it, but were accepting it as normal behaviour. We were the normal couple, not the people next door, because they'd grown up with it from birth.

This made it hard for her to leave: for 'if I said I wanted to go, I got the attitude "but why?" [from the children], it made it very difficult because they didn't understand that it is not normal behaviour.'

Women also spoke of their children experiencing various emotional and behavioural effects (for example, bed-wetting, 'feeling tense', refusing to eat, temper tantrums and outbursts of violence). One eight-year old-girl, after her father had left, went through a stage in which she thumped her mother, smashed the bannisters and tried to jump out of a window. In another case, a ten-year-old boy was bullying a boy at school (by humiliating and physically beating him) and his mother feared he was attempting to replicate his father's behaviour towards her. In a few cases violence was actually directed against children by the man. In one incident this only came to light after the relationship had ended: 'my son now talks about how he used to be bruised by his father as a small boy, he didn't tell me as he thought I would have taken my husband's side'.

However, many women said their partners were good fathers ('he idolised the children, they could have his last penny', 'he's devoted to the kids') and the children were, not surprisingly, very attached to them. The relationship between the children and their fathers serves to bind women into the relationship. In one case a woman went to a women's refuge, but her little boy, aged five years, missed his father so much that he became ill:

He lay in bed all weekend just burning up, I got a doctor to him, the doctor said there is nothing physically wrong with him, he is just pining. I felt I had no alternative but to go home. As he was only five I felt I couldn't just leave him with his father. There was no way out.

Having children usually means that when a relationship ends the majority of women have to remain in contact with their partners as a result of joint custody or access agreements.

Reporting of the violence

With regards to the reporting of violence, the predominant mode is private, to friends and relatives. Pahl (1985) has pointed out that it is only when these informal sources of support prove inadequate that women report to official agencies. Friends are, however, considerably more likely to be informed than relatives: 46 per cent in comparison to 31 per cent of women experiencing violence at some point in their lives. However, the response women received from friends and relatives varied: some were 'wonderful', 'very supportive', whereas, others expressed disbelief, blamed the woman and even coerced her into staying in the relationship. One woman who had been hospitalized on several occasions as a result of her husband's violence was told by her family that if she brought charges against him to consider herself on her own. Another reported that her family said to her that the 'woman's place is in the home and you married him for better or worse'. There is still today, despite our divorce statistics, an emphasis placed on preserving the image of the 'happy' family such as those presented in advertisements or the nuclear family idealized in present government policy.

Of the agencies, general practitioners and the police are the two front-line agencies: 22 per cent reported to general practitioners, 22 per cent to the police. The reporting to general practitioners is in line with the findings of the percentage of women who need medical attention and with the emphasis on keeping domestic violence private. For, given the restrictions placed on doctors with regards to confidentiality, what is revealed is seen as going no further than the consulting room. The finding that around one quarter of all life-time experiences are reported to the police is high compared to previous estimates. The Women's National Commission Report (1985), for example, suggests 2 per cent and Walker (1979) 10 per cent, but such differences may merely reflect different definitions of what constitutes domestic violence. The figures quoted in this section refer to a composite of domestic violence incidents, all of which are incontestably actual physical assaults; if a wider definition of domestic violence were used (including mental cruelty, threats and being 'grabbed or pushed or shaken') the figure for reporting to the police would fall to 11 per cent. Women who had been to the police prior to the changes in policy introduced in the late 1980s (for example, the setting up of Domestic Violence Units) were extremely critical of their response. Here are just some of their comments:

> The police were reluctant to do anything, they said because I was divorced they couldn't help.

> The police were very rude and uncooperative, in other words they didn't want to know.

They treated it like a joke.

They weren't very nice, in fact they were terrible. They spoke to me like I was an idiot.

They did nothing even when I ran to the police station after he threatened to kill me and was chasing me.

I rang the police but they said they didn't get involved in domestic problems.

Those women who had sought help in the more recent period were, in contrast, generally pleased with their treatment, particularly if they had been in contact with a Domestic Violence Unit.

However, although the finding that 22 per cent of those experiencing domestic violence (in accordance with our composite definition) report their assault to the police is high in terms of comparative estimates, it still reveals a hidden figure of violence which is a cause of concern. The Domestic Violence Units set up by the police across London since 1987,[6] with the intention of providing women with support and practical advice, were a major step forward. But it is vital not only that women should have confidence in these initiatives but also that they should *know* about them. As it is, only 41 per cent of women who had experienced domestic violence in the last 12 months had heard of the Units and only 37 per cent of women in general. Furthermore, where the police did come in for specific criticism was with respect to the length of time it took them to get to an incident – in one case it was over two hours before they arrived – and it emerged that there was still a tendency for the police to do little at the scene apart from mediate and refer the woman to the Domestic Violence Unit. A couple of women also mentioned the difficulties of getting through to the Domestic Violence Unit by telephone as they were either put through to an answer machine or the line was engaged. Some said they wished they were open 24 hours a day and at weekends – as incidents often happened at night or the weekend and they felt it was then that they needed advice on their options, although the Metropolitan Police argue that all police officers, that is, those attending the scene, should be able to give them the necessary advice. Two women, in addition, said the killing of Vandana Patel by her husband in Stoke Newington Police Station had not given them confidence in the recent police initiatives. The Patels had been given a room in the station, with a well-established Domestic Violence Unit, to discuss their problems. The police neglected to search Mr Patel, who was carrying a knife, and to supervise the situation adequately. In the aftermath of the killing, the Chief Superintendent defended their approach by stating that the, 'police were providing no more than a park bench on which they could talk, we were providing an extended social service'!

The proportion of women consulting a solicitor was also found to be high (21 per cent) and, once again, underlines the severity of the problem, whilst highlighting concerns about cutbacks in Legal Aid in Great Britain. Only a small proportion contacted a women's refuge (5 per cent) which is likely to reflect their restricted finances and the limited services they can provide. Those women who had gone to a women's refuge were almost without exception very impressed with the response they received. They were described as 'offering valuable support', 'a safe atmosphere'. One woman stated: 'it was so good to be among women who were on my side.'

Women's explanations for domestic violence

It is of great interest to know how the women themselves explained the violence they had suffered. Thus, women interviewed for the survey were presented with the following open-ended question: Why do you think some men use physical violence against their wives and girlfriends? The main replies from women who had experienced domestic violence were as follows: 'reinforces feelings of power' / 'makes them feel important' (36 per cent), 'they are insecure' / 'cannot deal with their feelings' (36 per cent), 'alcohol' (17 per cent). Thus a major reason why women see domestic violence as occurring is that of control. That is, it allows men to maintain power in their relationship, in situations where they feel insecure and unable to express and negotiate their feelings in non-violent ways. Undoubtedly, alcohol precipitates this violence but as other commentators have pointed out, it cannot be seen as a reason in itself (see Russell, 1982).

The factors that prevent women from leaving a violent relationship

Women were also asked what factors they thought prevented women from leaving a violent relationship. Women who had experienced domestic violence most frequently cited: economic dependence (27 per cent), hope that their partner will change (27 per cent), nowhere to go/ lack of affordable accommodation (26 per cent), children/break-up of family home (20 per cent) and fear of further violence (19 per cent). As can be seen, material circumstances (money, accommodation, children) are of great importance:

> It's difficult to walk out because of the children. It's humiliating to leave and it feels as if you've failed if you leave a marriage. I've just tried to stay and make it work.
>
> My children are young. If I left I'd need to earn a reasonable sum of money to keep us. But how? Because then I'd need childcare. It's impossible – its the lesser of the two evils, I just hope things will improve. Sometimes it's not so bad.

But there are also 27 per cent of women who hope their partner will change, that is, it is not material circumstances alone which keep them in the relationship. Indeed, the level of emotional involvement that exists in a relationship must not be underestimated,

> I love my husband, I've always done. I don't like being on my own, I've no family, he's all I've got.

It is not uncommon for there to be periods when no violence occurs. Men also frequently express remorse; they vow they will never do it again. A significant number of women, however, stay because they fear further violence: 'If I left he would always try to get me, hassle me'.

Finally, it should be noted that when a woman leaves, she is in many ways alone. It is she who has to bear the brunt both financially and emotionally of the break-up. As one woman commented:

> It's the bits when you are under pressure and you are on your own that you really feel like giving in … It would be nice if someone could be there 24 hours a day to help you through it. It's when you go to bed and close your eyes that the pressure is on. You think of things people have said to you. Children are used as a way of emotionally blackmailing you to stick in with someone.'[7]

7
What Do the Men Say? Male Attitudes to Domestic Violence

It is men who commit domestic violence against women so it is justifiable and indeed necessary not only to interview women but to focus on male attitudes and perspectives if we are to understand the phenomenon. Stage one of the survey therefore included a section addressed solely to male respondents concerning their attitudes to and use of violence against wives and girlfriends. With this in mind a series of vignettes were constructed detailing stereotypical 'conflict' situations. As noted earlier, it was thought that if men were asked directly whether they would use violence, their likely response would be negative, but if presented with a 'conflict' situation – which could be interpreted as an excuse for such behaviour – this might encourage a more honest and higher rate of response. The vignettes were based on the findings of previous studies (e.g. Dobash and Dobash, 1992) and also from in-depth interviews conducted in the pilot stage of the study, in which women were asked how their husbands or boyfriends had justified or rationalised their behaviour.

Each man was asked whether he would use violence in a situation where his partner had been unfaithful with a close friend of his, unfaithful with someone he did not know, arrived home late at night without having told him she would be late, neglected household duties, 'nagged' him, neglected the children, hit him or when they were both in the heat of a quarrel. Men were allowed to choose from four responses: 1. 'I could see myself hitting her even though it would not be the right thing to do'; 2. 'I could see myself hitting her and I would be justified'; 3. 'I would not hit her'; 4. I have actually hit her in this situation (more than one response, of course, being possible). As we have seen from the qualitative work with women, many report their partners as irrationally sexual jealous ('I had to give up working in the pub because he said in between pulling pints I'd go out the back to have sex with someone and go back to pulling another pint. It was so ridiculous'). Liz Kelly (1988a) comments that accusations of 'nagging' and 'arguing back' are often used by violent men to justify their behaviour. The utilization of a wide range of situations in the vignettes enables us to break out of the conception that only a minority of men are capable of violence towards their partners. Many men, as I shall show, would be likely to be violent in several of the situations.

An immediate objection to this approach is simply that the male respondents will lie in the presence of an interviewer. That is, their actual behaviour would be much more violent than the responses. This may well be true, but it has to be stressed that such data give us a base-line. It enables us to say that *at least* this proportion of men would be prone to violence. Moreover, it allows us to ascertain the group that see violence as a legitimate response. That is, they would not only see violence as a likely outcome but as a legitimate action on their part to be freely admitted in a survey. Thus it makes the useful sociological distinction between behaviour and values. A proportion of the respondents are avowedly violent: they see it not just as a lapse in behaviour, but a value or norm which they would ascribe. This group, of course, are extremely likely to be violent when confronted with actual or perceived situations. All of this, of course, would be of little interest if very few respondents were willing to admit their liability to violence. But a considerable proportion of men were willing to admit that they would be violent. It thus provides a significant baseline concerning the propensity to violence in our sample of men.

The common nature of violence

Tables 7.1 and 7.2 reveal the percentage of men perceiving themselves as likely to hit their partner and the percentage admitting they have actually hit their partner, analysed in terms of the vignettes.

From Table 7.1 the likelihood of violence can be divided into three groups:

1. **Sexual Infidelity** (A and B): here just under one third of all men say they would be liable to hit their partners. There is no difference between sex with a stranger or with a close friend. Of these 1 in 8 would see the assault as justified: these men clearly view their wives or girlfriends as their sexual property.

Table 7.1 Percentage of men perceiving themselves as likely to hit their partner, by vignette

Vignette	Total likely to hit %	Hit: justified %	Hit: unjustified %	Wouldn't hit %	Don't know/ refused %
A. Sex with a close friend	29	12	17	54	17
B. Sex with someone unknown to him	28	12	16	56	17
C. Arrives back late at night without telling him she was going to be late	3	2	1	86	12
D. Persistent neglect of household duties	3	1	2	87	11
E. Persistent 'nagging'	5	3	2	83	12
F. Persistent neglect of children	11	7	4	74	15
G. Hits you	24	15	9	60	16
H. Heat of a quarrel	12	5	7	68	20

$n = 429$.

2. **Quarrels** (G and H): a quarter of men say they would hit their partner if she hit them and 15 per cent of all men would see this as justified. In fact, this is the most justified violence of the vignettes. A smaller proportion (12 per cent) would be liable to commit violence in the heat of a quarrel. As we saw in examining the qualitative data, it is not unusual for women to use violence against their abusive partners and for this to be subsequently used by the man to excuse his behaviour.

3. **Domestic disputes** (C, D, E and F). This is the least likely category for assault to be perceived as liable to occur. The one exception is neglect of children.

However, if we turn to the question of whether the men interviewed have hit their partners in each vignette, a slightly different pattern emerges (Table 7.2). Quarrels become the most frequent situation (1 in 10 admit to violence), sexual infidelity is second (1 in 20) and least common is domestic disputes where between 1 and 4 per cent have hit their partners. This divergence in pattern between actual violence and

Table 7.2 Percentage of men hitting their partner, by vignette

Vignette	Have hit their partners %
A. Sex with a close friend	5
B. Sex with someone unknown to him	5
C. Arrives back late at night without telling him she was going to be late	1
D. Persistent neglect of household duties	2
E. Persistent 'nagging'	4
F. Persistent neglect of children	3
G. Hits you	10
H. Heat of a quarrel	12

$n = 429$.

Table 7.3 Percentage of men who would see themselves as liable to act violently, by number of vignettes

No. of vignettes	%
0	37
1	10
2	10
3	9
4	10
5	5
6	1
7	2
8	17
Average	2.9

$n = 429$.

perceptions of likelihood of violence is, of course, to be expected because of the differences in frequency of such occasions. Quarrels are much more likely than sexual transgressions, whether actual or perceived, of the type listed in the vignettes. Nevertheless the occurrence of physical violence is obviously very common, confirming the other findings presented in this book. Once again, we are talking of a baseline; no doubt there will be a considerable underestimation of actual violence because of lying or indeed questioning whether the assault was serious enough to mention.

The range of violence

It is of interest to discover over what range of the vignettes men would estimate their likelihood of acting violently. To do this the responses from each vignette have been added to create a nine-point scale. Thus, if a respondent would act violently in none of the vignettes he scored 0; if in all 8 (see Table 7.3).

From this we can see that only 37 per cent of men would claim that they would never act violently, about half would respond violently in up to two of the vignettes and 17 per cent would act violently to every example. The average score is just under three instances. It goes without saying that the 17 per cent of men who would act violently on every occasion represent a considerable number of men.

This scoring system can also be used on men who admit to hitting their partners in the situations of the various vignettes (see Table 7.4).

It should be noted that this is a prevalence rate, not an incidence rate. Many of these men would have hit their partners several times. It does, however, show that 19 per cent of men have acted violently to their partners at least once within the range of incidents presented to them, 7 per cent in two or more of the situations. This scoring system allows the examination of the class position of the men who admit to hitting their partners on at least one occasion.

Table 7.4 Percentage of men who have hit their partners, by number of vignettes

No. of vignettes	%
0	81
1	12
2	3
3	1
4	1
5 6 7 8	2
Average	0.38

$n = 429$.

Table 7.5 Actual use of violence in one or more of the vignettes, by class

Class	Had hit %
Professional	20
Lower-middle-class	17
Working-class	21

$n = 429$.

Men's class position

The data on men's actual use of violence was broken down by class in the light of the controversies in this area. The findings are presented in Table 7.5. As can be seen, no evidence was found to support the position of many previous researchers that domestic violence is largely a working-class phenomenon (McClintock, 1963; Straus, 1977; Gelles and Cornell, 1985; Young, 1986; Schwartz, 1988; DeKeseredy and Hinch, 1991). As Table 7.5 shows, violent men are found fairly equally in all parts of the class structure, with the rates for professional and working-class men almost identical (lower middle class men were somewhat less likely to be violent).

This finding underlines the fact that domestic violence can occur and at equal frequency throughout the class structure. It is not just a lower-class phenomenon. I began this book with a quotation from Sara Dylan, as this and other high-profile celebrity cases indicate, domestic violence knows no class or economic boundaries. O.J. Simpson's violence against his wife, Nicole Brown Simpson, and Tommy Lee's attacks on actress Pamela Anderson have recently been headline news, as have the violence of footballers Paul Gasgoine and Stan Collymore against their partners. Bea Campbell's fascinating book *Diana, Princess of Wales* (1998) documents the domestic violence experienced by Princess Diana's mother Frances Shand-Kydd from Earl Spencer.

Comparative work on attitudes to violence

Studies conducted elsewhere likewise reveal widespread acceptability of violence against women. In Edinburgh, research conducted by the Zero Tolerance Trust (Burton *et al.*, 1998) on young people aged between 14 and 21 years showed 1 in 5 young men and 1 in 10 young women to believe that violence against women was sometimes 'OK'. Almost 1 in

4 young men thought it could be acceptable if she has 'slept with' someone else. One in 8 young men if she were 'nagging'. In New Zealand a study revealed that 65 per cent of men blamed the woman for being hit in at least one of the circumstances presented to them, with infidelity being the most commonly cited (Leibrich *et al.*, 1995). In a New Jersey survey of male and female college students, 78 per cent approved of 'a man slapping his wife' in self-defence, 37 per cent in response to infidelity (Greenblat, 1985).

Women's responses to the vignettes

The vignettes in our survey were, in addition, presented to 100 women who were asked if they could envisage their partner hitting them in any of the 'conflict' situations and whether they thought the violence was justified. As we have seen from the in-depth interviews, many women blame themselves for the violence. The results are detailed in Table 7.6.

Table 7.6 Percentage of women perceiving themselves likely to experience violence, by vignette

Vignette	Total to be hit %	Hit: justified %	Hit: unjustified %	Wouldn't be hit %	Don't know/ Refused %
Sex with a close friend	34	21	13	47	19
Sex with someone unknown to him	30	18	12	50	21
Arrives back late at night without telling him was going to be late	7	4	3	83	10
Persistent neglect of household duties	6	6	0	79	15
Persistent 'nagging'	11	7	4	75	14
Persistent neglect of children	16	12	4	65	19
You hit him	28	21	7	55	18
Heat of a quarrel	13	4	9	67	20

n = 100.

Table 7.7 Perceived likelihood of hitting or being hit by a partner, men and women in rank order in terms of each vignette

Vignette	Men[a] %	Women[b] %
Sex with a close friend	29 (1)	34 (1)
Sex with someone unknown to him	28 (2)	30 (2)
She hit you/you hit him	24 (3)	28 (3)
Heat of a quarrel	12 (4)	13 (5)
Persistent neglect of children	11 (5)	16 (4)
Persistent 'nagging'	5 (6)	11 (6)
She arrives back late at night without telling him she was going to be late	3 (7)	7 (7)
Persistent neglect of household duties	3 (8)	6 (8)

[a]$n = 429$; [b]$n = 100$.
Rank order in brackets.

The immediate fact which strikes one is that women have almost identical assessments of their likelihood of being assaulted as men's of their liability to assault (see Table 7.2 above). The exception is the least likely assault category: disputes over domestic duties, where women see assault more likely compared to men. In Tables 7.7 and 7.8 the male and female responses have been put in rank order, to illustrate their general similarity.

What is apparent from these findings is that very many women see violence as the likely outcome of 'transgressions' on their part. The role of male violence as a control mechanism for women's behaviour is obvious. But the social dimension of this mechanism is further revealed if we look at Table 7.8, where male and female assessments of whether the assault is justified are compared. Once again the rank order is similar, with the exception of the least likely causes of assault. But more importantly, women are willing to accept that such attacks are

Table 7.8   Perception of hitting by male partner being *justified* for men and women in rank order in terms of each vignette

Vignette	Men[a] %	Women[b] %
She hits you/you hit him	15 (1)	21 (=1)
Sex with close friend	12 (=2)	21 (=1)
Sex with someone unknown to him	12 (=2)	18 (3)
Persistent neglect of children	7 (4)	12 (4)
Heat of a quarrel	5 (5)	4 (=7)
Persistent 'nagging'	3 (6)	7 (5)
She arrives back late at night without telling him she was going to be late	2 (7)	4 (=7)
Persistent neglect of household duties	1 (8)	6 (6)

[a]$n = 429$; [b]$n = 100$.
Rank order in brackets.

justified. That is, as a control mechanism it is strengthened by being seen not only to be behaviourally likely but to be normatively justified.

Indeed, superficially, many women would seem to see the assault as more justified than do men. This latter finding is undoubtedly flawed when one considers the psychology of answering this question by gender. Men, on being asked their likelihood of violence, will undoubtedly be put on the defensive. They may well admit that they would act violently, but they are more likely to claim that it would be an act 'on the spur of the moment' and not morally justified. Hence, the lower levels of justified violence by vignette than those of women.

But conversely, a significant proportion of women do view violence as being justified. This group do not, as one might have expected, see it merely as likely but unjustified. It is, however, important to consider this finding in the context of the fact that a *majority* of women would not see violence as justified. For given that over half of women in every

Table 7.9 Percentage of women who see their partner as liable to act violently, by number of vignettes

No. of vignettes	%
0	35
1	5
2	7
3	14
4	10
5	3
6	5
7	3
8	18
Average	4.9

$n = 100$.

circumstance would see themselves as not likely to be hit and very many of these would see violence as unjustified, these added to those who, although they see themselves as liable to violence view it as wrong, would constitute a clear majority.

The range of violence

The scoring system used for men (see above) was also applied to women's responses, to allow us to look at the number of incidents in which women would perceive themselves as liable to be the subjects of violence (see Table 7.9).

Thus, 35 per cent of women said their partners would not act violently in any of the situations, 18 per cent said they would in every example, 61 per cent in two or more of the vignettes. This, remarkably, is identical to the findings of the male survey: and clearly and dramatically corroborates the validity of the findings.

Note that of those women who responded to this section who had *not* reported on the supplementary questionnaires that they had been threatened with violence or experienced actual physical violence, slightly over half said they would expect their partner to hit them if one or more of the situations occurred. That there has been no violence of this nature may well be due to avoidance of such 'conflict' situations, which indicates that the behaviour of some women in domestic relationships is controlled by the *possibility* of male violence.

In addition, these findings may be taken to indicate that, contrary to popular myth, women who experience physical violence from their male partners are not weak and passive, but are those who, in word and deed, have challenged male power and refused to allow their behaviour to be curtailed by the threat of male violence. These results clearly illustrate not only widespread use of violence against wives and girlfriends by men, but also high levels of acceptance of violence against women. Furthermore, the threat of physical violence even where it has never occurred shapes women's behaviour. Women are well aware of the parameters beyond which violence is likely.

Part III

8
Violence, Space and Gender: Testing the Theories

So far I have concentrated on violence women experience from male partners or ex-partners. I wish now to widen this out to examine the social and spatial parameters of violence against both women *and men* from known and unknown persons. That is to delineate the overall level and patterning of violence, the social characteristics of victims of violence and perpetrators, and the location of violence, in terms of public and private space. This enables the testing of various hypotheses derived from the theoretical literature about the nature of violence in contemporary society.

In stage one of the survey women and men were asked whether anyone, including close friends or members of their family, had threatened them or used any form of physical violence against them in their home or in a public place in the last year. A sample of all violent incidents was then obtained by asking about the last incident that had occurred. This facilitated the collecting of more detailed information regarding the specific nature of the violence, its impact and the relationship of the victim to the perpetrator.

The focus of violence as presented in the literature

Let us recapitulate the main points made by new administrative criminologists, left realists, family violence theorists and radical feminists on the focusing of violence.

Liberal criminology: new administrative criminology

New administrative criminologists have tended to minimize the problem of crime. The findings of the various sweeps of the national British Crime Survey conducted by the Home Office have shown the risk of violent victimization to be low and less common than non-violent property offences, which are themselves presented as infrequent occurrences. Thus, one of the conclusions of the 1984 survey was that:

> Offences involving violence are very heavily outweighed by offences involving theft and damage to property. Some undercounting of non-stranger violence in the survey is likely, but present figures show wounding, robbery, sexual offences and common assaults to comprise only 17% of all BCS offences (excluding common assaults, the figure was 5%).
>
> (Hough and Mayhew, 1985: 16)

The 1998 Survey confirms this:

> The most common offences involve some type of theft (62% of total). Vandalism against vehicles and other household and personal property makes up a further 18% of offences ... a minority of crimes are categorised as violent offences (21%) and the majority of these are common assaults and involve at most minimal injury (14%); only 4% involve significant injury ... and 2% are muggings.
>
> (Mirrlees-Black *et al.*, 1998: 3)

With respect to the focusing of violence, the 'typical' victim is presented, particularly in the earlier British Crime Surveys, not as someone who is 'defenceless' or elderly but as a man, aged under 30 years, single, widowed or divorced, who spends several evenings out a week, drinks heavily and has assaulted others. Victims and offenders are, therefore, most likely to resemble each other and in a significant number of cases will be known to each other (Hough and Mayhew, 1982; Gottfredson, 1984). For example, in the 1988 survey, victims knew their assailants in about half of the cases (Mayhew *et al.*, 1989). Whilst it is acknowledged that the surveys under-count domestic violence and sexual offences, the risk of violence for women is generally presented by the Home Office as slight. And, in line with the apparent maleness of the phenomenon and life-style characteristics of the victims, violence is seen as a feature of public space, occurring mostly in pubs, clubs and other places of entertainment. According to Michael Gottfredson, 'those who stay in and around the home have lower likelihoods [of personal victimization] than those working outside the home' (1984: 18).

Left realists

On the overall focus of the level of violence, left realists have been critical of the incidence figures produced by the national crime surveys. Surveys of local areas conducted by left realists have yielded much higher incidence figures of interpersonal violence for women and the elderly, as well as for men. Further, they reverse the focus from men to women. Indeed, the first Islington Crime Survey uncovered higher assault rates for women than men: in the year of study there were 213 incidents for women, 152 for men per 1,000 households (Jones *et al.*, 1986).

The spectrum of violence experienced by women, particularly young women, is seen by left realists to be much wider than that for men, ranging from harassment to more serious assault. Violence against men is more likely to be experienced at the more serious end of the spectrum. Indeed, women encounter harassment on a level that is unknown to most men, as Young has pointed out:

> The equivalent experience of sexual harassment for men would be if every time they walked out of doors they were met with catcalls asking if they would like a fight. And the spectrum which women experience is all the more troublesome in that each of the minor incivilities could escalate to more serious violence. Sexual harassment could be a prelude to attempted rape; domestic verbal quarrels could trigger off domestic violence.
>
> (1992a: 50)

On the invisibility of violence, it has been stressed by left realists that much violence against women is, in fact, concealed. It does not appear in agency statistics and is less likely than property crime to be picked up using the conventional survey method. This is believed to be particulary true for domestic violence and sexual offences (Young, 1988a; Crawford *et al.*, 1990; Young, 1992a).

Finally, from a left realist perspective, people are seen as having a differential vulnerability to crime and, therefore, to talk of a general risk, the experiences of the 'average' person, assumes that everyone is equal in their capacity to resist the impact of such experiences. For left realists there is no such thing as an equal victim: people are more or less vulnerable, depending on their place in society: those who are poor with little political power will suffer the most from crime (Lea and Young, 1984; Kinsey *et al.*, 1986; Young, 1992a). And the relatively powerless situation of women – economically, socially and physically – is seen to make them more unequal victims than men (Young, 1988a).

Positivism: the family violence approach

The work of Straus *et al.* in the United States is solely concerned with emphasizing the problem of violence in the family. In the introduction to *Family Violence*, Richard Gelles writes:

> Twenty years ago, when people were concerned about violence they feared violence in the streets at the hands of a stranger. Today we are aware of the extent, impact and consequences of private violence.
>
> (1987: 13)

Violence between husbands and wives is seen as part of a pattern of violence occurring amongst all family members. The family violence approach is an attempt to look at the whole picture of family violence (see Gelles and Cornell, 1985).

The family violence researchers have conducted two national surveys in the United States, in 1975 and 1985 respectively, which have not only uncovered high levels of domestic violence but, in terms of focusing, have resulted in the highly controversial finding that men are as much at risk of violence from their wives as women are from their husbands (Straus, 1980; Straus and Gelles, 1988).[1] This is seen to contrast to women's behaviour outside the family, where it is said they are much less likely to use violence (Straus and Gelles, 1988). Thus, on the basis of the 1975 survey, Steinmetz (1977–8) concluded that there was a 'battered husband syndrome' which had not previously been acknowledged:

> violence between husband and wife is far from a one way street. The old cartoons of the wife chasing the husband with a rolling pin or throwing pots and pans are closer to reality than most (and especially those with feminist sympathies) realize.
>
> (1977–8: 488)

Radical feminists

Radical feminist research has centred on violence against women. The studies conducted by radical feminists in Britain, like those of left realists, have highlighted the myriad forms of violence experienced by women and have been used to challenge the figures produced by the

British Crime Surveys conducted by the Home Office. In the *Violence Against Women – Women Speak Out Survey* carried out in the London Borough of Wandsworth by feminist researchers, 44 per cent of women, for example, reported being the target of a violent attack within the past year. This, together with other findings uncovered by the research, was said by its co-ordinator, Radford, to 'cast real doubt on the figures cited in the British Crime Survey which reported a very low rate of offences against women' (1987: 35).

On the focusing of violence, feminists have emphasized the gender dimensions of violence against women; that is, it is made clear that violence is largely perpetrated *by men on women*. Whilst there has recently been an acknowledgement of women's violence against other women, particularly in the context of lesbian relationships (Lobel, 1986; Kelly, 1991a; Mann, 1993), female on male violence is presented as rare and, when it does occur, is seen as mainly in self-defence (Dobash and Dobash, 1979; Breines and Gordon, 1983; Kurz, 1993). The impact of violence against women in terms of psychological trauma, avoidance behaviours, injuries experienced and the difficulties inherent in their structural positions is, in addition, stressed by feminists.

With respect to the relationship to the perpetrator and locality of the violence, women are generally seen to be more likely to be assaulted by men who are known to them in their homes than by strangers in a public space:

> By far, most violence and threat arises from those who are familial and familiar. Rather than the street constituting the greatest threat to personal security, violence often happens in places such as the home or worksite.
>
> (Stanko, 1992: 3)

This position has led radical feminists to be critical of official crime prevention literature which tends to be fixated on the problem of 'stranger-danger' (*ibid.*: 3). Violence from known men, however, is seen as less likely to be reported to an interviewer due to its intrinsically personal nature (Hanmer and Saunders, 1984; Radford and Laffy, 1984). Indeed when Hanmer and Saunders (1984) found that 78 per cent of violence against women was by *unknown* men and more than half of violent incidents occurred in public space, they questioned the validity of their own results. They noted that when women were asked about violence they had witnessed in the neighbourhood, 69 per cent was between people known to each other, with a higher proportion occurring in the home. And when the pilot for the Wandsworth survey failed to uncover any violence on women by their husbands, brothers and boyfriends, Radford and Laffy commented: 'our conclusion is not that this has not occurred, as that contradicts what we know of domestic violence from Women's Aid but rather ours was not the right type of survey to explore such very personal and possibly continuing experiences' (1984: 113). On the location of the violence in terms of public and private space, Hanmer and Saunders make the point that incidents in public space may not necessarily be from strangers:

> Arguments and assaults between acquaintances, friends or married couples may begin and/or end outside the home or in any public location ... specific violent events are not sealed off into private versus public domains.

> (1984: 45)

Testing the theories

The various theoretical positions on the focus of violence suggest a series of propositions to be tested against the data.

Overall level of violence

1. The risk of violent victimization is low in comparison to property crimes (New Administrative Criminology)

The results presented in this book show violence against women by their husbands and boyfriends to be a relatively common occurrence. This chapter reveals this to be true *for violence overall*. As Table 8.1 demonstrates, nearly 20 per cent of the total sample (both men and women) had experienced a threat or some form of physical violence against them in the last 12 months, with equal proportions having

Table 8.1 Overall level of violence in the last twelve months by location, % of total sample ($n = 1,142$, weighted data)[2]

Location	n	%
Home	111	9.7
Public Place	109	9.5
Both Places*	214	18.7

*Both places does not equal the sum of home and public because some people were victimized in both spheres.

occurred in the home or in a public place. Three women and three men, in addition, had incidents against them in both the private *and* public spheres. This study has, therefore, refuted the finding of the British Crime Surveys conducted by the Home Office which show the risk of violent victimization to be low in comparison to property offences. It is likely that the use of highly trained, sensitive interviewers, together with the general emphasis placed on violence in the survey, has encouraged the reporting not only of domestic but of non-domestic violence.

Gender and age relation of overall violence

2. Men are the predominant victims of violence (New Administrative Criminology)
3. Men are the predominant perpetrators of violence (New Administrative Criminology, Left Realism, Radical Feminism)

Tables 8.2 and 8.3 show the women and men in this survey to be at fairly equal risk of violence against them. The supposition of the new administrative criminologists that it is men who are the predominant

Table 8.2 Overall focus of violence in the last twelve months by gender, % of total sample ($n = 1,142$, weighted data)

Victim	Home		Public		Both places	
	n	%	*n*	%	*n*	%
Women	67	11.7	39	6.8	103	18.0
Men	44	7.7	70	12.3	111	19.4
All people	111	9.7	109	9.5	214	18.7

Table 8.3 Overall focus of violence in the last twelve months by gender and locality, % of those experiencing violence ($n = 214$)

Victim	Home		Public		Both places	
	n	%	*n*	%	*n*	%
Women	67	60.4	39	35.8	103	48.1
Men	44	39.6	70	64.2	111	51.9
All people	111	100.0	109	100.0	214	100.0

*Both places does not equal the sum of home and public because some people were victimized in both spheres.

victims of violence is obviously based on an underestimation of violence in the home.

Respondents were asked further details about the last incident of violence that they had experienced. With respect to the perpetrator of the violence, the general assumption of radical feminist work, where it is made particularly explicit, and that of new administrative criminology and left realism, is that the perpetrator is most likely to be a man. The findings for the last incident, presented in Table 8.4, confirm this proposition: in 85 per cent of cases the assailant was found to be a man.

4. Young men are the predominant victims of violence (New Administrative Criminology)
5. Young women are more at risk of violence than older women (Left Realism)

The findings detailed in Tables 8.2 and 8.3 refute the new administrative criminologist's position with respect to the usual gender of the victim. However, as Table 8.5 demonstrates, when men are looked at as a category *by themselves*, it is younger men (aged 16–24 years) who are most likely to be victimized both in the home and in a public place. Further, it is of interest to note that, within this age group, 90 per cent of those who had experienced violence in a public place from an unknown man estimated his age to be under 25 years. New administrative criminology

Table 8.4 The perpetrator of the violence by gender and locality, % of those experiencing violence (*n* = 206)

Perpetrator	Home	Public	Both
Male	85.2	84.7	85.0
Female	14.8	15.3	15.0

Table 8.5 Violence against men by age and locality, % of total sample (*n* = 571)

Age	Home	Public
16–24	19	27
25–34	6	11
35–44	5	13
45+	4	9

Table 8.6 Violence against women by age and locality, % of total sample (*n* = 571)

Age	Home	Public
16–24	13	7
25–34	15	8
35–44	17	7
45+	7	9

is, therefore, correct when the focus is specifically on young men's experiences: violence on young men is largely perpetrated by other young men.

Table 8.6 shows the age profile for women. In the home the risk for women decreases significantly after the age of 45 years, which must, at least in part, relate to the increased number in this age group who live alone (divorced, separated or widowed and whose children have left home). In public spaces women of all ages had similar levels of victimization against them.

Locality of violence

6. Most violence occurs in public space (New Administrative Criminology)
7. Most violence occurs in pubs, clubs and other places of entertainment (New Administrative Criminology)

As Table 8.1 shows, this survey found violence to be equally distributed between the private and public spheres. Again, the position held by the new administrative criminologists is based on an underestimation of violence against women, a large proportion of which is domestic. When focusing specifically on violence in public places, the most common location for both women and men was found to be the street. Thus neither of the above propositions is supported (see Table 8.7).

The gendered distribution of the locality of violence

8. Most violence against men occurs in public space (New Administrative Criminology)
9. Most violence against women occurs in the private sphere (New Administrative Criminology, Left Realism, Radical Feminism)

Table 8.7 Location of the violence in public space by
gender, % of those experiencing violence (*n* = 109)

Location	Women %	Men %	All people %
Street	44	47	46
Pub/restaurant	13	11	12
Shop	8	10	9
Housing estate	21	16	17
Work	3	–	1
Other	11	16	15
All	100	100	100

10. Men are the predominant perpetrators of violence in public space (All Perspectives)
11. Men are the predominant perpetrators of violence in the private sphere (New Administrative Criminology, Left Realism, Radical Feminism)

This study confirms that most violence against women is private, most violence against men is public. However, as is apparent from Tables 8.2 and 8.3, in neither instance is the focus overwhelming. Table 8.3 shows 36 per cent of violence against women occurred in a public place, while 40 per cent of violence against men occurred in the home. Furthermore, it is interesting to note that the ratio of violence against women in the home compared to the public sphere is nearly equal to the ratio of violence against men in the public sphere compared to the home. Propositions 10 and 11 are additionally confirmed. As demonstrated in Table 8.4, men are the predominant perpetrators of violence in the domestic sphere and to an identical level (85 per cent) in public.

Inter- and intra-gender distribution of violence

12. Most male violence is against men (New Administrative Criminology)
13. Most female violence is against men (Family Violence Researchers)

Table 8.8 shows that male violence is directed more against women than men, although not by a great extent. Twice as much female violence is, however, against men than women, albeit on a much smaller scale. The first proposition is, therefore, refuted; the second is substantiated.

Table 8.8 The inter- and intra-gender distribution
of violence (*n* = 206)

Relationship	Home %	Public %	Both places %
Male to male	26	56	40
Male to female	59	29	45
Female to male	13	7	10
Female to female	2	8	5
All	100	100	100

Inter- and intra-gender distribution of violence by locality

14. Most male violence in public space is against men (New Administrative Criminology)
15. Most male violence against women is in the private sphere (Radical Feminism)
16. Most female violence against men is in the private sphere (Family Violence Researchers)

It is apparent from Table 8.8 that most male violence in the public sphere is against men although the ratio of 1.9 : 1 male to female victims is not perhaps as high as might have been expected. The new administrative criminologists' position is, therefore, supported. Indeed, it is of interest that there is a degree of symmetry here, with male violence in the private sphere being 2.3 : 1 female to male victims, almost the mirror image of the public sphere. The amount of male violence against males in the private sphere is likewise not insignificant. But, overall, twice as much male violence against women occurs in the private compared to the public sphere. The radical feminist position is thus substantiated. Female violence – *which is much less common* – does not have such a symmetry between the two spheres. An equal proportion of female violence in the public sphere is against men and women. In the private sphere, however, female violence is directed at men (6.5:1); thus the last position is validated.

Overall severity of violence

17. Most violence is minor (New Administrative Criminology)

Respondents encountered a wide range of violent behaviours against them, most commonly being punched and slapped. A weapon was involved in 15 per cent of cases and 34 per cent resulted in some form of injury. Nearly a third of those experiencing a threat of, or any form of, violence had experienced more than one incident. On the impact of the violence, a significant number sought medical treatment and experienced various emotional and psychological effects after the last incident. In the light of these findings, violence cannot be considered to be minor.

Severity of violence by gender

18. Violence against men is likely to be more severe (New Administrative Criminology, Left Realism)
19. Violence has a greater impact on women (Left Realism, Radical Feminism)

Overall women and men were found to experience a similar range of violence against them and similar injuries. However, in the home, women were 56 per cent more likely to experience more than one incident than men. With regards to impact, whilst men's experiences were not insignificant, violence was found generally to have a greater effect on women. For example, 4 per cent of women had stayed overnight in hospital (which underscores the seriousness of the injuries inflicted) in comparison to no men, and 49 per cent reported feeling depressed or losing self-confidence in comparison to 25 per cent of men. The degree of impact experienced by women is, of course, hardly surprising given the inter-gendered nature of violence against women. Thus, the results fail to support the first proposition, but substantiate the second.

Severity of violence by locality

20. Violence is more severe in public space (New Administrative Criminology)
21. Violence is more severe against men in public space (New Administrative Criminology)
22. Violence is more severe against women in the private sphere (Radical Feminism)

With respect to the range of violent behaviours used, the survey found little difference between the home and public space. In the home, however, the risk of injury was greater (36 per cent) and respondents were 71 per cent more likely to experience more than one incident. In public space there was a higher risk of the incident involving a weapon. The impact of violence was significantly greater in the home. When looking at the psychological effects of violence in particular, this is

Table 8.9 Overall violence by relationship and gender, % of
those experiencing violence (*n* = 214)

Perpetrator	Women %	Men %	All people %
Unknown male	15	32	24
Unknown female	5	–	3
Current partner	23	7	15
Ex-partner	10	6	8
Other male family member	7	9	8
Other female family member	2	1	2
Male friend	11	9	10
Female friend	–	1	1
Male acquaintance	22	23	23
Female acquaintance	2	3	3
Not specified	2	7	4
All	99	98	101

hardly surprising given that the home is where one is supposed to feel
safe and secure ('a haven in a heartless world'). Violence in the home is,
in addition, more likely to be carried out by a known person and, as the
incidence data show, may be part of a continuing experience. Finally,
there was little difference in the nature of the violence experienced by
men and women, either overall or in public and private space.

The relationship between victims and perpetrators

23. Most violence is committed by someone who is known to the vic-
    tim (New Administrative Criminology, Radical Feminism)
24. Violence against women in public space is more likely to be from
    an unknown man (Conventional Wisdom)
25. Violence against women in public space is likely to be from a
    known man (Radical Feminism)

The new administrative criminologists and radical feminists have suggested that the surveys they have conducted undercount non-stranger
violence due to the methods used. The assumption generally made in
their writing is that violence from known people is much greater than
that reported. The findings presented in Table 8.9 support the notion
that violence is usually perpetrated by a known person. This is not to

say, however, that violence from a stranger is insignificant, Tables 8.10 and 8.11 show that it accounts for 32 per cent of violence against men and 20 per cent of violence against women. The figure uncovered for women is even more notable given the extraordinary avoidance behaviours adopted by women to prevent such victimization (see, for example, Painter, 1988; Painter *et al.*, 1990). It is clearly important in highlighting the reality of domestic violence that women's experience of violence from unknown men is not forgotten.

Table 8.10 shows women were found to be at greatest risk in the home from, first, their current partner (34 per cent), second, a male friend (18 per cent) or male acquaintance (18 per cent), and third, an ex-partner (13 per cent). In public, the assailant was most likely to be an unknown male (38 per cent), a male acquaintance (29 per cent) or an unknown female (12 per cent). For men, the perpetrator in the home was most likely to be another male family member (24 per cent), second, a male friend (20 per cent), third, a male acquaintance (17 per cent), and fourth, a current partner (15 per cent). The 'other male family member' most usually cited by men was a brother. In public, men were most likely to be victimized by an unknown male (51 per cent) and second, by a male acquaintance (27 per cent).

If we analyse non-stranger and stranger violence in public we find that both women and men have about a 50 per cent chance of

Table 8.10   Violence against women: relationship to the perpetrator by locality, % of those experiencing violence (*n* = 103)

Perpetrator	Home %	Public %	Both places %
Unknown male	–	38	15
Unknown female	–	12	5
Current partner	34	5	23
Ex-partner	13	7	10
Other male family member	12	–	7
Other female family member	3	–	2
Male friend	18	–	11
Female friend	–	–	–
Male acquaintance	18	29	22
Female acquaintance	–	5	2
Not specified	2	4	2
All	100	100	99

Table 8.11 Violence against men: relationship to the perpetrator by locality, % of those experiencing violence ($n = 111$)

Perpetrator	Home %	Public %	Both places %
Unknown male	2	51	32
Unknown female	–	–	–
Current partner	15	1	7
Ex-partner	9	4	6
Other male family member	24	–	9
Other female family member	3	–	1
Male friend	20	1	9
Female friend	–	1	1
Male acquaintance	17	27	23
Female acquaintance	2	4	3
Not specified	7	9	7
All	99	98	98

the attacker being a stranger. For men this stranger is invariably male and for women there is a three to one chance of the assailant being male. These findings refute the notion that violence against women in public space is more likely to be from an unknown man – he is just as likely to be known as unknown. And, of course, it refutes the opposite assertion often occurring in the radical feminist literature.

Violence between husbands and wives/boyfriends and girlfriends

26. Most violence in the private sphere is between husbands and wives/boyfriends and girlfriends (All Perspectives)

Table 8.12 indicates that most violence in the home was found to be perpetrated by a current partner. However, it is important to point out that violence in the home from non-family members is not insubstantial, particularly by a male friend (19 per cent) or male acquaintance (18 per cent).

27. Men are as likely to experience violence from wives/girlfriends as women are from husbands/boyfriends (Family Violence Researchers, 1996 British Crime Survey finding)

Table 8.12 Overall violence in the home by relationship, % of those experiencing violence (*n* = 111)

Perpetrator	All people %
Unknown male	1
Unknown female	–
Current partner	25
Ex-partner	12
Other male family member	17
Other female family member	3
Male friend	19
Female friend	–
Male acquaintance	18
Female acquaintance	1
Not specified	4
All	100

28. Women are more likely to experience violence from their husbands/boyfriends than men from their wives/girlfriends (Radical Feminism)
29. Women use violence against their husbands/boyfriends in self-defence and are more likely to be injured and experience a greater degree of impact (Radical Feminism)

The findings detailed in Tables 8.10 and 8.11 suggest the risk to women from their current partners was over three times greater than that for men. Moreover, methods used at this stage of the project probably underestimate domestic violence against women; that is face-to-face interviews as opposed to self-complete questionnaires. Thus these data clearly contradict the findings of Straus *et al.* and undermine Steinmetz's notion of the 'battered husband syndrome'. Proposition 27 is, therefore, dismissed and proposition 28 confirmed.

This survey also shows that women were more likely to endure a wide range of violent behaviours, be injured and have a weapon used against them by their partners or ex-partners than was the case for men. In fact, no man was found to have had a weapon used against him by a partner. Women were also more likely to experience multiple incidents and the impact on them was, not surprisingly, worse. Qualitative work shows further that women who experience violence from their partners often use violence in self-defence. Thus, as occurred above, the radical feminist position on this form of violence is found to be valid.

Furthermore, as left realists in particular have stressed, there is no such thing as an equal victim; people have a differential vulnerability to crime. Thus violence against women, because of their structural position, is likely to be worse and have a greater effect than that against men.

Summary of findings and conclusion

Summary of findings

This chapter set out to explore the social and spatial parameters of violence. Its main findings are as follows:

- Violence is a relatively common occurrence.
- Women and men have fairly equal risks of violence against them.
- Men are the predominant perpetrators of violence.
- Violence is equally distributed between the public and private spheres.
- Most violence against men occurs in public, most violence against women occurs in private, but in neither instance is the focus overwhelming.
- Men are the predominant perpetrators of violence in both the private and public spheres.
- Most male violence in the public sphere is against men, most male violence in the private sphere is against women, although male violence against women in the public sphere and male violence against men in the private sphere is not insignificant.
- Violence is serious; respondents experienced a wide range of violent behaviours against them; injuries and the impact was correspondingly severe.
- Women and men experienced a similar range of violent behaviours against them, use of weapons and injuries. Violence had a greater impact on women.
- There was little difference between the home and public space with respect to the range of violent behaviours. In the home the risk of injury was slightly greater and the impact was worse.
- Most violence is committed by someone who is known to the victim, although violence from a stranger is not insignificant in public space. Violence from strangers entering the home is negligible.
- Women were most at risk from their current partners, followed by male acquaintances and then unknown men.
- Men were most at risk from unknown men, followed by male acquaintances and then male friends.

- The perpetrator of violence in a public space is equally likely to be a non-stranger as a stranger whether the victim is a woman or man.
- Violence from partners or ex-partners in public space was relatively infrequent.
- Women are at much greater risk of violence from partners or ex-partners. Violence against men from partners or ex-partners was relatively uncommon. Women are more likely to use violence against their partners or ex-partners in self-defence, are more likely to be injured, have a weapon used against them and experience a greater degree of impact.

Conclusion

These findings with regards to the distribution of violence cut across the predictions of the major theories, invalidating many whilst supplying answers where there has previously only been conjecture. In particular, they contradict the widespread notion that violence is a relatively infrequent occurrence which focuses on men in public space and is perpetrated by strangers. On the contrary, violence is a common event and not the 'poor cousin' of property offences in the criminological agenda; it focuses equally on men and women and occurs in equal proportions in the public and private spheres and is frequently committed by non-strangers.

Patterns of victimization have been found to be clearly gendered. For a man the public sphere is twice as likely to be the arena of risk in comparison to the home; for a woman the pattern is exactly the opposite. For a man, strangers are the greatest risk, followed by acquaintances and then partners: the risk decreases with intimacy. For a woman the reverse is true: partners are by far the greatest perpetrators of violence, followed by acquaintances and then strangers. However, for men and women the one constant factor is that it is *men* who pose the greatest threat. Thus, this survey to a large extent has validated the radical feminist arguments, although, in highlighting the problem of domestic violence for women, we must not underestimate the danger they face in public space from male acquaintances and strangers; this has also proved to be not insignificant.

Postscript: abused men? the controversy bubbles on

'One in four women abused' shouted a page-three headline in The *Guardian* on Thursday, citing a report from the British Medical Association published the previous day.

According to the newspaper, a BMA survey in North London questioned 571 women and 429 men about domestic violence. It reported that one in three of the women said they suffered some form of domestic violence and a quarter of them said they had been forced to have sex against their will. There is no mention in the paper of any result from the questioning of 429 men.

In fact, the men were questioned only about whether or not they had physically or sexually abused women. The BMA researchers failed to ask the men if they considered themselves victims of domestic violence.

(Pizzey, 1998: 24)

On first glancing at this article by Erin Pizzey in *The Observer* I was annoyed by the headline 'MEN ARE STRONG, MEN ARE BULLIES AND MEN ARE VIOLENT. MEN DONT CRY WHEN THEIR WIVES BEAT THEM UP – THIS IS THE UNREPORTED FACE OF DOMESTIC VIOLENCE'. Annoyed because the 'revelation' of domestic violence against men is a perennial in the newspapers and particularly on documentary television (a recent Channel 4 flyer announced 'Scared to go home to your wife tonight? ('Battered Men', *Dispatches*). However, on reading the article, my annoyance was transformed into bemusement. It seemed almost miraculous that the British Medical Association survey had interviewed 571 women and 429 men about domestic violence – exactly the same number I had and in North London to boot. I telephoned the British Medical Association to talk to the researchers only to be told that the 'study' of domestic violence was a literature review and, of course, the survey was my own. It had merely been given a spin and emerged refreshed in the columns of *The Guardian* newspaper as a new survey. But what was really excruciating was not the way my research had been hijacked like a commodity and cast into cyberspace without time, place or author, but the overbearingly confident assertion of Erin Pizzey that, 'in fact' men had only been interviewed about their violence to women and that violence from women had been ignored as if by an act of automatic political correctness. Of course, this was not so as this book shows. Indeed, one of the controversies I sought to examine was precisely the comparison of domestic violence against women and men.

Part IV

9
Tackling Domestic Violence: From Theory to Policy

This book has been concerned with four themes: one empirical, one methodological, one theoretical and the last a concern about policy. First of all the examination of the distribution of violence, in public and private space, between men and women and in terms of age, class and ethnicity. In doing so I have stressed the need, particularly in terms of domestic violence, to develop a sensitive methodology. As we have seen, numerous conventional large-scale surveys fall short in their ability to uncover the extent of violence and indeed distort its distribution. The methodological aspect is of extreme importance as without reasonable data the most refined and well thought out theory is erected on shifting sands – it is as impermanent as the next survey. Third this book sets out to test theory and to see how the fit and disjunction between findings and theory allows us to move to a more satisfactory understanding of violence – domestic or otherwise. Finally, a book written from a perspective of commitment to tackling domestic violence must move from theory to policy and this forms the basis of my conclusions.

Testing theory

I have analysed four major criminological traditions which attempt explanation of domestic violence, namely, classicism (including the new administrative criminology), positivism, feminism and left realism. I have delineated their main principles and shown how each has been applied to explain, research and combat domestic violence, and identified the strengths and weaknesses of each position. Furthermore, the empirical data generated by the research project enabled the testing of various hypotheses derived from the theoretical literature about the nature of violence in general, particularly with regards to its social and

215

spatial patterning. These findings invalidated many of the predictions derived from theory. For example, it showed the 'battered husband syndrome' of the positivist, family violence approach to be largely a myth and countered the claim of the new administrative criminology that violence is relatively uncommon in comparison to property offences. It also supplied answers where there had previously only been conjecture as to the distribution of violent behaviour.

On examination, the approaches of radical feminism and left realism were found to provide the most useful framework for understanding the phenomenon. It is necessary to build on their contribution and attempt to achieve a synthesis of their positions: a *feminist realism* within criminology. The insights gained from radical feminism and left realism were utilized to inform the research methodology. For example, the exploration of definitional differences and the generation of consensus definitions was derived from left realism and the use of sensitive research techniques from radical feminism. Many of the findings resulting from the research support the common positions of radical feminism and left realism, for example, with respect to the gendered distribution and widespread nature of violence against women. However, some of the predictions derived from radical feminism and left realism are divergent and here the empirical results provide a basis on which to develop a feminist realism.

The endemic nature of domestic violence

Both radical feminism and left realism are constructionist in that they see human beings as being constituted by the structures and discourses of patriarchy and capitalism respectively. The causes of domestic violence are, therefore, to be found not as blemishes in an otherwise satisfactory social system but as endemic to the core structures of present day society.

Of great importance in terms of the theoretical backcloth to this thesis has been the radical feminist contention that violence is central to the maintenance of patriarchal order. Violence is seen as a powerful means of subordinating women, thus serving as a key mechanism of social control. This position has been consistently verified by the empirical findings at every stage of the research study. Violence against women is widespread, it exists throughout the class structure and is viewed by both men and women as a means of control. A significant finding was that even in those relationships where violence did not occur, the women were well aware of the types of behaviour which would be *likely* to evoke violence from their partners. Indeed women's predictions of those behaviours which would elicit violence concurred with those in which men suggested they would be likely to be violent. All this confirms the radical feminist position, but what it does not suggest is that violence is the main method of patriarchal dominance (economic superiority is of great importance) nor that it is true for all heterosexual relationships (a minority of men and women would not use or expect violence in any situation).

This construction can be readily melded with the left realist stress on capitalism as creating differential levels of vulnerability within society. Capitalism generates massive inequalities in the social structure. Women, in particular, have less access to money and resources, and are frequently economically dependent on men and/or the state. In the Ladywood Crime Survey, for example, realists drew attention to how cuts in public sector expenditure, changes in the structure and organization of the housing market and the social benefit system have increased women's unemployment and dependence (Painter *et al.*, 1990b). These changes also reinforce women's restricted access to community facilities such as child care, transport, education and health. Thus, if radical feminism points to the causes of domestic violence within the social order, realism can help explain the factors that prevent women from leaving violent men and why men are able to get away with such violence. Substantive inequalities make women financially dependent on men and/or the welfare state. Factors such as women's lack of work opportunities, low pay and resulting economic dependence on men are likely to influence their decision to leave or return to violent partners, particularly if they have children. As we have seen, structural reasons in the study were commonly given by women for staying with violent men: 27 per cent cited economic dependence, 26 per cent 'nowhere to go/lack of affordable accommodation', 20 per cent 'children/break-up of family home'.

But it is not only economic dependence but spatial divisions which facilitate domestic violence. For the liberal state on which capitalism is founded is noted for its division of society into public and private spheres, with the private sphere relatively immune from state interference. Within this sanctuary of privacy, opportunities for violence regularly occur and deterrence is low. Furthermore, during the twentieth century the family has become more private and thus less susceptible to informal controls over behaviour. As Laslett (1973) has pointed out, this is due to changes in household composition (for example, there has been a decrease in the number of children born per family and it is less likely to be composed of extended family members) and developments in architectural styles and practices. Thus behaviour is less visible and less prone to detection than it was in the past.

The social construction of domestic violence

Radical feminism highlights the fact that what constitutes 'domestic violence' is not a given, taken-for-granted, construct but one that is subject to male-oriented definitions. As Liz Kelly comments, conventional definitions of violence and legal categories, 'reflect men's ideas and limit the range of male behaviour that is deemed unacceptable to the most extreme, gross and public forms' (1988a: 138). Radical feminists note that when conventional definitions are utilized, women find themselves caught between their own experience which they regard as abusive, and the dominant male discourse which defines such behaviour as normal or to be expected.

Realism concurs with radical feminism, but places even greater emphasis on the problematic nature of all social problems. Definition is always up for grabs: for the central premise of realism is the dyadic nature of crime and deviance. There are no absolute or monolithic definitions of what constitutes a problem: rather, it depends on whose base one takes as defining domestic violence, whether it be that of men, women or any subgroup therein. Definitions of domestic violence vary according to the values and the perceptions of the group doing the defining. What is violence to one person may not necessary be to another. The process of defining what constitutes violence is likely to be affected by such factors as gender, age, ethnicity, class, education and the context of the violence. An initial task therefore of the study was to establish to what *extent* there is a consensus of definition amongst women and the *limits* of this consensus. The demarcation of a consensus definition enabled the creation of a general rate of violence termed 'composite domestic violence'. This allowed the exploration of variations in the rates of domestic violence across subsections of the population. The use of such a consensus definition countered the argument that violence rates are simply a reflection of definitional variations between different parts of the population.

The extent and distribution of domestic violence

Both radical feminism and left realism agree as to the widespread nature of violence against women and its gendered distribution. They have argued that it is much more prevalent than official statistics or conventional victimization surveys would have us believe. Both concur 'that women's fear of crime is based in an accurate assessment of risk rather than overactive imaginations or hysterical tendencies of females' (Ahluwalia, 1992: 246). This contention has been extensively borne out by the empirical findings presented in this study. There has, however, been a lack of clarity as to how such violence is distributed by class, age and ethnicity. For example, there is a tendency in radical feminism to view domestic violence as evenly spread throughout the social structure, whereas, realists point to a differential distribution stressing an inverse relationship with class. The findings of this study illuminate this debate. A key differentiation made is between the class position of the male perpetrator and the female victim. Thus, if we examine the class position of the man, we find domestically violent men occur in all sections of the class structure. Professional and working-class men were equally as likely to be violent to their partners (lower-middle-class men somewhat less so). Taking the woman's class position into account, however, professional women did have significantly lower rates against them. This seemed to relate to their greater access to resources. Professional women are likely to be more able to get out of a relationship before it becomes violent. They were also less likely to have children, which would serve to bind them to the relationship. Of further relevance here is that professional women were more likely to define mental cruelty as domestic violence than other groups of women, mental cruelty being found to be a feature in the early stages of a violent relationship before the onset of physical violence. Thus they were not only more able to leave a violent relationship, they were also more likely to move out early in that relationship.

Such findings do not corroborate the realist notion of a class link, which is a function of displaced economic deprivation amongst lower-class men. On the contrary they suggest that it is the class of the victim rather than the offender which is paramount and that this is a product not of victim precipitation but of victim mobility. Nor do they concur with a radical feminist notion of equal levels of victimization irrespective of class, although the finding here is of less significance theoretically, being predicated merely on the differential ability of better off women to move away from aggressive men.

The impact of domestic violence

Both radical feminists and realists stress the considerable impact of violence on women's lives but, whereas radical feminists tend to see male violence as a central pillar in patriarchy and in the control and restriction of all women, realists stress a greater differentiation of impact. With this in mind, the contours of the impact of domestic and non-domestic violence on women's lives by class, age and ethnicity and public and private space have been examined in this study. In terms of spatial distribution, violence of all forms had a greater impact when it occurred in the home as opposed to that inflicted by a stranger in public. This is undoubtedly because it is less likely to be a one-off and occurs within an emotional relationship. No matter what the social circumstances of women domestic violence was found to have a long-lasting impact. However, as we have seen, women with more access to money and other resources and support systems were able to get out quicker, thus lessening the overall impact. Social circumstances obviously compound the problems women face, particularly if they have children. Thus, although, contrary to the expectations of left realism, domestic violence occurs across class lines, its impact is greatly mediated by class. Lastly, following the approach suggested in the radical feminist literature, the coping and resistance strategies adopted by women in response to domestic violence were explored in order to gain a fuller picture of how women deal with their experiences.

Utilizing both qualitative and quantitative methods

There has been a tendency for radical feminists to favour qualitative methods and realists to emphasize the utility of the quantitative victimization study, although both stress the use of sensitive methods. There is, however, nothing inherent in either position to generate such a dichotomous approach and the emphasis in this research is on the use of both quantitative and qualitative approaches. The need to use multiple methods has been stressed throughout this book.

Policy: the politics of redistribution and recognition

Let me conclude with a discussion of policy. What does our delineation of the empirical parameters of domestic violence and the theoretical architecture which attempts to circumscribe this space tell us about what we can do to combat this problem? For is this not the litmus test of the usefulness of research and investigation?

The key finding in terms of policy is the widespread nature of domestic violence. That is, it is not an unusual act restricted to men who are psychologically unstable or wantonly wicked. Yet it is often portrayed as that and the policy implications are considerable. Iris Marion Young, in her pathbreaking *Justice and the Politics of Difference,* spells out this in terms of violence in general:

> Given the frequency of violence in our society, why are theories of justice usually silent about it? I think the reason is that theorists do not typically take such incidents of violence and harassment as matters of social injustice ...
>
> What makes violence a face of oppression is less the particular acts themselves, though they are often utterly horrible, than the social context surrounding them, which makes them possible and even acceptable. What makes violence a phenomenon of social injustice, and not merely an individual moral wrong, is its systematic character, its existence as a social practice ... It is a social given that everyone knows it happens and will happen again. It is always on the horizon of social imagination, even for those who do not perpetrate it. According to the prevailing social logic, some circumstances make such violence more 'called for' than others
>
> (1990: 61–2)

She refers here to racist attacks and homophobia as well as violence against women. The findings of our study of domestic violence clearly show that 'everyone knows' it happens, that there are generally understood expectations of what circumstances elicit it and that it exists as an institutionalised practice prevalent within our society. Thus its endemic nature suggests its institutional basis, and this in turn points to such violence being engendered within the core structure of society. Such a finding fits well with both radical criminology (left realism) and radical feminism – both which stress the root rather than superficial nature of the phenomenon. The policy imperatives which such an analysis generates are perennials of radical politics, namely what is the nature of the fundamental changes we must make in order to tackle the problem and which are the immediate policies we must advocate in pursuit of this aim? Both radical feminism and left realism have, as we have seen, addressed these questions. Left realism, however, is perhaps clearer in the relationship between short- and long-term reforms, whilst radical feminism is more in a quandary about this: it opposes 'band aid reform' yet, at the same time, is actively involved in short-term campaigns. In fact, the very basis of left realism is an attempt to navigate between establishment criminology (which sees crime as peripheral and short-term reform all that is necessary) and critical criminology (which sees crime as endemic and denies that any change can be made without fundamental reform). Rather, realism argues that immediate reform is necessary in order to ameliorate the problem of those suffering violence *and* in order to pave the way for change. That is, short-term gains and long-term transformations.

Left realism with its notion of the square of crime has, correspondingly, four points of possible intervention. This can involve the mobilization of state agencies (usually the police) or public bodies (voluntary agencies or the public at large) directed either at the control of offenders or the relief and protection of the victim. Further, this multi-agency range of interventions must deal with immediate problems and the structural problems which give rise to crime in the first place – this priority being given in the long run to the latter. This being said there was a tendency in early left realist work (for example, *What is to be Done About Law and Order?* (Lea and Young, 1984) and *Losing the Fight Against Crime* (Kinsey *et al.*, 1986)) to focus on state interventions in terms of the police, and to see control as tackling the offender. That is to marginalize public mobilization, consigning the victim, somewhat ironically, to the mapping out of the problem and to cast structural change to a rather hazy backcloth of the argument. In short, to adopt a rather conventional approach which was radical only in terms of the call for democratic control of the police and the need to shift the focus of police resources away from the prioritization of men, the middle class and the defence of property towards the safety needs of women, the working class and problems of violence. Radical feminist practice differed in that it focused overwhelmingly on the victim of male violence and mobilized, famously, voluntary agencies in the creation of women's refuges. This was coupled with a rhetorical demand on the police to tackle the problem, muted significantly by doubts as to whether such a male-dominated organization, with its internal problems of sexism and harassment, could ever deliver the goods.

In more recent years both positions have changed and widened their scope but there still remains some confusion. The argument of this book is quite simply that:

1. The focus must be on both offenders and victims – the long-term must be changing the behaviour and attitudes of offenders, the short-term that of ameliorating the plight of victims.
2. All agencies should be mobilized, but the solution to the problem of domestic violence does not, in the long term, lie with the police (they can at best hold the problem at bay), but in structural change, in particular, that directed at changing gender relationships.

Thus far I have sketched the problem of policy with regards the various modes of intervention and their long- or short-term nature. More fundamentally, we must now examine the basis of reform; that is, what sort of changes we must envisage and how effective they will be in making profound changes in the social fabric.

Nancy Fraser, in *Justice Interruptus* (1997), provides us with an extremely useful and pertinent classification of reform. First, she distinguishes between reform that is redistributive and reform that involves recognition. Gender, for example, involves both economic divisions and cultural differences. Women are the inferior part of a series of economic divisions, between 'productive' and domestic labour, that between higher-paid and lower-paid occupations, primary and secondary labour markets, and so on. As a result, they are economically much more vulnerable than men. To take an example from this research, they are much less capable of moving home when under duress, especially if they have children. Any changes here must involve policies of *redistribution*. But this is only half the story. They also suffer the cultural injustice of androcentrism. That is the 'feminine' is disparaged, trivialized, objectified and demeaned in a stereotypical fashion. These harms Fraser terms *recognition*. This has a close relationship with domestic violence because we know that the ability to act violently towards another commonly involves denying their full humanity (see I. Young, 1990). 'This devaluation', as Fraser puts it 'expressed in a range of harms suffered by women, including sexual assault, sexual exploitation, and pervasive domestic violence...' (1997: 20). Economic inequality, then, renders women more vulnerable to domestic violence, misrecognition facilitates them becoming a target of aggression.

On this division between distributive and cultural justice, Fraser superimposes those reforms which simply reaffirm the divisions and those which transform the situation of injustice. Affirmative measures of redistribution involve the surface transfer of resources in a band aid fashion. To take the case of class: the transfer of resources from the employed to the unemployed without changing the relationships of class, for example, by social security payments or housing subsidy. With regards gender, this would involve equal opportunities and attitudinal change, but it would not, for example, allow for the changing of jobs so that they facilitate childrearing. It would not alter the distribution of domestic labour. It would involve the state subsidy of women who were separated rather than a transformation of their job opportunities. Affirmative recognition would, similarly, involve only superficial changes: it would involve the revaluation of femininity *as it now is*, that is an attempt to equalize the cultures of the masculine and the feminine. The result would be quite similar to a conservative ideal: the redrawing of the division of labour between the sexes with each in their 'equal' spheres. Presumably in this instance femininity would seem to have a special calling towards childrearing and masculinity to breadwinning, etc. Equal respect between unequal cultures does not result in equality. Nothing would change and presumably this bicentric culture of masculine and feminine would deem women who strayed out of their cultural 'destiny' to have violated their duty, so that domestic violence would continue to be a possibility.

Transformative remedies attempt to transcend these binaries of economic and cultural roles. Thus transformative redistribution would tackle the deep structures which make women as a group economically inferior to men. In this respect it would allow women much more easily to leave an abusive partner, whereas transformative recognition would attempt to deconstruct femininity by destabilizing gender dichotomies.

To destabilize the gender binary is an easy phrase but there is much controversy about what this means. Critics might cynically suggest that such a dissolution of difference between men and women might lead to assimilation. That is the dominant culture of masculinity would simply encompass femininity, generating, at best, a culture of androgyny, at worst, a rejigged monoculture of masculinity (I. Young, 1996). Surely, one does not want in the process of transforming gender differences to lose what is distinctly feminine? For there are clearly differences between the economic and the cultural. Whilst the politics of redistribution will clearly seek to abolish economic divisions, the politics of recognition will want to maintain both difference and equality (see Phillips, 1998). Indeed, much feminist scholarship over the last decade has been concerned with basically this problem (see Barrett and Phillips, 1992). Nancy Fraser's solution is threefold: one should seek to eliminate such cultural differences which are the result of oppression or which rest on claims of dominance or superiority, others such as feminine nurturing should be valued and universalized throughout society, whilst other differences should remain as valued variations within the human condition (Fraser, 1997: 203–4). Such a programme ('a differential view of difference') may be somewhat pragmatic, but it provides clear guidelines for what differences should be valued and which, for positive and negative reasons, should be abolished (see J. Young, 1999).

Domestic violence occurs in situations of the economic inferiority of women and where they are seen as culturally inferior to men or, more precisely, when they challenge the stereotypes of inferiority and appropriate behaviour. The pursuit of transformative policies which involve both redistribution and recognition between the sexes is the key to tackling the problem at its core.

Conclusion

This book started by indicating the dearth of satisfactory data on the extent of domestic violence. Its first aim was to remedy this and, by implication, develop the methodological tools which would make the generation of reliable data in a sensitive area possible. I have been concerned, however, not only with data but with theory. The methodological problems of definition confronted at the very onset of this project immediately threw up problems of theory and the subsequent findings themselves serve to validate or invalidate many of the presuppositions held in contemporary theories of domestic violence. The theoretical discussion which ensued has elucidated both problems of feminist theory in its understanding of violence and of recent criminology in its dialogue with feminist theory.

Finally, this book has focused not only on method and theory, but on policy. The size of the problem revealed and its endemic nature poses difficulties of a considerable magnitude. To try to alleviate the extent of domestic violence, let alone make a sizeable reduction in its incidence, demands a substantial political commitment at both national and local government levels. It might be argued that such intervention will prove too costly. However, given the levels of domestic violence that have been uncovered by this study and the impact that it has on a wide spectrum of women, the social costs are already high and damaging to the fabric of our society. We cannot afford to do nothing. Justice demands a major social initiative and the experience of the many women who have cooperated in this research project makes it imperative that something be done. If this book in giving voice to these women and proposing a solution contributes to raising public concern and fuelling this demand for action, then its aim will have been realized.

Notes

Introduction

1 In Britain, for example, we have had surveys on a national level (see Hough and Mayhew, 1983; Chambers and Tombs, 1984; Hough and Mayhew, 1985; Mayhew *et al.*, 1989; Kinsey and Anderson, 1992; Mayhew *et al.*, 1993, Mayhew *et al.*, 1994; Mirrlees-Black *et al.*, 1996; Mirrlees-Black *et al.*, 1998) and on a local level (see Kinsey, 1985; Jones *et al.*, 1986; Lea *et al.*, 1986; Lea *et al.*, 1988; Painter *et al.*, 1989; Painter *et al.*, 1990a; Painter *et al.*, 1990b; Crawford *et al.*, 1990; Jones *et al.*, 1990; Mooney, 1992).

2 Self-complete questionnaires were used in *Manchester's Crime Survey of Women for Women* (Bains, 1987) and McGibbon *et al.*'s (1989) survey of domestic violence for Hammersmith and Fulham Council.

3 This framework is derived from that utilized by Young (1981; 1994) in order to analyse traditional and contemporary paradigms of criminological theory and that of Jaggar (1983) in relation to feminist political theory. However, it should be pointed out that this structure will result to some extent in the creation of ideal types – we must be aware that there are theorists who lack consistency and others whose work falls between the different theoretical strands.

2 Positivism: Scientific Explanations of Violence

1 Other early biological determinist work on female criminality includes that of Adams (1910), Thomas (1923) and Pollak (1950).

2 In *Crime: Its Causes and Remedies*, Lombroso did, however, comment on other factors that might be relevant. For example, on women and urban crime: 'women are more criminal in the more civilized countries. They are almost always drawn into crime by a false pride about their poverty, by a desire for luxury, and by masculine occupations and education, which give them the means and opportunity to commit crimes such as forgeries, crimes against the laws of the press and swindling' (1918 ed : 54).

3 Prior to this Wilson worked for the Nixon government: in 1972 he was Chair of the National Advisory Council for Drug Abuse Prevention, the prelude to the modern 'War Against Drugs'.

4 However, as we shall see, contemporary positivist accounts of domestic violence, those of evolutionary theory and the family violence approach – which includes the work of Gelles and Cornell (1985) – confront the fact that domestic violence is much more widespread than traditional individual positivism would countenance.

5 This is not to suggest that all individual positivist explanations of domestic violence support the view that it is predominantly located in the lower socio-economic groups. Gayford (1978), for example, found no class relationship in his study.

6 As we have seen in discussing Lombroso, the application of the basic tenets of evolutionary theory to criminal behaviour in general is not a new idea. Further, as Janet Sayers has pointed out in *Biological Politics*, evolutionary theory was frequently utilized in the late nineteenth and early twentieth centuries to justify sex-role specialization. This is particularly evident in the work of social Darwinists such as Spencer (1873, 1884) and feminist essentialists (e.g. Blackwell, 1875; Gilman, 1898; Addams, 1922). 'Nature', as noted in our previous criticisms of traditional classicist thinkers, was at this time commonly presented as having fitted the two sexes for their current social roles – women as child-rearers and therefore confined to the private sphere (i.e. the home) and men as workers in the public sphere.

3 Violence and the Three Feminisms

1 In 1891 it became illegal following the *R* v *Jackson* ruling for a husband to beat or imprison his wife. Prior to this a husband had in common law the right to confine and exercise reasonable chastisement of his wife; however, how far this 'right' extended is unclear (see Clark, 1992; Doggett, 1992).

2 At this time, the property a woman owned on marriage or acquired afterwards became the property of her husband: 'at common law ... a woman effectively had nothing during marriage' (Doggett, 1992: 38). And as Brophy and Smart (1981) note, until the middle of the nineteenth century it was only conceivable to refer to father's rights, never the mother's rights, with respect to legitimate children. Indeed Caroline Norton's husband gave their children to his mistress to look after (Smart, 1989).

3 This is not to imply that there had not been earlier forms of collective opposition to domestic violence, however, these had taken place more on the level of the community. For example, violence against wives certainly met with disapproval amongst Puritans who saw it as disruptive of family life (Taves, 1989) and it has been pointed out that 'charivaris', a public shaming ritual, was used against wife-beaters (Dobash and Dobash, 1979; Doggett, 1992).

4 In the United States, many nineteenth century feminists campaigned against wife-beating through the temperance movement (Gordon, 1988).

5 Cobbe, towards the end of her life, became prominent in the anti-vivisection movement, creating The British Union for the Abolition of Vivisection Society in 1898.

6 Chiswick Women's Aid split from the National Women's Aid Federation (NWAF) at their inaugural meeting: according to Dobash and Dobash, the majority of Women's Aid groups wished 'to form a democratic, egalitarian organisation (NWAF) and Chiswick, in the person of Erin Pizzey, wish[ed] to maintain central control, power, publicity and exclusive access to funds donated by the public' (1992: 33).

7 This debate has also been considered in criminology (Heidensohn, 1994); indeed Allison Morris and Loraine Gelsthorpe repeatedly put forward the view (see Morris, 1987; Gelsthorpe and Morris, 1988; Gelsthorpe and

Morris, 1990) that a 'feminist criminology' cannot exist because neither criminology nor feminism presents a unified set of principles and practices:

> Criminology, like feminism, encompasses disparate and sometimes conflicting perspectives. The history of criminology well reflects these. In contrast, the tensions and conflicts within feminism are seen as indicative of an inchoate, unrigorous and 'indisciplined' discipline. There is no one specific feminism just as there is no one specific criminology.
>
> (1990: 2)

Thus Gelsthorpe and Morris believe the phrase 'feminist perspectives in criminology' more accurately describes the body of feminist work that has contributed to the subject.

8 It should be pointed out, however, that patriarchy has not been utilized in either political (see Pateman, 1988) or feminist theory in a simple or unified manner (Walby, 1990; Stacey, 1993; Heidensohn, 1994). And there has been debate, particularly amongst socialist feminists, over the usefulness of the term (Barrett, 1980; Rowbotham, 1982; Wilson and Weir, 1986; Messerschmidt, 1993).

9 Of course, the three feminisms reflect the arena of debate in the second wave of feminism of the 1970s, since then massive discussion has occurred with the postmodernist development of a feminism which concentrated on differences between women (Fraser, 1997). That is one which is suspect of the universalising voice of second-wave feminism accusing it of speaking, in fact, for white, middle-class, First World women. The axes of ethnicity, class and sexuality come into play interesecting and fragmenting the universal woman. The problem of going too far down this path is well put by Anne Phillips:

> The argument suggests a very radical pluralism, in which seemingly endless differences by sex, race, age, class, culture... all have to be taken into account. An obvious complaint would be that this emphasis leads us away from being able even to think of equality, for if people are so complex and diverse it seems impossible to conceive of them as in any sense being treated the same.
>
> (1992: 20)

The feminist realist position set out in this book is sensitive to the differences between women; indeed it goes out of its way to examine differences of attitude and experience by all of the major social axes, but it notes that there is a considerable overlap of agreement and shared experience. Such a degree of consensus is not in essence unalterable over time but changes with the vicissitudes of male–female relationships and the differences in the social construction of what constitutes 'domestic violence'. Lastly, the analysis presented here takes issue with the form of postmodernism that seeks to confine itself to the study of the representation of violence and is seemingly unconcerned with the actual occurrence and patterning of violence in the real world (e.g. Young and Rush, 1994).

10 Indeed this introduction shows Barrett to have retreated from many of her original arguments; for example, she comments, 'although *Women's Oppression Today* begins from the proposition that marxism and feminism have not been integrated, it is written with a much greater sense of the desirability of this at a political level than I would now express' (*ibid.*: xxiii). For Barrett, 'the arguments of post-modernism already represent...a key position around which feminist theoretical work in the future is likely to revolve' (*ibid.*: xxxiv). And, as Bryson notes, post-modernism with its emphasis on the multiplicity of experiences and subjectivities that exist can, 'provide a salutary warning against simplistic certainties and over-inclusiveness...it can in principle avoid the incipient racism of much feminist thought, whereby all women are seen as subject to the same processes, and the very different experiences of different groups ignored' (1992: 254).

11 Racism both on an individual and institutional level is considered by many commentators to compound the problems of black women experiencing domestic violence. And immigration law exacerbates the situation of immigrant women by, for example, forcing them to stay with violent husbands in order to fulfil immigration requirements (Mama, 1989; Kohli, 1992).

12 Walby sees a 'proper synthesis' as including waged work, housework, sexuality, culture, violence and the state (1990: 7).

13 First published in 1969, *Sexual Politics* and Firestone's *The Dialectics of Sex*, 1970, made major contributions to the development of radical feminist theory.

14 Brownmiller was attacked by black feminists, for example, Alison Edwards and Angela Davis, for not putting 'the white myth of the black rapist into an adequate historical context' (Humm, 1992: 70). Her novel *Waverley Place* (1989a) also encountered controversy. Based on the true Joel Steinberg case, she raises the question of whether the battered woman, Hedda Nussbaum, was a victim or an accomplice in their adopted daughter's death, as she did not take steps to protect the child from Steinberg's violence. In a subsequent article for *Ms* magazine Brownmiller describes Nussbaum as a 'participant in her own and Lisa's [the daughter's] destruction' and argues, 'victimhood must no longer be an acceptable or excusable model of female behaviour' (1989b: 61).

15 As Edwards notes, Brownmiller, like many other radical feminists at this time, in contrast, for example, to MacKinnon and, as we shall see, other recent contributors to the violence discussion, makes, 'a distinction between "deviant" and "normal" heterosexuality, placing the former in the category of violence, and the latter in that of sexuality' (1987: 19).

16 Andrea Dworkin and Catherine MacKinnon formulated a civil law which would have enabled women in the USA to take direct legal action in dealing with pornography (the Dworkin–MacKinnon Ordinance). Dworkin argues that pornography is 'a violation of women's civil rights' and the Ordinance was designed to recognise, 'the injury that pornography does: how it hurts women's rights of citizenship through sexual exploitation and sexual torture both' (1993a: 533). Dworkin and MacKinnon were successful in getting their law passed in Minneapolis and Indianapolis. However, it was later declared unconstitutional by the Supreme Court. Although Dworkin and MacKinnon's proposals have won a certain amount of support in this country (Kelly 1988b; Itzin, 1993), many feminists are opposed to anti-pornography

legislation. The organisation Feminists Against Censorship, for example, argue that it is likely to lead to the ' "policing" of diverse sexualities' (Power, 1993: 289) when what is needed is 'a much more wide-ranging debate about sex' (Rodgerson and Wilson, 1991: 15). Further the pro-legislation/anti-legislation debate can be seen as one between radical and socialist feminists (see Kelly, 1988b) – many of those who are against further legislation, for example, Mary McIntosh, Elizabeth Wilson and Lynne Segal, have contributed to socialist feminism. Hence, the first Feminists Against Censorship leaflet proclaimed,

We need a feminism willing to tackle issues of class and race and to deal with a variety of oppressions in the world, not to reduce all oppressions to pornography.

(1989)

17 In some accounts, following, as we have noted, the centrality awarded to heterosexuality in understanding women's oppression (e.g. Rich, 1980; MacKinnon, 1989), the term 'hetero-patriarchy' is preferred to 'patriarchy', 'to signify a system of social relations based on male dominance, or supremacy, in which men's structured relationships to women underpin all other systems of exploitation' (Hanmer *et al.*, 1989: 2).

18 The utilizing of predetermined definitions of violent behaviours in this survey contradicts Kelly's (1987; 1988a; 1988c) earlier insistence on the importance of using women's definitions.

19 The relative merits and disadvantages of qualitative and quantitative methods in social science research has been subject to much debate (see Glaser and Straus, 1967; Bryman, 1988).

20 That is a parallel to Left idealists, that is fundamentalist socialists who see such interim measures as mere reformism (see Chapter 4).

4 Feminist Realism: a Synthesis

1 Despite using the term 'realism', left realism did not initially explore the philosophical realism of writers such as Sayer, Harre, Bhaskar (see Walklate, 1992c and d; Carlen, 1992). More recent work (see Young, (forthcoming) has turned its attention in this direction.

2 This quotation is, however, taken out of context: Box argues that men of *all classes* rape but, 'income inequality ... helps us to understand why men commit one type of rape rather than another' (1983: 152). Successful men (i.e. those with wealth, organisational power and social status) are able to use different forms of coercion to achieve 'sexual access' – rather than actual physical violence. Further, Box suggests:

economic inequality between men helps us to understand why the official population of rapists, that is those legally adjudicated and imprisoned, are characterised by an over-representation of men from oppressed ethnic minorities and the lower or economically marginalized social class. These are just the men who are much more likely to commit those types of rapes – mainly 'anger' and less so 'domination' – which the law recognises as rape and is prepared sometimes, depending on the social characteristics of the victim and the suspect, to prosecute. Commenting on the fact that mainly poor and black men go to prison for rape, whilst others, mainly powerful men get away with it, Greer says that (1975: 379): 'neither the judges nor the prosecuting attorneys are hampered in their dealings by the awareness that they, too, are rapists, only they have more sophisticated methods of compulsion'.

(Ibid.: 152–3).

3 For example, the Merseyside Crime Survey (Kinsey, 1985), Islington Crime Survey (Jones *et al.*, 1986), Broadwater Farm Survey (Lea *et al.*, 1986), Hilldrop Environmental Improvement Project (Lea *et al.*, 1988; Jones *et al.*, 1991), Hammersmith and Fulham Crime and Policing Survey (Painter *et al.*, 1989), the West Kensington Estate Survey (Painter *et al.*, 1990a), Second Islington Crime Survey (Crawford *et al.*, 1990), Ladywood Crime and Community Survey (Painter *et al.*, 1990b) and Mildmay Crime Survey (Jones *et al.*, 1990).

4 For instance, the first Islington (Jones *et al.*, 1986), Hilldrop (Lea *et al.*, 1988; Jones *et al.*, 1991) and Mildmay (Jones *et al.*, 1990) Crime Surveys were financed by Islington Council; Broadwater Farm Survey (Lea *et al.*, 1986) by Haringey Council; the Hammersmith and Fulham (Painter *et al.*, 1989) and West Kensington Estate (Painter *et al.*, 1990a) Surveys by Hammersmith and Fulham Council.

5 However, many of the local surveys conducted by left realists, including the first Islington Crime Survey (Jones *et al.*, 1986), retain the word 'rape'.

6 This section focuses on realism's treatment of violence against women. Criticisms of other aspects of left realism have been dealt with in detail elsewhere (see Sim *et al.*, 1987; Jefferson *et al.*, 1991; Matthews and Young, 1992b; Young and Matthews, 1992b; Mawby and Walklate, 1994).

7 Currie (1991) and DeKeseredy (1991, 1992) also note that left realism has neglected crimes of the powerful against 'women ... are killed annually as a direct result of contraceptive and other unsafe "feminine" products' (Currie, 1991: 25).

8 This is not, of course, to suggest that radical feminists overlook the impact that women's structural and material circumstances have on their victimisation, it is just that realists link this more systematically to the capitalist social order.

9 It was Edwards who first utilized the terms 'feminist realist' to describe this group.

5 Researching Violence

1 Jan Pahl, however, argues that 'violent husbands' might be more appropriate than 'battered wives'; for in using the latter term, 'it is rather as though the problem of international terrorists hijacking aeroplanes was described as 'the problem of hostages' (1985: 5). She sees 'battered wives' as serving

to shift attention from the instigators of the violence to its victims, and the shift tends to make it easy to blame the victim for the problem and to encourage a search for solutions among the victims rather than among violent partners. (And) this misnaming is probably no accident. A great many people hold to the view that battered women are somehow responsible for what has happened to them, and this view is expressed in statements as 'the woman must have done something to deserve it' or 'the woman must enjoy it really, otherwise she would leave'.

(ibid.)

This argument is of interest in that it explicitly places the causality of the violence on the masculine side of the relationship.

2 Previous research shows that repeated contacts on postal surveys dramatically improve the response rate (see Fox *et al.*, 1988; Yammarino *et al.*, 1991). Given the nature of the research, the follow-ups were, of course, carried out in a discrete manner.

3 This method is distinct from the Conflict Tactic Scales used by the family violence researchers, which does not suggest specific scenarios (Straus, 1979; Straus *et al.*, 1980).

4 Brokowski *et al.* (1983) also used vignettes to explore how different practitioners defined domestic violence.

6 Revealing the Hidden Figure

1 As many commentators have pointed out (Estrich, 1987; Hall, 1985; Clark and Lewis, 1977) many rapes are accompanied by non-physical forms of coercion (i.e. not by overt threats of violence or actual physical force or violence e.g. bruising, broken bones, etc.). Social and economic forms of coercion, for example, are likely to occur, particularly when rape takes place in the context of a relationship. It must also be stressed that rape is a violent act in itself whether or not achieved by threats of or actual physical violence. Unfortunately, whilst being made to have sex without giving consent is defined in law as 'rape', it is often only when physical forms of coercion are involved that society and particularly the criminal justice system – and then not always (see Lees and Gregory, 1993) – is prepared to accept that a rape has taken place.

2 It should be noted that threats of violence and actual physical violence are not mutually exclusive as some women will be threatened and/or have physical violence used against them in different incidents.

3 It must be noted that several women found it difficult to quantify their experiences, some could only reply 'lots and lots'. One woman said, 'too many over too long a period to remember'. In these cases an average figure was taken. See the discussion in Genn (1988).

4 Caution must be exercised in detailing the coping and resistance strategies adopted by women to ensure that the emphasis is not placed on the women themselves to do something about the violence. There is always the danger that women will be blamed for their actions or lack of action in dealing with the situation.

5 See Chapter 7 for the scenarios in which men see their behaviour as justified.

6 In 1999 the Domestic Violence Units were disbanded and their work incorporated into Community Safety Units. These new units – although dealing

with a wider range of crimes, for example, sexual and racial violence – are still expected to operate in a similar way to the Domestic Violence Units.

7   Many of the women had made several attempts to leave, but returned for the reasons cited in this section.

8   Violence, Space and Gender: Testing the Theories

1   Such findings of equal rates of domestic violence between the sexes occur throughout the literature. We have already encountered such a statistic in the results of the 1996 British Crime Survey (see Chapter 6). As I noted, the concurrence is probably the result of lack of anonymity in the interview situation.

2   The numbers in the tables refer to threats of, or actual, physical violence.

References

Abbott, P. and Sapsford, R., 1987, *Women and Social Class*, London: Tavistock.

Addams, J., 1922, *Peace and Bread in Time of War*, New York: Macmillan.

Ahluwalia, S., 1992, 'Counting what Counts: The Study of Women's Fear of Crime', in J. Lowman and B. MacLean, eds, *Realist Criminology: Crime Control and Policing in the 1990s*, Toronto: University of Toronto Press.

Alexander, F. and Healy, W., 1935, *Roots of Crime*, New York: Knopf.

Allen, F., 1960, 'Raffaele Garofalo', in H. Mannheim, *Pioneers in Criminology*, London: Stevens and Sons Ltd.

Amir, M., 1971, *Patterns of Forcible Rape*, Chicago: University of Chicago Press.

Anderson, S. and Leitch, S., 1996, *Main Findings from the 1993 Scottish Crime Survey*, Edinburgh: Scottish Office.

Andrews, B., 1987, 'Violence in Normal Families', Paper presented at the *Marriage Research Centre Conference on Family Violence*, London, April.

Appleton, W., 1980, 'The Battered Woman Syndrome', *Ann. Emergency Medicine*, 9, 84: 91.

Archer, J., ed., 1994, *Male Violence*, London: Routledge.

Astell, M., 1986, 'Reflections on Marriage and Other Writings' in B. Hill, ed., *The First English Feminist*, Aldershot: Gower.

Bains, S., 1987, *Manchester's Crime Survey of Women for Women*, Manchester Council: Police Monitoring Unit.

Ball, M., 1977, 'Issues in Family Violence Casework', *Social Casework*, 58: 3–12.

Barash, D.P., 1977, *Sociobiology and Behaviour*, New York: Elsevier.

Barnett, V., 1991, *Sample Survey: Principles and Methods*, London: Edward Arnold.

Barrett, M., 1988, *Women's Oppression Today*, London: Verso, original edn. 1980.

Barrett, M., and Phillips, A., eds, 1992, *Destabilizing Theory: Contemporary Feminist Debates*, Cambridge: Polity Press.

Bart, P. and Moran, E., eds, 1993, *Violence Against Women*, Newbury Park: Sage.

Becker, H., 1967, 'Whose Side Are We On?', in H. Becker, ed., *Sociological Work*, London: Allen Lane.

Beechey, V., 1977, 'Some Notes on the Female Wage Labourer in Capitalist Production', *Capital and Class*, 3: 45–66.

Bewley, C. and Gibbs, A., 1997, 'The Role of the Midwife', in Bewley, S., Friend, J. and Mezey, G., eds, *Violence Against Women*, London: Royal College of Obstetricians and Gynaecologists.

Bhavani, K.-K. and Coulson, M., 1986, 'Transforming Socialist-feminism: the Challenge of Racism', *Feminist Review*, 20: 81–92.

Binney, V., Harkell, G. and Nixon, J., 1981, *Leaving Violent Men: A Study of Refuges and Housing for Battered Women*, London: Women's Aid Federation England.

Blackman, J., 1989, *Intimate Violence*, New York: Columbia University Press.

Blackwell, A.B., 1875, *The Sexes Throughout Nature*, New York: Putnam's.

Blake, M., 1892, 'Are Women Protected?', *Westminister Review*, 137: 43.

Bloch, H. and Geis, G., 1970, *Man, Crime and Society*, New York: Random House.

Bograd, M., 1988, 'Feminist Perspectives on Wife Abuse: An Introduction', in K. Yllo and M. Bograd, eds, *Feminist Perspectives on Wife Abuse*, Newbury Park: Sage.

Bouchier, D., 1978, *Idealism and Revolution: New Ideologies of Liberation in Britain and the United States*, London: Edward Arnold.

Bouchier, D., 1983, *The Feminist Challenge*, London: Macmillan.

Bowker, L., 1983, *Beating Wife Beating*, Lexington, Mass.: Lexington Books.

Box, S., 1983, *Power, Crime and Mystification*, London: Tavistock.

Braithwaite, J., 1979, *Inequality, Crime and Public Policy*, London: Routledge & Kegan Paul.

Breines, W. and Gordon, L., 1983, 'The New Scholarship on Family Violence', *Signs*, 8, 3: 490–531.

British Medical Association, 1998, *Domestic Violence: A Health Care Issue?*, London: British Medical Association.

Brokowski, M., Murch, M. and Walker, V., 1983, *Marital Violence: The Community Response*, London: Tavistock.

Brophy, J. and Smart, C., 1981, 'From Disregard to Disrepute: The Position of Women in Family Law', *Feminist Review*, 9: 3–16.

Brown, C. and Ritchie, J., 1981, *Focused Enumeration: the Development of a Method of Sampling Ethnic Minorities*, London: Social and Community Planning Research.

Brown, D. and Hogg, R., 1992, 'Law and Order Politics – Left Realism and Radical Criminology: a View from Down Under', in R. Matthews and J. Young, eds, *Issues in Realist Criminology*, London: Sage.

Brownmiller, S., 1975, *Against Our Will: Men, Women and Rape*, New York: Simon & Schuster.

Brownmiller, S., 1989a, *Waverley Place*, London: Hamish Hamilton.

Brownmiller, S., 1989b, 'Madly in Love', *Ms*, April, 56–61.

Bruegal, I., 1979, 'Women as a Reserve Army of Labour: a Note on Recent British Experience', *Feminist Review*, 3: 12–23.

Brush, L., 1993, 'Violent Acts and Injurious Outcomes in Married Couples: Methodological Issues in the National Survey of Families and Households' in P. Bart and E. Moran, eds, *Violence Against Women*, Newbury Park: Sage.

Bryman, A., 1992, *Quantity and Quality in Social Research*, London: Routledge.

Bryson, V., 1992, *Feminist Political Theory*, London: Macmillan.

Burgess, R. and Draper, P., 1989, 'The Explanation of Family Violence: the Role of Biological, Behavioral and Cultural Selection', in L. Ohlin and M. Tonry, eds, *Family Violence*, Chicago: University of Chicago Press.

Burton, S., Kitzinger, J., Kelly, L. and Regan, L., 1998, *Young People's Attitudes Towards Violence, Sex and Relationships*, Glasgow: Zero Tolerance Charitable Trust.

Campbell, B., 1993, *Goliath*, London: Methuen.

Campbell, B., 1998, *Diana, Princess of Wales: How Sexual Politics Shook the Monarchy*, London: The Women's Press.

Cameron, D., 1997/8, 'Back to Nature', *Trouble & Strife*, 36, 6–15.

Carby, H., 1982, 'White Women Listen! Black Feminism and the Boundaries of Sisterhood', in Centre for Contemporary Cultural Studies, eds, *The Empire Strikes Back*, London: Hutchinson.

Carlen, P., ed., 1985, *Criminal Women*, Cambridge: Polity Press.

Carlen, P., 1992, 'Criminal Women and Criminal Justice: the Limits to, and Potential of, Feminist and Left Realist Perspectives', in R. Matthews and J. Young, eds, *Issues in Realist Criminology*, London: Sage.

Chambers, G. and Tombs, J., 1984, *The British Crime Survey: Scotland*, Edinburgh: HMSO.

Clark, L. and Lewis, D., 1977, *Rape: The Price of Coercive Sexuality*, Ontario: The Women's Press.

Clarke, A., 1992, 'Humanity or Justice? Wifebeating and the Law in the Eighteenth and Nineteenth Centuries', in C. Smart, ed., *Regulating Womanhood: Historical Essays on Marriage, Motherhood and Sexuality*, London: Routledge.

Clarke, R., 1980, 'Situational Crime Prevention: Theory and Practice', *British Journal of Criminology*, 20, 2: 136–147.

Clarke, R., 1984, 'Opportunity-based Crime Rates', *British Journal of Criminology*, 24, 1: 74–83.

Clarke, R. and Cornish, D., eds, 1983, *Introduction to Crime Control in Britain*, Albany: SUNY Press.

Clarke, R. and Felson, M., eds, 1993, *Routine Activity and Rational Choice*, New Brunswick, NJ: Transaction.

Cloward, R. and Ohlin, L., 1960, *Delinquency and Opportunity*, New York: Free Press.

Cobbe, F.P., 1904, *Life of Frances Power Cobbe, As Told by Herself*, London: Swan Sonnenschein & Co.

Cobbe, F.P., 1878, 'Wife-torture in England', *Contemporary Review*, 55–87.

Cohen, A.K., 1965, 'The Sociology of the Deviant Act: Anomie Theory and Beyond', *American Sociological Review*, 30: 5–14.

Coole, D., 1993, *Women in Political Theory*, London: Harvester Wheatsheaf.

Corrigan, P., Jones, T., Lloyd, J. and Young, J., 1988a, *Socialism, Merit and Efficiency*, London: Fabian Society.

Corrigan, P., Jones, T. and Young, J., 1988b, 'Citizen's Gains', *Marxism Today*, August, 18–21.

Corrigan, P., Jones, T. and Young, J., 1989, 'Rights and Obligations', *New Socialist*, February–March, 16–17.

Coulson, M., Branka, M. and Wainwright, H., 1975, 'The Housewife and her Labour under Capitalism – a Critique', *New Left Review*, 89: 59–72.

Crawford, A., 1998, *Crime Prevention and Community Safety*, Harlow: Longman.

Crawford, A., Jones, T., Woodhouse, T. and Young, J., 1990, *The Second Islington Crime Survey*, Middlesex Polytechnic: Centre for Criminology.

Crawford, M.S., 1893, 'Maltreatment of Wives', *Westminster Review*, 139: 292–9.

Currie, D., 1990, 'Battered Women and the State: From the Failure of Theory to a Theory of Failure', *Journal of Human Justice*, 1, 2: 77–96.

Currie, D., 1991, 'Realist Criminology, Women, and Social Transformation in Canada', in B. MacLean and D. Milovanovic, eds, *New Directions in Critical Criminology*, Vancouver: The Collective Press.

Currie, D., 1992, 'Feminism and Realism in the Canadian Context', in J. Lowman and B. MacLean, eds, *Realist Criminology: Crime Control and Policing in the 1990s*, Toronto: University of Toronto Press.

Currie, D., 1998, 'Violent Men or Violent Women? Whose Definition Counts?', in R.K. Bergen, ed., *Issues in Intimate Violence*, Thousand Oaks, CA: Sage.

Currie, E., 1985, *Confronting Crime*, New York: Pantheon.

Daly, M. and Wilson, M., 1988, 'Evolutionary Social Psychology and Family Homicide', *Science*, 242: 519–24.

Daly, M. and Wilson, M., 1994, 'Evolutionary Psychology of Male Violence, in J. Archer, ed., *Male Violence*, London: Routledge.

Darwin, C., 1871, *Descent of Man*, London: John Murray.

Dawkins, R., 1976, *The Selfish Gene*, New York: Oxford University Press.

DeKeseredy, W. 1991, 'Confronting Woman Abuse: a Brief Overview of the Left Realist Approach', in B. MacLean and D. Milovanovic, eds, *New Directions in Critical Criminology*, Vancover: The Collective Press.

DeKeseredy, W., 1992, 'Confronting Woman Abuse in Canada: a Left Realist Approach', in J. Lowman and B. MacLean, eds, *Realist Criminology: Crime Control and Policing in the 1990s*, Toronto: University of Toronto Press.

DeKeseredy, W. and Hinch, R., 1991, *Woman Abuse: Sociological Perspectives*, Ontario: Thompson.

DeKeseredy, W. and Schwartz, M., 1991, 'British Left Realism and the Abuse of Women: a Critical Appraisal', in H. Pepinsky and R. Quinney, eds, *Criminology as Peacemaking*, Indianapolis: Indiana University Press.

DeKeseredy, W. and Schwatrz, M., 1996, *Contemporary Criminology*, Belmont, CA: Wadsworth.

Denzin, N., 1970, *The Research Act*, Chicago: Aldine.

Dewsbury, A., 1975, 'Family Violence seen in General Practice', *Royal Society of Health Journal*, 6: 290–4.

Dobash, R.E. and Dobash, R.P., 1979, *Violence Against Wives: a Case Against the Patriarchy*, New York: The Free Press.

Dobash, R.E. and Dobash, R.P., 1992, *Women, Violence and Social Change*, London: Routledge.

Dobash, R.E., Dobash, R.P., Wilson, M. and Daly, M., 1992, 'The Myth of Sexual Symmetry in Marital Violence', *Social Problems*, 39, 1: 71–91.

Doggett, M., 1992, *Marriage, Wife-Beating and the Law in Victorian England*, London: Weidenfeld & Nicolson.

Donovan, J., 1997, *Feminist Theory*, New York: Continuum.

Downes, D. and Rock, P., 1988, *Understanding Deviance*, Oxford: Clarendon Press.

Dutton, D.G., 1995, 'Intimate Abusiveness', *Clinical Psychology: Science and Practice*, 2, 207–24.

Dworkin, A., 1981, *Pornography: Men Possessing Women*, London: Women's Press.

Dworkin, A., 1983, *Right-Wing Women. The Politics of Domesticated Females*, London: Women's Press.

Dworkin, A., 1993a, 'Against the Male Flood: Censorship, Pornography and Equality', in C. Itzin, ed., *Pornography: Women, Violence and Civil Liberties*, Oxford: Oxford University Press.

Dworkin, A., 1993b, 'Living in Terror, Pain: Being a Battered Wife', in P. Bart and E. Moran, eds, *Violence Against Women*, Newbury Park: Sage.

Edwards, A., 1987, 'Male Violence in Feminist Theory: an Analysis of the Changing Conceptions of Sex/Gender Violence and Male Dominance', in J. Hanmer and M. Maynard, eds, *Women, Violence and Social Control*, London: Macmillan.

Edwards, S., ed., 1985, *Gender, Sex and the Law*, London: Croom Helm.

Edwards, S., 1986, *The Police Response to Domestic Violence in London*, London: Polytechnic of Central London.

Edwards, S., 1989, *Policing 'Domestic' Violence*, London: Sage.

Ehrlich, I., 1975, 'The Deterrent Effect of Capital Punishment: a Question of Life or Death', *American Economic Review*, 65.

Eisenstein Z., ed., 1979, *Capitalist Patriarchy and the Case for Socialist Feminism*, New York and London: Monthly Review Press.

Estrich, S., 1987, *Real Rape*, London: Harvard University Press.

Evans, R. J., 1977, *The Feminists: Women's Emancipation Movements in Europe, America and Australasia 1840–1920*, London: Croom Helm.

Eysenck, H., 1964, *Crime and Personality*, London: Paladin.

Eysenck, H. and Gudjonsson, G., 1989, *The Causes and Cures of Criminality*, New York: Plenum Press.

Faulk, M., 1974, 'Men Who Assault Their Wives, *Medicine, Science and the Law*, 14: 180–3.

Felson, M., 1994, *Crime and Everyday Life*, Thousand Oaks CA: Pine Forge Press.

Freeman, M., 1979, *Violence in the Home*, Farnborough: Saxon House.

Finch, J., 1987, 'The Vignette Technique in Survey Research', *Sociology*, 21: 105–14.

Finkelhor, D., 1981, 'Common Features of Family Violence', Paper presented at the *National Conference for Family Violence Researchers*, Durham, NH, USA.

Firestone, S., 1970, *The Dialectics of Sex*, New York: Bantam Books.

Fitch, F. and Papantonio, M.A., 1983, 'Men Who Batter: Some Pertinent Characteristics', *Journal of Nervous and Mental Disease*, 171, 3: 190–2.

Flynn, J., 1977, 'Recent Findings Related to Wife Abuse', *Soc. Casework*, 58: 13–20.

Foreman, A., 1978, *Femininity as Alienation*, London: Pluto Press.

Fotjik, K.M., 1977–8, 'The N.O.W. Domestic Violence Project', *Victimology*, 2: 655–7.

Fox, R., Crask, M. and Kim, J., 1988, 'Mail Survey Response Rate: a Meta-analysis of Selected Techniques for Inducing Response', *Public Opinion Quarterly*, 52: 467–91.

Fraser, N., 1997, *Justice Interruptus*, London: Routledge.

Gardiner, J., 1975, 'Women's Domestic Labour', *New Left Review*, 89: 47–58.

Gayford, J., 1975, 'Wife Battering: a Preliminary Survey of 100 Cases', *British Medical Journal*, January, 194–7.

Gayford, J., 1976, 'Ten Types of Battered Wives', *Welfare Officer*, 25, 1: 5–9.

Gayford, J., 1978, *Battered Wives: The Study of the Aetiology and Psychosocial Effects among One Hundred Women*, MD Thesis, University of London.

Gayford, J., 1979, 'Battered Wives', *British Journal of Hospital Medicine*, November, 496–503.

Gelles, R., 1987, *Family Violence*, Newbury Park: Sage.

Gelles, R., 1993, 'Through a Sociological Lens: Social Structure and Family Violence', in R. Gelles and D. Loseke, 1993, *Current Controversies on Family Violence*, Newbury Park: Sage.

Gelles, R. and Cornell, C., 1985, *Intimate Violence in Families*, Beverly Hills: Sage.

Gelles, R. and Loseke, D., eds, 1993, *Current Controversies on Family Violence*, Newbury Park: Sage.

Gelles, R. and Straus, M., 1979, 'Determinants of Violence in the Family: Toward a Theoretical Integration', in W.R. Burr, R. Hill, F.I. Nye and I.L. Reis, eds, *Contemporary Theories about the Family*, New York: Free Press.

Gelles, R. and Straus, M., 1988, *Intimate Violence*, New York: Simon & Schuster.

Gelsthorpe, L. and Morris, A., 1988, 'Feminism and Criminology in Britain', in P. Rock, ed., *A History of British Criminology*, Oxford: Clarendon Press.

Gelsthorpe, L. and Morris, A., eds, 1990, *Feminist Perspectives in Criminology*, Milton Keynes: Open University Press.

Genn, H., 1988, 'Multiple Victimisation', in M. Maguire and J. Pointing, eds, *Victims of Crime: a New Deal*, Milton Keynes: Open University Press.

Giles-Sims, J., 1983, *Wife-Beating: A Systems Theory Approach*, New York: Guilford.

Gilman, C.P., 1966, *Women and Economics*, New York: Harper & Row, original edn 1898.

Glaser, B. and Straus, A., 1967, *The Discovery of Grounded Theory*, Chicago: Aldine.

Glueck, S. and Glueck, E., 1950, *Unravelling Juvenile Delinquency*, New York: Commonwealth Fund.

Gordon, L., 1988, *Heroes of Their Own Lives: the Politics and History of Family Violence*, London: Virago.

Gottfredson, M., 1984, *Victims of Crime: the Dimensions of Risk*, London: HMSO.

Graham, D., Rawlings, E. and Rimini, N., 1988, 'Survivors of Terror: Battered Women, Hostages and the Stockholm Syndrome', In Yllo K. and Bograd, M., *Feminist Perspectives on Wife Abuse*, Newbury Park: Sage.

Greenblat, C.S., 1985, 'Don't Hit Your Wife … Unless', *Victimology*, 10: 221–41.

Greer, G., 1975, 'Seduction is a Four-letter Word', in L.G. Schultz, ed, *Rape Victimology*, Illinois: C.C. Thomas.

Gregory, J., 1986, 'Sex, Class and Crime', in R. Matthews and J. Young, eds, *Confronting Crime*, London: Sage.

Griffin, S., 1971, 'Rape: the All-American Crime', *Ramparts*, 10: 26.

Guettel, C., 1974, *Marxism and Feminism*, Toronto: The Women's Press.

Guze, S., 1976, *Criminality and Psychiatric Disorders*, New York: Oxford University Press.

Hague, G., Harwin, N., McMinn K., Rubens, J. and Taylor, M., 1989, 'Women's Aid: Policing Male Violence in the Home', in C. Dunhill, ed., *The Boys in Blue: Women's Challenge to the Police*, London: Virago.

Hague, G. and Malos, E., 1993, *Domestic Violence: Action for Change*, Cheltenham: New Clarion Press.

Hale, M., 1778, *The History of the Pleas of the Crown*, Vol. 1, London: Sollom Emlyn.

Hall, R., 1985, *Ask Any Woman*, Report of the Women's Safety Survey conducted by Women Against Rape, Bristol: Falling Wall Press.

Hampton, R., Gelles, R. and Harrop, J., 1989, 'Is Violence in Black Families Increasing? A Comparison of 1975 and 1985 National Survey Rates', *Journal of Marriage and the Family*, 51: 969–80.

Hanmer, J. and Maynard, M., eds, 1987, *Women, Violence and Social Control*, London: Macmillan.

Hanmer, J., Radford, J. and Stanko, E., eds, 1989, *Women, Policing and Male Violence*, London: Routledge.

Hanmer, J. and Saunders, S., 1984, *Well-Founded Fear*, London: Macmillan.

Hanmer, J. and Stanko, B., 1985, 'Stripping away the Rhetoric of Protection: Violence to Women, Law and the State in Britain and the USA', *International Journal of the Sociology of Law*, 13, 4: 357–74.

Harding, S., ed., 1986, *The Science Question in Feminism*, Milton Keynes: Open University Press.

Harding, S., ed., 1987, *Feminism and Methodology*, Milton Keynes: Open University Press.

Hartmann, H., 1979, 'The Unhappy Marriage of Marxism and Feminism: Towards a More Progressive Union', *Capital and Class*, Summer, 1–33.

Hartmann, H., 1983, 'Capitalism, Patriarchy and Job Segregation by Sex', in Abel, E. and Abel, E.K., eds, *The Signs Reader: Women, Gender and Scholarship*, Chicago: University of Chicago Press, original edn 1976.

Harwin, N., 1998, *Families without Fear*, Bristol: Women's Aid.

Heal, K. and Laycock, G., eds, 1986, *Situational Crime Prevention*, London: HMSO.

Heidensohn, F., 1985, *Women and Crime*, London: Macmillan.

Heidensohn, F., 1989, *Crime and Society*, London: Macmillan.

Heidensohn, F., 1994, 'Gender and Crime', in M. Maguire, R. Morgan and R. Reiner, eds, *The Oxford Handbook of Criminology*, Oxford: Clarendon Press.

Hester, M., Kelly, L. and Radford, J., 1996, *Women, Violence and Male Power*, Buckingham: Open University Press.

Heylin, C., 1991, *Dylan: Behind the Shades*, London: Penguin.

Hirschi, T., 1969, *The Causes of Delinquency*, Berkeley: University of California Press.

Home Office, 1998, *Criminal Statistics, England and Wales, 1997*, London: HMSO.

hooks, b., 1982, *Ain't I a Woman: Black Women and Feminism*, London: The Women's Press.

hooks, b., 1984, *Feminist Theory: From Margin to Center*, Boston: South End Press.

Hooton, E., 1939, *Crime and the Man*, Cambridge, MA: Harvard University Press.

Hope, T., 1985, *Implementing Crime Prevention Measures*, London: HMSO.

Horley, S., 1988, 'A Pioneering Police Plan to Help Battered Women, *Social Work Today*, March 24.

Hotaling, G., Finkelhor, D., Kirkpatrick, J. and Straus, M., eds, 1988. *Family Abuse and its Consequences*, Newbury Park: Sage.

Hough M, 1986, 'Victims of Violent Crime: Findings from the First British Crime Survey', in E. Fattah, ed., *From Crime Policy to Victim Policy*, London: Macmillan.

Hough, M. and Mayhew, P., 1983, *The British Crime Survey: First Report*, London: HMSO.

Hough, M. and Mayhew, P., 1985, *Taking Account of Crime: Key Findings from the 1984 British Crime Survey*, London: HMSO.

Hughes, G., 1998, *Understanding Crime Prevention*, Buckingham: Open University Press.

Humm, M., ed, 1992, *Feminisms: A Reader*, London: Harvester Wheatsheaf.

Island, D. and Letellier, P., 1991, *Men Who Beat the Men Who Love Them*, New York: Haworth Press.

Itzin, C., ed., 1993, *Pornography: Women, Violence and Civil Liberties*, Oxford: Oxford University Press.

Jackson, S., 1993, 'Feminist Social Theory', in S. Jackson *et al.*, eds, *Women Studies: a Reader*, London: Harvester Wheatsheaf.

Jackson, S., Atkinson, K., Beddoe, D., Brewer, T., Faulkner, S., Hucklesby, Pearson R., Power, H., Prince, J., Ryan M., and Young, P., eds, 1993, *Women's Studies: a Reader*, London: Harvester Wheatsheaf.

Jacobs, P., Brunton, M. and Melville, M., 1965, 'Aggressive Behaviour, Mental Abnormality and the XYY Male, *Nature*, 208: 1351-2.

Jaggar, A., 1983, *Feminist Politics and Human Nature*, Brighton: Harvester Press.

James, S. and Dalla Costa, M., 1973, *The Power of Women and the Subversion of the Community*, Bristol: Falling Wall Press.

James-Hanman, D., 1993, 'Policy Recommendations for Islington Council, the Inter-Agency Domestic Violence Working Party and Other Agencies', in J. Mooney, *The Hidden Figure: Domestic Violence in North London*, Middlesex University: Centre For Criminology.

Jefferson, T., Sim, J. and Walklate S., 1991, 'Europe, the Left and Criminology in the 1990s: Accountability, Control and the Social Construction of the Consumer', paper presented to the *British Criminology Conference*, York, July.

Jeffreys, S., 1990, *Anticlimax*, London: The Woman's Press.

Jeffreys, S., 1994, *The Lesbian Heresy*, London: The Women's Press.

Jesperson, A., 1987, 'The "Domestics" ' Dilemma', *Police Review*, July, 1328-9.

Jones, T., MacLean, B. and Young, J., 1986, *The First Islington Crime Survey*, Aldershot: Gower.

Jones, T., Lea, J., Woodhouse, T. and Young, J., 1990, *The Mildmay Crime Survey* Islington: Islington Council.

Jones, T., Woodhouse, T. and Young, J., 1991, *The Second Hilldrop Estate Survey*, Islington: Islington Council.

Jupp, V., 1989, *Methods of Criminological Research*, London: Unwin Hyman.

Kaluzynska, E., 1980, 'Wiping the Floor with Theory: a Survey of Writings on Housework', *Feminist Review*, 6: 27-54.

Kashani, J. and Allan, W., 1998, *The Impact of Family Violence on Children and Adolescents*, Thousand Oaks, CA: Sage.

Kelly, L., 1987, 'The Continuum of Sexual Violence', in J. Hanmer and M. Maynard, eds, *Women, Violence and Social Control*, London: Macmillan.

Kelly, L., 1988a, *Surviving Sexual Violence*, Cambridge: Polity Press.

Kelly, L., 1988b, 'The US Ordinances; Censorship or Radical Law Reform?', in G. Chester and J. Dickey, eds, *Feminism and Censorship*, Bridport: Prism Press.

Kelly, L., 1988c, 'How Women Define their Experiences of Violence', in K. Yllo and M. Bograd, eds, *Feminist Perspectives on Wife Abuse*, Newbury Park: Sage.

Kelly, L., 1989, Letter on Segal's 'The Beast in Man'. *New Statesman & Society*, 29 September, 7.

Kelly, L., 1990, 'Journeying in Reverse: Possibilities and Problems in Feminist Research on Sexual Violence', in L. Gelsthrope and A. Morris, eds, *Feminist Perspectives in Criminology*, Milton Keynes: Open University Press.

Kelly, L., 1991a, 'Unspeakable Acts: Women who Abuse', *Trouble and Strife*, no. 23.

Kelly, L., 1991b, 'Women's Refuges: 20 Years on', *Spare Rib*, 221: 32-5.

Kelly, L., Burton, S. and Regan, L., 1994. 'Researching Women's Lives or Studying Women's Oppression? Reflections on What Constitutes Feminist Research', in M. Maynard and J. Purvis, eds, Researching *Women's Lives from a Feminist Perspective*, London: Taylor Francis.

Kelly, L. and Radford, J., 1987, 'The Problem of Men: Feminist Perspectives on Sexual Violence', in P. Scraton, ed., *Law, Order and the Authoritarian State*, Milton Keynes: Open University Press.

Kelly, L. and Radford, J., 1997, ' "Nothing Really Happened": the Invalidation of Women's Experiences of Sexual Violence' in M. Hester, L. Kelly and J. Radford, eds, *Women, Violence and Male Power*, Buckingham: Open University Press.

Kemp, S. and Squires, S., 1997, *Feminisms*, Oxford: Oxford University Press.

Kennedy, H., 1992, *Eve was Framed: Women and British Justice*, London: Chatto & Windus.

Kinsey, R., 1985, *First Report of the Merseyside Crime Survey*, Liverpool: Merseyside County Council.

Kinsey, R., Lea, J. and Young, J., 1986, *Losing the Fight against Crime*, Oxford: Basil Blackwell.

Kinsey, R., and Anderson, S., 1992, *Crime and the Quality of Life: Public Perceptions and Experiences of Crime in Scotland*, Edinburgh: Scottish Office.

Kish, L., 1965, *Survey Sampling*, New York: Wiley.

Koedt, A., 1992, 'The Myth of the Vaginal Orgasm', in Humm, M., ed., *Feminisms: a Reader*, London: Harvester Weatsheaf, original edn. 1970.

Kohli, S., 1992, 'Ruled by Time and Custom', *The Guardian*, 28 October. 30–1.

Kourany, J., Sterba, J. and Tong, R., 1993, *Feminist Philosophies*, London: Harvester Wheatsheaf.

Kurz, D., 1993, 'Social Science Perspectives on Wife Abuse: Current Debates and Future Directions' in P. Bart and E. Moran, eds, *Violence Against Women*, Newbury Park: Sage.

Kurz, D., 1998, 'Old Problems and New Directions in the Study of Violence against Women', in R.K. Bergen, ed., *Issues in Intimate Violence*, Thousand Oaks, CA: Sage.

Labell, L.S., 1979, 'Wife Abuse: a Sociological Study of Battered Women and Their Mates, *Victimology*, 4: 258–65.

Laslett, B., 1973, 'The Family as a Public and Private Institution: an Historical Perspective', *Journal of Marriage and the Family*, August, 480–92.

Lea, J., 1987, 'Left realism: a Defence', *Contemporary Crises*, Vol. 11, 4: 357–70.

Lea, J., 1992, 'The Analysis of Crime', in J. Young and R. Matthews, eds, *Rethinking Criminology: the Realist Debate*, London: Sage.

Lea, J., Jones, T. and Young, J., 1986, *Saving the Inner City: Broadwater Farm*, Middlesex Polytechnic: Centre for Criminology.

Lea, J., Jones T., Woodhouse, T. and Young, J., 1988, *Preventing Crime: The Hilldrop Experiment*, Middlesex Polytechnic: Centre for Criminology.

Lea, J. and Young, J., 1984, *What is to be Done About Law and Order?*, London: Penguin.

Lee, R., 1993, *Doing Research on Sensitive Topics*, London: Sage.

Leeds Revolutionary Feminist Group, 1981, 'Political Lesbianism: the Case against Heterosexuality', in Onlywomen Press, eds, *Love Your Enemy? The Debate between Heterosexual Feminism and Political Lesbianism*, London: Only-women Press.

Lees, S., 1989, Letter on Segal's Beast in Man', *New Statesman & Society*, 22 September, 6.

Lees, S. and Gregory, J., 1993, *Rape and Sexual Assault: a Study of Attrition*, Islington Council: Police and Crime Prevention Unit.

Leibrich, J., Paulin, J. and Ransom, R., 1995, *Hitting Home*, Wellington: Department of Justice.

Lewis, M.L., 1954, 'Initial Contact with Wives of Alcoholics', *Soc Casework*, 35: 8–14.

Lilly, J.R., Cullen, F. and Ball, R., 1989, *Criminological Theory: Context and Consequences*, Newbury Park: Sage.

Lobel, K., ed., 1986, *Naming the Violence: Speaking Out About Lesbian Battering*, London: Seal.

Locke, J., 1690, *Two Treatises of Government*, London: Dent (Rpr. 1924).

Lombroso, C. and Ferrero, G., 1895, *The Female Offender*, London: Unwin.

Lombroso, C., 1911, 'Introduction' in G. Lombroso Ferrero's Summary of *Criminal Man*, London: GP Putnam's Sons.

Lombroso, C., 1918 edn, *Crime: Its Causes and Remedies*, Boston: Little, Brown.

Lombroso, Ferrero G., 1911, *Criminal Man*, London: GP Putnam's Sons.

London Strategic Policy Unit, 1986, *Police Response to Domestic Violence*, Police Monitoring and Research Unit Briefing Paper 1, London: London Strategic Policy Unit.

Lovenduski, J. and Randall, V., 1993, *Contemporary Feminist Politics*, Oxford: Oxford University Press.

Lowman, J., 1992, 'Rediscovering crime', in J. Young and R. Matthews, eds, *Rethinking Criminology: the Realist Debate*, London: Sage.

Lowman, J. and Maclean B., eds, 1992, *Realist Criminology: Crime Control and Policing in the 1990s*, Toronto: University of Toronto Press.

McCarthy, A, 1994, 'Talking Loud', *Everywoman*, May, 103: 20–1.

McClintock, D., 1963, *Crimes of Violence*, London: Macmillan.

McGibbon, A., Cooper, L. and Kelly, L., 1989, *What Support?*, Polytechnic of North London: Child Abuse Studies Unit.

MacKinnon, C., 1979, *Sexual Harassment of Working Women*, New Haven: Yale University Press.

MacKinnon, C., 1982a, 'Feminism, Marxism, Method and the State: an Agenda for Theory, *Signs*, 7, 3: 515–44.

MacKinnon, C., 1982b, 'Violence against women: a perspective', *Aegis*, 33, 52.

MacKinnon, C., 1989, *Toward a Feminist Theory of the State*, Cambridge, MA: Harvard University Press.

MacKinnon, C., 1993, 'Feminism, Marxism and the State: Toward a Feminist Jurisprudence', in Bart, P. and Moran, E., eds, *Violence Against Women*, Newbury Park: Sage.

MacLean, B., 1985, 'Review of *Ask Any Woman* by Ruth Hall, *British Journal of Criminology*, 25: 390–1.

Mama, A., 1989, *The Hidden Struggle: Statutory and Voluntary Sector Responses to Violence against Black Women in the Home*, London: London Race and Housing Unit.

Mann, L., 1993, 'Domestic Violence in Lesbian Relationships', Paper Presented at *British Sociological Association Annual Conference*, Essex.

Mannheim, H., 1965, *Comparative Criminology*, Vols 1 and 2, London: Routledge and Kegan Paul.

Martin, D., 1976, *Battered Wives*, San Francisco: Gide Publications.

Matthews, R. and Young, J., eds, 1986, *Confronting Crime*, London: Sage.

Matthews, R. and Young, J., 1992a, 'Reflections on Realism', in J. Young and R. Matthews, eds, *Rethinking Criminology: The Realist Debate*, London: Sage.

Matthews, R. and Young, J., eds, 1992b, *Issues in Realist Criminology*, London: Sage.

Mawby, R. and Walklate, S., 1994, *Critical Victimology*, London: Sage.

Mayhew, P. and Hough, M., 1988, 'The British Crime Survey: Origins and Impact', in M. Maguire and J. Pointing, eds, *Victims of Crime: A New Deal?*, Milton Keynes: Open University Press.

Mayhew, P., Elliot, D. and Dowds, L., 1989, *1988 British Crime Survey*, London: HMSO.

Mayhew, P., Maung, N.A., Mirrlees-Black, C., 1993, *The 1992 British Crime Survey*, London: HMSO.

Mayhew, P., Mirrlees-Black, C. and Aye Maung, N., 1994, *Trends in Crime: Findings from the 1994 British Crime Survey*, London: HMSO.

Mayhew, P. and van Dijk, J., 1997, *Criminal Victimisation in Eleven Industrialised Countries*, Amsterdam: WODC.

Maynard, M., 1989, *Sociological Theory*, London: Longman.

Maynard, M., 1993, 'Violence towards Women', in D. Richardson and V. Robinson, eds, *Introducing Women's Studies*, Basingstoke: Macmillan.

Maynard, M., 1994, 'Methods, Practice and Epistemology: the Debate about Feminism and Research', in M. Maynard and J. Purvis, eds, *Researching Women's Lives from a Feminist Perspective*, London: Taylor Francis.

Medea, A. and Thompson, K., 1974, *Against Rape*, New York: Farrar, Straus & Giroux.

Merton, R., 1938, *Social Theory and Social Structure*, New York: Free Press.

Messerschmidt, J., 1993, *Masculinities and Crime*, Maryland: Rowman and Littlefield.

Messerschmidt, J., 1997, *Crime as Structured Action*, Thousand Oaks: Sage.

Metropolitan Police, 1987, *Metropolitan Police Force Order on Domestic Violence*.

Metropolitan Police, 1987, *Summary of the Report of the Metropolitan Police Working Party into Domestic Violence*.

Mezey, G., 1998, 'Domestic Violence in Pregnancy', in Bewley, S., Friend, J. and Mezey, G., eds, *Violence against Women*, London: Royal College of Obstetricians and Gynaecologists.

Mies, M., 1986, *Patriarchy and Accumulation on a World Scale: Women in the International Division of Labour*, London: Zed Books.

Mill, J.S., 1992, 'The Subjection of Women', in Collini, S., ed., *J.S. Mill: On Liberty and Other Writings*, Cambridge: Cambridge University Press, original edn 1869.

Millett, K., 1977, *Sexual Politics*, London: Virago, original edn 1969.

Mirrlees-Black, C., 1999, *Domestic Violence: Findings from a New British Crime Survey Self-completion Questionnaire*, London: HMSO.

Mirrlees-Black, C., Mayhew, P. and Percy, A., 1996, *The 1996 British Crime Survey*, London: HMSO.

Mirrles-Black, C., Budd, T., Partridge, S. and Mayhew, P., 1998, *The 1998 British Crime Survey*, London: HMSO.

Mitchell, J., 1987, 'Women and Equality', in A. Phillips, ed., *Feminism and Equality*, Oxford: Basil Blackwell.

Mitchell, J. and Oakley, A., eds, 1986, *What is Feminism?*, Oxford: Basil Blackwell.

Mooney, J., 1993, *The Miranda Crime and Community Survey*, Middlesex University: Centre for Criminology.

Morley, R. and Mullender, A., 1992, 'Hype or Hope? The Importation of Pro-arrest Policies and Batterers' Programmes from North America to Britain as

Key Measures for Preventing Violence against Women in the Home', *International Journal of Law and the Family*, 6: 265–88.

Morris, A., 1987, *Women, Crime and Criminal Justice*, Oxford: Basil Blackwell.

Naffine, N., 1990, *Law and the Sexes*, Sydney: Allen and Unwin.

Naffine, N., 1997, *Feminism and Criminology*, Cambridge: Polity.

Nicoloson, D. and Sanghvi, R., 1993, 'Battered Women and Provocation: the Implications of *R V. Ahluwalia*', *Criminal Law Review*, 728–38.

Norton, C., 1982, *Caroline Norton's Defense: English Laws for Women in the Nineteenth Century*, Chicago: Academy of Chicago, original ed. 1854.

Oakley, A., 1981, *Subject Women*, Oxford: Martin Robinson.

O'Donovan, K., 1985, *Sexual Divisions in Law*, London: Weidenfeld and Nicolson.

O'Donovan, K., 1991, 'Defences for Battered Women who Kill', *Journal of Law and Society*, 18: 219.

O'Malley, P., 1992, 'Risk, Power and Crime Prevention', *Economy and Society*, 21 (3), 252–75.

Ohlin, L. and Tonry, M., eds, 1989, *Family Violence*, Chicago: University of Chicago Press.

Okin, S.M., 1989, *Justice, Gender and the Family*, New York: Basic Books.

Okin, S.M., 1998, 'Gender, the Public and Private', in A. Phillips, ed., *Feminism and Politics*, Oxford: Oxford University Press.

Okun, L., 1986, *Woman Abuse*, New York: SUNY Press.

O'Leary, K.D. and Arias, I., 1988, 'Assessment Agreement of Reports of Spouse Abuse', in G. Hotaling, D. Finkelhor, J. Kirkpatrick and M. Straus, eds, *Family Abuse and its Consequences*, Newbury Park: Sage.

O'Leary, K.D., 1993, 'Through a Psychological Lens: Personality Traits, Personality Disorders and Levels of Violence', in Gelles, R. and Loseke, D., eds, *Current Controversies on Family Violence*, Newbury Park: Sage.

Pagelow, M., 1984, *Family Violence*, New York: Praeger.

Pahl, J., ed., 1985, *Private Violence and Public Policy*, London: Routledge and Kegan Paul.

Painter, K., 1988, *Lighting and Crime: The Edmonton Project*, Middlesex Polytechnic: Centre for Criminology.

Painter, K., Lea, J., Woodhouse, T. and Young, J., 1989, *Hammersmith and Fulham Crime and Policing Survey*, Middlesex Polytechnic: Centre for Criminology.

Painter, K., Lea, J., Woodhouse, T. and Young, J., 1990a, *The West Kensington Estate Survey*, Middlesex Polytechnic: Centre for Criminology.

Painter, K., Woodhouse, T. and Young, J., 1990b, *The Ladywood Crime Survey*, Middlesex Polytechnic: Centre for Criminology.

Pateman, C., 1988, *The Sexual Contract*, Cambridge: Polity Press.

Pateman, C., 1989, *The Disorder of Women*, Cambridge: Polity Press.

Pfohl, S., 1985, *Images of Deviance and Social Control: a Sociological History*, New York: McGraw-Hill.

Phillips, A., 1992, 'Universal Pretensions in Political Thought', in M. Barrett and A. Phillips, eds, *Destabilizing Theory*, Cambridge, Polity.

Phillips, A., ed., 1987, *Feminism and Equality*, Oxford: Basil Blackwell.

Phillips, A., ed., 1998, *Feminism and Politics*, Oxford: Oxford University Press.

Phillips, A. and Taylor, B., 1980, 'Sex and Skill: Notes towards a Feminist Economics', *Feminist Review*, 6: 79–83.

Pizzey, E., 1974, *Scream Quietly or the Neighbours Will Hear*, Harmondsworth: Penguin.

Pizzey, E., 1998, 'Men are Strong, Men are Bullies and Men are Violent. Men Don't Cry when their Wives Beat them up – This is the Unreported Face of Domestic Violence', *The Observer*, 5 July: 24.

Pizszey, E. and Shapiro, J., 1981, 'Choosing a Violent Relationship', *New Society*, 23 April, 133.

Pollak, O., 1950, *The Criminality of Women*, New York: A.S Barnes/Perpetuo.

Popkin, R., Stroll, A. and Kelly, A., 1981, *Philosophy*, Heinemann: London.

Power, H., 1993, 'Women and the law', in S. Jackson *et al.*, eds, *Women Studies: A Reader*, London: Harvester Wheatsheaf.

Prescott, S. and Letko, C., 1977, 'Battered Women, a Sociological Perspective', in M. Roy, ed., *Battered Women: a Psychosociological Study of Domestic Violence*, New York: Van Nostrand Reinhold.

Price, W.H. and Whatmore, P.B., 1967, 'Behaviour Disorders and Patterns of Crime among XYY Males Identified at a Maximum Security Hospital', *British Medical Journal*, I: 533–6.

Quinney, R. and Wildeman, J., 1977, *The Problem of Crime*, New York: Harper & Row.

Radford, J., 1987, 'Policing Male Violence – Policing Women', in J. Hanmer and M. Maynard, eds, *Women, Violence and Social Control*, London: Macmillan.

Radford, J. and Laffy, C., 1984, 'Violence against Women: Women Speak out', *Critical Social Policy*, 11: 111–18.

Radford, J. and Stanko, E., 1991, 'Violence against Women and Children: the Contradictions of Crime Control under Patriarchy', in K. Stenson and D. Cowell, eds, *The Politics of Crime Control*, London: Sage.

Radford, L., 1993, 'Pleading for Time: Justice for Battered Women who Kill', in H. Birch, ed., *Moving Targets: Women, Murder and Representation*, London: Virago.

Rapoport, R. and Rapoport, R., 1976, *Dual Career Families Re-examined*, London: Martin Robertson.

Reinharz, S., 1979, *On Becoming a Social Scientist*, San Francisco: Jossey-Bass.

Renzetti, C., 1992, *Violent Betrayal: Partner Abuse in Lesbian Relationships*, Newbury Park: Sage.

Reynolds, J., 1974, 'Rape as Social Control', *Catalyst*, 8: 62–7.

Rich, A., 1992, 'Compulsory Heterosexuality and Lesbian Existence', in Humm, M., ed., *Feminisms: A Reader*, London: Harvester Wheatsheaf, original edn 1980.

Rights of Women, 1992, *Proposals for Amending the 1957 Homicide Act*, London: Rights of Women.

Roberts, E., 1984, *A Woman's Place: an Oral History of Working Class Women 1890–1940*, Oxford: Basil Blackwell.

Roberts, H., 1984, 'Putting the Show on the Road: the Dissemination of Research Findings', in C. Bell and H. Roberts, eds, *Social Researching: Politics, Problems, Practice*, London: Routledge & Kegan Paul.

Rodgerson, G, and Wilson, E., eds, 1991, *Pornography and Feminism: The Case against Censorship*, London: Lawrence & Wishart.

Rose, S., Lewontim, R.C., Kamin, L., 1990, *Not in Our Genes: Biology, Ideology and Human Nature*, Harmondsworth: Penguin (3rd edn).

Roshier, B., 1989, *Controlling Crime*, Milton Keynes: Open University Press.

Rounsaville, B., 1978, 'Theories of Marital Violence: Evidence from a Study of Battered Women', *Victimology*, 3: 11–31.

Rousseau, J.–J., 1911, *Emile*, London: Dent (rpr. 1974).

Rowbotham, S., 1982, 'The Trouble with Patriarchy', in M. Evans, ed., *The Woman Question*, Oxford: Fontana.

Roy, M., 1977, 'A Current Survey of 150 Cases', in M. Roy, ed., *Battered Women: A Psychosociological Study of Domestic Violence*, New York: Van Nostrand Reinhold.

Ruggiero, V., 1992, 'Realist Criminology: a Critique', in J. Young and R. Matthews, eds, *Rethinking Criminology: The Realist Debate*, London: Sage.

Russell, D., 1982, *Rape in Marriage*, New York: Macmillan.

Rushton, P, 1995, *Race, Evolution and Behaviour* New Jersey: Transaction.

Sachs, A. and Hoff Wilson, A., 1978, *Sexism and the Law*, Oxford: Martin Robertson.

Saunders, D., 1988, 'Wife Abuse, Husband Abuse or Mutual Combat?' in K. Yllo and M. Bograd, eds, *Feminist Perspectives on Wife Abuse*, Newbury Park: Sage.

Savitz, L., Turner S. and Dickman, S., 1977, 'The Origin of Scientific Criminology: Franz Joseph Gall as the First Criminologist', in R Meier, ed, *Theory in Criminology*, London: Sage.

Sayers, A., 1984, *Method in Social Science: a Realist Approach*, London: Hutchinson.

Sayers, J., 1982, *Biological Politics*, London: Tavistock.

Schecter, S., 1982, *Women and Male Violence*, Boston: South End Press.

Schwartz, M., 1988, 'Universal Risk Theories of Battering', *Contemporary Crises*, 12, 4: 373–92.

Schwartz, M. and DeKeseredy, W., 1993, 'The return of the "Battered Husband Syndrome" through the typification of Women as Violent', *Crime, Law and Social Change*, 20, 3: 249–65.

Scraton, P., 1990, 'Scientific Knowledge or Masculine Discourses? Challenging Patriarchy in Criminology', in L. Gelsthorpe and A. Morris, eds, *Feminist Perspectives in Criminology*, Milton Keynes: Open University Press.

Seccombe, W., 1973, 'The Housewife and her Labour under Capitalism', *New Left Review*, 83: 3–24.

Seccombe, W., 1975, 'Domestic Labour: a Reply to the Critics', *New Left Review*, 94: 85–96.

Segal, L., 1987, *Is the Future Female? Troubled Thoughts on Contemporary Feminism*, London: Virago.

Segal, L., 1989, 'The Beast in Man', *New Statesman & Society*, 8 September, 21–3.

Segal, L., 1990, *Slow Motion: Changing Masculinities, Changing Men*, London: Virago.

Sheldon, W., 1949, *Varieties of Delinquent Youth: An Introduction to Constitutional Psychiatry*, New York: Harper & Brothers.

Sim, J., Scraton, P. and Gordon, P., 1987, 'Introduction: Crime, the State and Critical Analysis', in P. Scarton, ed., *Law, Order and the Authoritarian State*, Milton Keynes: Open University Press.

Slattery, M., 1986, *Official Statistics*, London: Tavistock.

Smart, C., 1976, *Women, Crime and Criminology*, London: Routledge and Kegan Paul.

Smart, C., 1989, *Feminism and the Power of the Law*, London: Routledge.

Smart, C., 1990, 'Feminist Approaches to Criminology or Postmodern Woman Meets Atavistic Man', in L. Gelsthorpe and A. Morris, eds, *Feminist Perspectives in Criminology*, Buckingham: Open University Press.

Smith, L., 1989, *Domestic Violence*, London: HMSO.

Snell, J., Rosenwald, R. and Robey, A., 1964, 'The Wifebeater's Wife: a Study of Interaction', *Archives of General Psychiatry*, 11: 107–13.

Sparks, R., 1981, 'Surveys of Victimisation: an Optimistic Assessment', in N. Morris, ed., *Crime and Justice Review*, Vol. 3.

Sparks, R., 1992, 'Reason and Unreason in "Left realism": Some Problems in the Constitution of the Fear of Crime', in R. Matthews and J. Young, eds, *Issues in Realist Criminology*, London: Sage.

Spencer, H., 1873, 'Psychology of the Sexes', *Popular Science Monthly*, 4: 30–8.

Spencer, H., 1884, *Social Statics*, New York: Appleton.

Stacey, J., 1993, 'Untangling Feminist Theory', in D. Richardson and V. Robinson, *Introducing Women's Studies*, London: Macmillan.

Stanko, E., 1985, *Intimate Intrusions: Women's Experience of Male Violence*, London: Routledge and Kegan Paul.

Stanko, E., 1987, 'Typical Violence, Normal Precaution: Men, Women and Interpersonal Violence in England, Wales, Scotland and the USA', in J. Hanmer and M. Maynard, eds, *Women, Violence and Social Control*, London: Macmillan.

Stanko, E., 1990, *Everyday Violence*, London: Pandora.

Stanko, E., 1992, 'The Image of Violence', *Criminal Justice Matters*, Summer, 8: 3.

Stanley, L. and Wise, S., 1983, *Breaking Out: Feminist Consciousness and Feminist Research*, London: Routledge & Kegan Paul.

Steinmetz, S., 1977–8, 'The Battered Husband Syndrome', *Victimology*, 2, 3–4: 499–509.

Steinmetz, S. and Straus, M., eds, 1974, *Violence in the Family*, New York: Harper & Row.

Stewart, M.A. and deBlois, C.S., 1981, 'Wife Abuse among Families Attending a Child Psychiatry Clinic', *J. Am. Acad. Child Psychiatry*, 20: 845–62.

Stinchcombe, A., 1964, 'Institutions of Privacy in the Determination of Police Administrative Practice', *American Journal of Sociology*, 69: 150–60.

Straus, M., 1973, 'A General Systems Theory Approach to the Development of a Theory of Violence between Family Members', *Social Science Information*, 12: 105–25.

Straus, M., 1977, 'A Sociological Perpective on the Prevention and Treatment of Wife-beating', in M. Roy, ed., *Battered Women*, New York: Van Nostrand Reinhold.

Straus, M., 1997–8, 'Wife-beating: How Common and Why?', *Victimology*, 2, 3/4: 443–58.

Straus, M., 1979, 'Measuring Intrafamily Conflict and Violence: the Conflict Tactics Scales', *Journal of Marriage and the Family*, 41: 75–88.

Straus, M., 1980, 'A Sociological Perspective on the Causes of Family Violence', in M.R. Green, ed., *Violence and the Family*, Boulder, CO: Westview.

Straus, M., 1998, 'Foreword', in J. Jasinski and L.Williams eds, *Partner Violence: A Comprehensive Review of 20 years of Research*, Thousand Oaks, CA: Sage.

Straus, M. and Gelles, R., 1986, 'Societal Change and Change in Family Violence from 1975 to 1985 as Revealed by Two National Surveys', *Journal of Marriage and the Family*, 48: 465–79.

Straus, M. and Gelles, R., 1988, 'How Violent are American Families? Estimates from the National Family Violence Resurvey and Other Studies', in G. Hotaling, D. Finkelhor, J. Kirkpatrick and M. Straus, eds, *Family Abuse and its Consequences*, Newbury Park: Sage.

Straus, M. and Gelles, R., 1990, *Physical Violence in American Families*, New Brunswick: Transaction.

Straus, M., and Gelles, R. and Steinmetz, S., 1976. 'Violence in the Family: an Assessment of Knowledge and Risk Needs', Paper presented at the American Association for the Advancement of Science, Boston.

Straus, M., Gelles, R. and Steinmetz, S., 1980, *Behind Closed Doors: Violence in the American Family*, New York: Anchor/Doubleday.

Straus, M., and Hotling, G., eds, 1979, *The Social Causes of Husband–Wife Violence*, Minneapolis: University of Minnesota Press.

Straus, M. and Smith, C., 1990, 'Violence in Hispanic Families in the United States: Incidence Rates and Structural Interpretations', in M. Straus and R.Gelles, eds, *Physical Violence in American families*, New Brunswick: Transaction.

Streatham Police Division, 1989, *Streatham Division Report: Domestic Violence Deferred Decision Proceedure*.

Sutherland, E. and Cressey, D., 1966, *Principles of Criminology*, Philadelphia: JP Lippincott.

Szinovacz, M.E., 1983, 'Using Couple Data as a Methodological Tool: the Case of Marital Violence', *Journal of Marriage and the Family*, 45: 633–44.

Tappan, PW., 1947, 'Who is the Criminal?', *American Sociological Review*, 12: 96–102.

Taves, A., ed., 1989, *Religion and Domestic Violence in Early New England: The Memoirs of Abigail Abbot Bailey*, Indianapolis: Indiana University Press.

Taylor, I., 1992, 'Left Realist Criminology and the Free Market Experiment in Britain', in J. Young and R. Matthews, eds, *Rethinking Criminology: The Realist Debate*, London: Sage.

Taylor, I., 1997, 'The Political Economy of Crime', in M. Maguire, R. Morgan and R. Reiner, eds, *The Oxford Handbook of Criminology*, 2nd edn, Oxford: Clarendon Press.

Taylor, I., Walton, P. and Young, J., 1973, *The New Criminology*, London: Routledge and Kegan Paul.

Taylor, I., Walton, P. and Young, J., eds, 1975, *Critical Criminology*, London: Routledge and Kegan Paul.

Thomas, W.I., 1923, *The Unadjusted Girl*, Boston: Little, Brown.

Todd, S. and Butcher, B., 1982, *Electoral Registration in 1981*, OPCS, London: HMSO.

Tolmie, J., 1991, 'Add Women and Stir: an Australian Perspective on Defences to Murder for Women who Kill their Violent Husbands', Paper Presented *Law & Society Conference*, Amsterdam.

Tomes, N., 1978, ' "A Torrent of Abuse": Crimes of Violence between Working-class Men and Women, 1840–1875', *Journal of Social History*, 11: 238–345.

Trivers, R.L., 1972, 'Parental Investment and Sexual Selection', B. Campbell, ed., *Sexual Selection and the Descent of Man 1871–1971*, Chicago: Aldine.

Van den Haag, E., 1975, *Punishing Criminals*, New York: Basic Books.

Van Dijk, J. and Mayhew, P., 1993, *Criminal Victimisation in the Industrialised World: Key Findings of the 1989 and 1992 International Crime Survey*, The Hague: Directorate of Crime Prevention, Ministry of Justice.

Victim Support, 1992, *Domestic Violence*, London: Victim Support.

Vold, G. and Bernard, T. 1986, *Theoretical Criminology*, Oxford: Oxford University Press.

Wages for Housework, 1993, 'European Parliament Votes to Count Women's Unwaged Work', *Wages for Housework Campaign Bulletin*, 25 June.

Walby, S., 1990, *Theorizing Patriarchy*, Oxford: Blackwell.

Walker, L.E., 1979, *The Battered Women*, New York: Harper & Row.

Walklate, S., 1989, *Victimology*, London: Unwin Hyman.

Walklate, S., 1992a, *The Kirkby Inter-Agency Response to Domestic Violence*, University of Salford: Department of Sociology.

Walklate, S., 1992b, Re*sponding to Domestic Violence*, University of Salford: Department of Sociology.

Walklate, S., 1992c, 'Researching Victims of Crime: Critical Victimology', in J. Lowman and B. MacLean, eds, *Realist Criminology: Crime Control and Policing in the 1990s*, Toronto: University of Toronto Press.

Walklate, S., 1992d, 'Appreciating the Victim: Conventional, Realist or Critical Victimology', in R. Matthews and J. Young, eds, *Issues in Realist Criminology*, London: Sage.

Walklate, S., 1995, *Gender and Crime*, Hemel Hempstead: Prentice Hall.

Weir, A., 1977, 'Battered Women: Some Perspectives and Problems', in M. Mayo, ed., *Women in the Community*, London: Routledge & Kegan Paul.

Weitzman, J. and Dreen, K., 1982, 'Wife-beating: a View of the Marital Dyad', *Social Casework*, 63, 5: 259–65.

West, C.M., 1998, 'Lifting the "Political Gag Order": Breaking, the Silence around Partner Violence in Ethnic Minority Families', in J. Jasinski and L. Williams, eds, *Partner Violence: a Comprehensive Review of 20 Years of Research*, Thousand Oaks, CA: Sage.

West, D., 1988, 'Psychological Contributions to Criminology', in P. Rock, ed., *A History of British Criminology*, Oxford: Clarendon Press.

Willis, P., 1977, *Learning to Labour*, Farnborough: Saxon House.

Wilson, E., 1983, *What is to be Done About Violence Against Women?*, Harmondsworth: Penguin.

Wilson, E. and Weir, A., 1986, *Hidden Agendas: Theory, Politics and Experience in the Women's Movement*, London: Tavistock.

Wilson, J.Q., 1975, *Thinking about Crime*, New York: Neintage Books.

Wilson, J.Q. and Herrnstein, R., 1985, *Crime and Human Nature*, New York: Simon and Schuster.

Wilson, M., 1989, 'Marital Conflict and Homicide in Evolutionary Perspective', in R.W. Bell and N.J. Bell, eds, *Sociobiology and the Social Sciences*, Lubbock: Texas Technical University Press.

Wilson, M. and Daly, M., 1992, 'The Man who Mistook his Wife for a Chattel', in J.H. Barkow, L. Cosmides and J. Tooby, eds, *The Adapted Mind*, New York: Oxford University Press.

Wilson, M. and Daly, M., 1998, 'Lethal and Nonlethal Violence against Wives and the Evolutionary Psychology of Male Sexual Proprietariness', in R.E. Dobash and R.P. Dobash, eds, *Rethinking Violence against Women*, Thousand Oaks, CA: Sage.

Wittig, M., 1992, *The Straight Mind and Other Essays*, London: Harvester Wheatsheaf.

Wolfgang, M., 1960, 'Cesare Lombroso', in H. Mannheim, ed., *Pioneers in Criminology*, London: Stevens & Son Ltd.

Women's National Commission, 1985, *Violence Against Women*, London: Cabinet Office.

Woodhouse, T. and Yaylali, E., 1990, *Domestic Burglary in Highbury Neighbourhood*, Islington: Islington Council.

Worral, A. and Pease, K., 1986, 'Personal Crime against Women: Evidence from the 1982 British Crime Survey', *Howard Journal*, 25, 2: 118–24.

Wright, S., 1993, 'Preliminary Findings on the Role of the Police in combating Domestic Violence', *British Criminology Conference*, Cardiff University.

Yammarino, F., Skinner, S. and Childers, T., 1991, *Public Opinion Quarterly*, 55: 613–39.

Yllo, K., 1988, 'Political and Methodological Debates in Wife Abuse Research', in K. Yllo and M. Bograd, eds, *Feminist Perspectives on Wife Abuse*, Newbury Park: Sage.

Yllo, K., 1993, 'Through a Feminist Lens: Gender, Power and Violence', in R. Gelles and D. Loseke, eds, *Current Controversies in Family Violence*, Newbury Park: Sage.

Yllo, K. and Bograd, M., eds, 1988, *Feminist Perspectives on Wife Abuse*, Newbury Park: Sage.

Young, A. and Rush, P., 1994, 'The Law of Victimage in Urbane Realism: Thinking Through Inscriptions of Violence', in D. Nelken, ed., *The Futures of Criminology*, London: Sage.

Young, I., 1990, *Justice and the Politics of Difference*, Princeton: Princeton University Press.

Young, J., 1975, 'Working-class Criminology', in I. Taylor, P. Walton and J. Young, eds, *Critical Criminology*, London: Routledge and Kegan Paul.

Young, J., 1979, 'Left Idealism, Reformism and Beyond', in B. Fine, R. Kinsey, J. Lea, S. Picciotto and J. Young, eds, *Capitalism and the Rule of Law*, London: Hutchinson.

Young, J., 1981, 'Thinking Seriously about Crime: Some Models of Criminology' in M. Fitzgerald, G. McLennan and J. Pawson, eds, *Crime and Society*, London: Routledge and Kegan Paul.

Young, J., 1986, 'The Failure of Criminology: The Need for Radical Realism', in R. Matthews and J. Young, eds, *Confronting Crime*, London: Sage.

Young, J., 1987, 'The Tasks of a Realist Criminology', *Contemporary Crises*, II: 337–56.

Young, J., 1988a, 'Risk of Crime and Fear of Crime: a Realist critique of survey-based assumptions' in M. Maguire and J. Pointing, eds, *Victims of Crime: a New Deal?*, Milton Keynes: Open University Press.

Young, J., 1988b, 'Recent Developments in Criminology', in M. Haralambos, ed., *Developments in Sociology*, Volume 4, Ormskirk: Causeway Press.

Young, J., 1988c, 'Radical Criminology in Britain: The Emergence of a Competing Paradigm', in P. Rock, ed., *A History of British Criminology*, Oxford: Clarendon.

Young, J., 1992a, 'Ten Points of Realism', in J. Young and R. Matthews, eds, *Rethinking Criminology: The Realist Debate*, London: Sage.

Young, J., 1992b, 'Realist Research as a Basis for Local Criminal Justice Policy', in J. Lowman and B. MacLean, eds, *Realist Criminology: Crime Control and Policing in the 1990s*, Toronto: University of Toronto Press.

Young, J., 1994, 'Incessant Chatter: Recent Paradigms in Criminology', in M. Maguire, R. Morgan and R. Reiner, eds, *The Oxford Handbook of Criminology*, Oxford: Clarendon Press.

Young, J., 1997, 'Left Realist Criminology: Radical in its Analysis, Realist in its Policy', in M. Maguire, R. Morgan and R. Reiner, eds, *The Oxford Handbook of Criminology*, Oxford: Clarendon Press (2nd edn).

Young, J., 1999, *The Exclusive Society*, London: Sage.

Young, J., forthcoming, *Realist Criminology*, London: Sage.

Young, J. and Matthews. R., 1992a, 'Questioning Left Realism', in R. Matthews and J. Young, eds, *Issues in Realist Criminology*, London: Sage.

Young, J. and Matthews, R., eds, 1992b, *Rethinking Criminology: The Realist Debate*, London: Sage.

Index

Abbott, P., 147–8
Addams, J., 228
Against Our Will (Brownmiller), 106
Ahluwalia, S., 134, 219
Allan, W., 141
Amir, M., 46
Anderson, S., 20, 227
Andrews, B., 47
Appleton, W., 45
Arias, I., 151
Astell, M., 26

Bains, S., 227
Ball, R., 6, 37–8, 40, 42–3, 52
Barash, D.P., 56
Barnett, V., 32
Barrett, M., 75, 80–3, 224, 229–30
Bart, P., 91
battered husbands, 50–1, 64–5,
   207–21
Beccaria, C., 15, 18
Becker, H., 100
Beechey, V., 80–1
Beirne, P., 18, 35
Bernard, T., 36–7
Bewley, C., 58
Bhaskar, R., 231
Bhavani, K.-K., 82
Blackman, J., 73
Blackwell, A.B., 228
Blake, M., 68, 70
Bloch, H., 39
Bograd, M., 52, 62, 91–2, 99–100,
   141–3
Bonger, W., 39
Bouchier, D., 75
Box, S., 118, 231–2
Braithwaite, J., 116
Branka, M., 79
Breines, W., 197
British Crime Survey, 4, 20–4, 33, 98,
   122, 133, 150, 164–5, 193–4, 197,
   199, 207, 227 n1, 234

British Medical Association, 3, 142,
   210–11
Brokowski, M., 3, 68, 73–4, 142, 233
Brown, D., 128
Brownmiller, S., 89–90, 106, 230
Bruegal, I., 80
Brush, L., 64
Bryson, V., 25, 27, 75, 77–80, 86, 107,
   230
Budd, T., 19–20, 22, 194, 227
Burgess, R., 40, 55–6
Burton, S., 101, 185
Butcher, B., 144

Cameron, D., 58
Campbell, B., 137, 185
Carby, H., 82
Chambers, G., 20, 227
Childers, T., 233
Chiswick Women's Aid, 45, 74, 228
   n6
Christie, A., 39
Clark, L., 233
Clarke, A., 2, 66–7
Clarke, R., 13, 16–18, 21–2
classicist contradiction, 27, 30, 77
classicist criminology, 13–34
   denial of causes, 16, 22, 30–1
   and the philosophy of the
      Enlightenment, 13–15, 25–7,
      76
   and positivism, 35
Cloward, R., 117
Cobbe, F.P., 68–73, 77, 228 n5
Cohen, A.K., 111
computer-assisted self-interviewing
   (CASI), 23, 32, 164–6
conflict tactics scale, 63–4, 233 n3
Connell, R., 107
Coole, D., 79
Cooper, L., 95, 97–8, 101, 227
Cornell, C., 4, 44–5, 50, 52–3, 60, 62,
   143, 170, 185, 196, 227